The Work of Psychoanal

Psychoanalysts working in clinical situations are constantly confronted with the struggle between conservative forces and those which enable something new to develop. Continuity and change, stasis and transformation, are the major themes discussed in *The Work of Psychoanalysis*, and address the fundamental question: How does and how can change take place?

The Work of Psychoanalysis explores the underlying coherence of the complex linked issues of theory and practice. Drawing on clinical cases from her own experience in the consulting room Dana Birksted-Breen focuses on what takes place between patient and analyst, giving a picture of the interlocking and overlapping vertices that make up the work needed in psychoanalysis. Some of the key topics covered include: sexuality; aspects of female identity; eating disorders; time; dreams; modalities of thought; and terminating psychoanalysis.

This book draws different traditions into a coherent theoretical position with consequences for the mode of working analytically. *The Work of Psychoanalysis* will appeal to psychoanalysts and academics in psychoanalysis, psychotherapists, as well as postgraduate students studying courses in these fields.

Dana Birksted-Breen is a Training and Supervising Psychoanalyst of the British Psychoanalytical Society, member of the IPA, and current Editor-in-Chief of the *International Journal of Psychoanalysis*. She was the Editor of the New Library of Psychoanalysis for 10 years, and is a psychoanalyst in private practice in London.

THE NEW LIBRARY OF PSYCHOANALYSIS
General Editor: Alessandra Lemma

The New Library of Psychoanalysis was launched in 1987 in association with the Institute of Psychoanalysis, London. It took over from the International Psychoanalytical Library which published many of the early translations of the works of Freud and the writings of most of the leading British and Continental psychoanalysts.

The purpose of the New Library of Psychoanalysis is to facilitate a greater and more widespread appreciation of psychoanalysis and to provide a forum for increasing mutual understanding between psychoanalysts and those working in other disciplines such as the social sciences, medicine, philosophy, history, linguistics, literature and the arts. It aims to represent different trends both in British psychoanalysis and in psychoanalysis generally. The New Library of Psychoanalysis is well placed to make available to the English-speaking world psychoanalytic writings from other European countries and to increase the interchange of ideas between British and American psychoanalysts. Through the *Teaching Series*, the New Library of Psychoanalysis now also publishes books that provide comprehensive, yet accessible, overviews of selected subject areas aimed at those studying psychoanalysis and related fields such as the social sciences, philosophy, literature and the arts.

The Institute, together with the British Psychoanalytical Society, runs a low-fee psychoanalytic clinic, organises lectures and scientific events concerned with psychoanalysis and publishes the *International Journal of Psychoanalysis*. It runs the training course in psychoanalysis which leads to membership of the International Psychoanalytical Association – the body which preserves internationally agreed standards of training, of professional entry, and of professional ethics and practice for psychoanalysis as initiated and developed by Sigmund Freud. Distinguished members of the Institute have included Michael Balint, Wilfred Bion, Ronald Fairbairn, Anna Freud, Ernest Jones, Melanie Klein, John Rickman and Donald Winnicott.

Previous general editors have included David Tuckett, who played a very active role in the establishment of the New Library. He was

TITLES IN THIS SERIES

Seeds of Illness and Seeds of Recovery: The genesis of suffering and the role of psychoanalysis Antonino Ferro

The Work of Psychic Figurability: Mental States Without Representation César Botella and Sára Botella

Key Ideas for a Contemporary Psychoanalysis: Misrecognition and Recognition of the Unconscious André Green

The Telescoping of Generations: Listening to the Narcissistic Links Between Generations Haydée Faimberg

Glacial Times: A Journey through the World of Madness Salomon Resnik

This Art of Psychoanalysis: Dreaming Undreamt Dreams and Interrupted Cries Thomas H. Ogden

Psychoanalysis and Religion in the 21ˢᵗ Century: Competitors or Collaborators? David M. Black

Recovery of the Lost Good Object Eric Brenman

The Many Voices of Psychoanalysis Roger Kennedy

Feeling the Words: Neuropsychoanalytic Understanding of Memory and the Unconscious Mauro Mancia

Constructions and the Analytic Field: History, Scenes and Destiny Domenico Chianese

Projected Shadows: Psychoanalytic Reflections on the Representation of Loss in European Cinema Edited by Andrea Sabbadini

Encounters with Melanie Klein: Selected Papers of Elizabeth Spillius Elizabeth Spillius

Yesterday, Today and Tomorrow Hanna Segal

Psychoanalysis Comparable and Incomparable: The Evolution of a Method to Describe and Compare Psychoanalytic Approaches David Tuckett, Roberto Basile, Dana Birksted-Breen, Tomas Böhm, Paul Denis, Antonino Ferro, Helmut Hinz, Arne Jemstedt, Paola Mariotti and Johan Schubert

Time, Space and Phantasy Rosine Jozef Perelberg

Rediscovering Psychoanalysis: Thinking and Dreaming, Learning and Forgetting Thomas H. Ogden

Mind Works: Techniques and Creativity in Psychoanalysis Antonino Ferro

Doubt Conviction and the Analytic Process: Selected Papers of Michael Feldman Michael Feldman

Melanie Klein in Berlin: Her First Psychoanalyses of Children Claudia Frank

The Psychotic Wavelength: A Psychoanalytic Perspective for Psychiatry Richard Lucas

Betweenity: A Discussion of the Concept of Borderline Judy Gammelgaard

The Intimate Room: Theory and Technique of the Analytic Field Giuseppe Civitarese

THE NEW LIBRARY OF PSYCHOANALYSIS

General Editor: Alessandra Lemma

The Work of Psychoanalysis

Sexuality, Time and the Psychoanalytic Mind

Dana Birksted–Breen

Routledge
Taylor & Francis Group

LONDON AND NEW YORK

First published 2016
by Routledge
2 Park Square, Milton Park, Abingdon, Oxon OX14 4RN

and by Routledge
711 Third Avenue, New York, NY 10017

Routledge is an imprint of the Taylor & Francis Group, an informa business

© 2016 Dana Birksted-Breen

The right of Dana Birksted-Breen to be identified as author of this work has been asserted by her in accordance with sections 77 and 78 of the Copyright, Designs and Patents Act 1988.

Trademark notice: Product or corporate names may be trademarks or registered trademarks, and are used only for identification and explanation without intent to infringe.

British Library Cataloguing in Publication Data
A catalogue record for this book is available from the British Library

Library of Congress Cataloging in Publication Data
A catalog record for this book has been requested

ISBN: 978-1-138-96339-9 (hbk)
ISBN: 978-1-138-96340-5 (pbk)
ISBN: 978-1-315-65880-3 (ebk)

Typeset in Bembo
by Wearset Ltd, Boldon, Tyne and Wear

Printed and bound in the United States of America by
Edwards Brothers Malloy on sustainably sourced paper

To my family for their love and support

Contents

Contents

ACKNOWLEDGEMENTS

The ideas in this book are the outcome of my thinking and my own 'psychic work' over a number of decades, and I am grateful to my former teachers and to the many colleagues and friends I have been in contact with over the years. I have benefited from having 'a home' in the British Psychoanalytical Society as well as from my contact with psychoanalysts from other psychoanalytic cultures. All my ideas emerge from my work in the consulting room and I am grateful to all my patients for this experience.

I thank Alessandra Lemma, the editor of the New Library for her continued encouragement for this book, her support and her comments.

I would like to thank the following for their kind permission to reproduce copyright material:

The *Journal of the American Psychoanalytic Association* for:
"Unconscious Representation of Femininity", Vol. 44S (1996).

The *International Journal of Psychoanalysis* for:
"Working with an Anorexic Patient", Vol. 70 (1989).
"Time and the *après-coup*", Vol. 84 (2003).
"'Reverberation Time', Dreaming and the Capacity to Dream", Vol. 90 (2009).
"Taking Time: The Tempo of Psychoanalysis", Vol. 93 (2012).
"Bi-ocularity, The Functioning Mind of the Psychoanalyst", Vol. 97 (2016).

INTRODUCTION

Psychical reality is a particular form of existence not to be confused with material reality.

(Freud, 1900, p. 620)

A felt need to convert the conscious rational experience into dream.

(Bion, 1992, p. 184)

Love in infant or mother or both increases rather than decreases the obstruction.

(Bion, 1962, p. 10)

Continuity and change, stasis and transformation, these are the themes which connect the various lines of enquiry I have pursued since the early 1970s. They are central to both clinical psycho-analysis and psychoanalytic theory.

Before becoming a psychoanalyst I was interested in looking at how change takes place through life events and in issues of positive mental health; that is, with that which is more than the absence of ill-health. I was not well acquainted with Winnicott's writing at the time but this would have been about the time when he wrote "that absence of psychoneurotic illness may be health, but it is not life" (1971, p. 100). This interest, coupled with an interest in identity, identifications and change, and in femininity as an aspect of it, led me to a research project on first pregnancies (Breen, 1975). There, I described two models I found in the literature: one which discusses pregnancy as a hurdle from which one recovers and returns to a pre-pregnancy state as one does an illness; and one which discusses it from the perspective of development. I looked at first pregnancies

1

as a time of necessary change, a time when a woman needs to make psychic changes if she is to become a mother without a breakdown of one kind or another. Particular moments in life require change if they are to be lived, not just gone through. Stasis signals problems. Pregnancy and early motherhood are such a time when internal object relationships and identifications need to be reworked and modified (Breen, 1975, 1981, 1986).

This interest in stasis and change has continued to focus my thinking. Temporality infuses psychoanalysis. It may be found at the metapsychological level, in such notions as the repetition compulsion, the balance between life and death drives and the role of objects in influencing that balance, in notions of regression, Nirvana, timelessness of the unconscious, and at the micro level of 'the clinic' in issues such as the timing of interpretations, intuition and anticipation, the repercussions of sessional and termly interruptions, terminability, fusion versus separateness, fixation points and psychic retreat.

Clinical psychoanalysis deals with those situations in which an individual has become stuck in repetitive patterns and cannot change over time due to being out of touch with aspects of him- or herself. Past ('reminiscences'; Breuer and Freud, 1893, p. 7), present ('here and now'), future (dreams and illusions) coalesce in the sessions in a 'now always' which needs to be transformed and separated into a 'then' and a 'now' in order to release a movement forward. The past can paralyse the present and the present can be persecuting when there is no sense of a future, or when the future is the catastrophe, or the impossible ideal. The terror of catastrophic change can lead to a withdrawal from objects. The clinical situation deals with the intersection between the timelessness of the unconscious and the time of the conscious, reality and development.

Working as a psychoanalyst in clinical situations, one is all the time confronted with the struggle between the conservative forces and those which enable something new to develop, and with the struggle between love and the forces of 'obstruction' (Bion, 1962 p. 10).[1]

It is with such issues in the consulting room that I have been primarily concerned. How does and how can change take place? Psychoanalysis rests on repetition but repetition without transformation leads at worst to re-traumatisation and at best to interminability. The aim is for repetition to gradually show an element of difference, which, however minute it may be at times, eventually leads to significant modification, making termination possible. These modifications rest on the process of symbolisation basic to the 'talking cure', since symbols are necessary for the storing of emotional experience and for conveying our affects to others and to ourselves (Da Rocha Barros and Da Rocha Barros, 2011), for processing past and present emotional experience, for the plasticity with which the past can be made sense of and the future anticipated. Representation comes in the place of the absent object but, as Roussillon notes (2001, p. 176), "it is when the object is *present* that the self has to discover the wherewithal to work at representation, not simply when the object is absent". Or, I would say, the self has to respond, with the help of the 'present object', the psychoanalyst, to the challenge of dealing with the continual movement between presence and absence.

Strachey spoke about the mutative aspect when the patient becomes aware, through interpretative work, of a distinction between his archaic phantasy object and the real external object (1934), while Bion emphasised the necessary transformation operated by the psyche of the 'object' which enables repetition to be, one could say, 'in a new key'.

When development is made possible, it is often not the one that analysands were expecting. They often discover that it is with 'living' as opposed to 'existing' that a change takes place, making life more meaningful, and with a greater sense of 'humanity'. This rests on a different emotional contact with their own internal world as well as with others, and with a wider range of emotional experience, including often the subtle experience of sadness. This sadness goes together with a different relationship to the past and a less split view of the world and of themselves.

Temporality and identity are interconnected themes. Continuity is the basis of a sense of identity. Identity is not in itself a psychoanalytic concept although disturbances of identity are described as central to the more severe pathologies, and projective identification "confuses the distinction between the self and the external object" (Bion, 1962a, p. 307). Transgenerational transmission and projections from objects are all part of what comes to be experienced as identity. Issues of temporality and symbolisation are also closely linked with questions of identity. In all pathologies one can find a temporal problematic and one of subjectivation, to which I include

3

sexuality, and representations of the body. Sexuality is part of, and a consequence of, identity. Sexuality is grounded in the body but its development takes place over time, and is intimately related to and modulated by the relationship to objects, and by the objects' own desires and experiences. Identifications with loved, hated and feared objects interact in complex ways so that parts of the self remain static while others develop, making up pathological, healthy and character-ological aspects of identity. Non-recognition and misrecognition by the primary objects are foundational to pathology and in particular contribute to narcissistic difficulties, to feelings of shame, and to rigid defence mechanisms which lead to stasis. All these experiences are present to varying degrees in everyone and contribute to fluctuations between positions and parts of the personality, between psychotic parts and non-psychotic parts, and will be reflected in different modal-ities of thought. As Denis (1995) writes, "All pathologies of temporal-ity are … (p. 1109) at the same time pathologies of subjectivation and of language." Pathology takes over when 'stuckness' predominates, and it is with this that Freud became preoccupied when he intro-duced the notion of the death drive. The danger clinically is always that stasis takes over, the analytic situation itself becoming a pathologi-cal organisation 'à deux' in which primitive anxieties and movements are avoided for fear of collapse, or in which the trauma is relived without any modification.

Temporality within the analytic situation is a complex issue. Events are continually resignified as described in the notion of après-coup (see Chapter 7). There is therefore no one-to-one rela-tionship between present and past and never a 'pure past', and yet, of course, the past has an effect on the present and needs to be 'owned' while at the same time the present of the analytic encoun-ter has an effect on the past so that the past becomes different. There is also the past that can never be known, that which is inscribed in the body with no representation, the place that is present by its absence, what Botella (2014) calls "memory without recollection" and the areas of psychic 'blank' which Green considers to be "the fundamental psychotic kernel" (Green, 1975). The understanding of 'memory', the role and nature of early trauma and whether and how its traces can be captured in the analytic setting, have been and still are important areas of debate.

Central to the clinical situation is the ambiguity between past and present: that of a present which thinks it has no past, or of a past which doesn't realise how present it is. The function of the analyst is to enable the 'then' to become now and the 'now' to become then. 'Here and now' is purely a reference to a technical approach which addresses the immediate experience as being the one which is most alive and where change can take place. However, it needs to be remembered that the 'here and now' is far from devoid of temporality and plays on the whole essential temporal basis on which psychoanalysis is constructed by creating the optimal conditions for the 'there and then' to come fully into view in the 'here and now' of the clinical encounter. More precisely it is the continually resignified past that we call the *internal world* which comes into view. The 'here and now' only makes sense insofar as it retains its temporal dimension and incorporates the ambiguity of the two dimensions of temporality. It is precisely the play of the various 'times' and 'locations' in the now of the session which fosters symbolisation, even while technically the transformative power is in the 'now'. Forgetting this is a source of impasse. It is the task of the analyst to keep hold of these different locations and these different times which appear to have disappeared from the scene even while interpreting that which is most alive in the room. In the consulting room everything has meaning in the here and now but none of it is simply here and now. Here and now always refers to that which is not apparently there, the unconscious, the lost connection, the absent other, the non-represented (see Chapter 11). This is the essence of psychoanalysis.

My focus on the development of symbolic capacity and its connection with temporality 'in the presence of the object' (that is, within the clinical situation) is the thread which runs throughout this book. I address, in particular, clinical situations in which awareness of emotions is not available and in which there is a significant lack of connection between emotion or sensation and idea, and in which necessary representation is unavailable. They pose a particular challenge and I suggest that they, above all, necessitate a particular mode of attentiveness in order to capture minute details of the patient's experience as and when it becomes available, both consciously and unconsciously, to both parties. In these more autistic and schizoid situations I see it as important not to confuse the patient's survival strategies and desperate attempts to maintain equilibrium with a destructive urge. Or put another way, the attack or refusal to take in is often linked in the first instance to a panic about the collapse of a vital equilibrium to deal with the 'incomprehensi-ble' outside and inside pieces of experience and sensation, or to protect from an expected catastrophe if change of any kind were to take place, or if an emotional experience and connection is pro-moted. This is not to deny the role of envy and extreme destructiveness.

The necessary 'presence of the object' is one which is of a par-ticular kind. It involves what Bion calls 'containment', as represent-ative of the analyst's (the mother's) love. To this I would add the role of pleasure, the importance of the mother's basic pleasure in the child's care and the psychoanalyst's basic pleasure in the psycho-analytic work, both of which involve a 'giving over', the soil from which the more intuitive aspects emerge and keep contact alive, in situations which can become empty or deathly.

This book is made up of some previously published and in most cases modified papers, and some new chapters.

Chapter 1, 'Setting the scene', is just that: it sets the scene for my own ideas by discussing those aspects which in my view are central and essential to the psychoanalytic situation, and sets out my own take on them. The viewpoint is a personal one, primarily the outcome of my clinical experience and the result of my engaging with authors whom I have found helpful to my thinking; in that sense, in Chapter 1 I am setting the scene for the later chapters, and hence it is a much longer chapter than the others which each focus on a particular and circumscribed issue. When discussing the liter-ature I do not aim to cover perspectives from parts of the world with which I am not as familiar and which have not had much influence on my development.

I have engaged in particular with the work of French psychoana-lysts, an interest which, helped by my bilingual and bicultural history, stems from their detailed and complex reading and rereading of Freud, 'making Freud work' as Sechaud put it, and the way in which that 'work' has led different French authors in inter-esting divergent directions (see Birksted-Breen *et al.*, 2010). In par-ticular, the reaction against Lacan and his removal of the body, of affect, of preverbal phenomena from psychoanalysis, has led French authors to develop their own concepts; for instance, Aulagnier's 'pictogram', Anzieu's 'formal signifiers', Roussillon's 'primary sym-bolisation', Cahn's and Roussillon's 'subjectivation'. I have found it of interest to follow these developments in an 'other' psychoanalytic culture; a culture which has been relatively insular until recently, albeit with an influence from Winnicott and Bion via Green in particular, and which has creatively forged its own theoretical developments and concepts while maintaining a strong basis in Freudian theory. Resonances and differences can lead to a fruitful dialogue between psychoanalytic cultures. This is always from the point of view of my own psychoanalytic background in 'British psychoanalysis'.

Chapter 2, to some extent, continues to 'set the scene' but focuses more specifically on questions of feminine and masculine identity. I develop my view that the construction of sexual identity is connected with issues of modalities of thought. This is developed clinically in subsequent chapters.

In Chapter 3, I focus on femininity and propose a duality at the heart of femininity. In Chapter 4, I consider sexuality as it manifests in the consulting room, making a distinction between 'noisy and silent sexuality'. Chapter 5 is about eating disorders, eating having a connection with sexuality and the body, and I look again specifically at its manifestation in the consulting room.

After focusing on women, and proposing a distinction between a 'positive' and a 'negative' femininity, I became interested in masculinity. As McDougall (2000, p. 158) writes:

> Freud, who was constantly preoccupied with the difficulties that faced the little girl-child on path to attaining adult femininity leaves us to suppose, by his silence in the respect, that the attainment of adult masculinity is an effortless achievement, which is far from being the case, as every analyst knows.

The development of masculinity is in fact very fragile and the relationship of boys to their fathers is much more complex than only the castration fear described by Freud. Cultural elements have often masked this fragility.

Looking at the masculine element (in men and women) led me to make a distinction between phallus and penis-as-link. This is the theme of Chapter 6, in which I introduce the notion of 'penis-as-link', a reference to the mental function of linking and structuring, to be distinguished both from the phallus and the penis in its purely bodily reality.

While questions of temporality never left the scene, I go on to focus specifically on temporality in all the remaining chapters, discussing it from different angles and in particular as it inheres in the analytic process itself and in processes of transformation. Intertwined with this is my focus on the development of symbolic thinking, intimately linked with temporality, with notions of containment and of *reverie* as a cornerstone of the psychoanalytic enterprise and that which promotes change. I turn to these, to the psychic processes and mode of attentiveness of the psychoanalyst, in the remaining chapters (Chapters 8, 9, 10 and 11). I discuss and elaborate on Bion's notion of *reverie*, in particular the significance of the visual image which comes unbidden into the analyst's mind and how the maximally receptive mode of attentiveness can offer a bridge with patients who are difficult to reach and those whose psychic space is restricted. This needs to take place in counterpoint with an 'analysing' function, in what I call 'bi-ocularity' in Chapter 11.

I chose to order the chapters not purely in terms of when they were written, but more in a way which makes sense as a book. In actual fact, the movement in the book, from sexuality to symbolisation, and to the psychic work of the psychoanalyst and phenomena of the psychoanalytic pair, reflects the development of my thinking and the movement of my focus of interest over the years such that a number of the earlier chapters tend on the whole to have been written earlier than the later ones. Chapters 6 to 11 were written in that order and reflect how my ideas built up over time.

Nevertheless, the various themes of temporality, sexuality, disturbances in the area of identity, disturbances in modalities of thought, stasis versus change, all interweave throughout the chapters, forming a thread. I approach these themes from different angles with one or the other being the overarching focus at a particular time – sexuality, temporality, modalities of thought, the mind of the psychoanalyst – but all these themes are involved throughout and form part of my thinking. They all derive from my work in the consulting room. The nodal points of my thinking are around the concepts I introduced of 'penis-as-link' (Chapter 6), of 'reverberation time' (Chapter 9) and of 'bi-ocularity' and polytemporal (Chapter 11). They address the psychic work required of both patient and psychoanalyst.

Continuity and change is something which is relevant to the very understanding of what makes up psychoanalysis as a theory and as a professional activity. Issues about conservatism versus innovation are central. The mushrooming of different schools as well as of the many therapies deriving from psychoanalysis make it necessary to identify the fundamental frame which makes up the boundaries of psychoanalysis. In my view these fundamentals would have to include the notions of psychic reality, of unconscious processes, of phantasy, of transference, of internal objects, of primal scene with its reference to the difference between the sexes and the generations and the positioning of the self in relation to it. Important developments since Freud have taken place within these parameters mostly in relation to primitive phenomena and borderline and psychotic structures, creating a potential for important dialogue: for instance, archaic and symbolic forms of representation within a Kleinian model in which phantasy is always present as the psychical representative of the drive, contrasting with notions of unrepresented states of mind, blank psychosis (Donnet and Green, 1973), "unrepresented forms of remembering" (Green, 2012a, p. 1246) and "memory of the id" (Botella, 2010).

Multilingualism in psychoanalysis can be enriching or dangerous: enriching when there is a deep understanding of the different languages, and dangerous when concepts are appropriated without consideration for the total 'grammar', leading to distortion, reductionism and misunderstandings.

As I wrote in an editorial for the *International Journal of Psychoanalysis*:

Deep knowledge about other theories is rare as it involves immersion in the specific analytic culture including its clinical practice. Few people are truly bilingual, and those who are will tell you that there is no equivalence between words and concepts due to the polysemy of meanings and associations. Concepts come with a web of associations and a specific framework. As White (2010) points out (p. 818): "The circles of meanings of words seldom completely coincide from one language to another". At best, perhaps, we can only find a 'transitional space' between 'languages' (Luepnitz, 2009), enhanced by each approach rather than succumbing to a reductive and impoverished attempt to do a 'literal' translation. To take a concept out of one body of theory without having a deep knowledge of that theory is in danger of distorting the concept. There is a fine line between distortion of a theory and valid elaboration. Being an 'outsider' has also its advantages, as the clinician knows, as long as the total 'grammar' of the other language is understood.

(Birksted–Breen, 2010)

Blass also points out the impossibility of dialogue if "concerns and different understandings of basic human nature and of what constitutes analytic change" are not acknowledged (2015). I would add that in my view analytic change often involves a changed way of thinking of 'humanity' (see Chapter 12).

'The Work of Psychoanalysis', the title of this book, puts the temporal factor and transformation centre stage, using 'work' in the original sense Freud used it to refer to a specific psychical activity as in 'psychic work' and 'the dream-work'. It implies a duration, the time of necessary psychical activity if transformation is to be achieved, as in 'the work of mourning' and 'working through'. It also implies something which goes beyond conscious activity. In that sense it differs from the usual notion of work which implies a deliberate conscious activity. On the contrary, this 'work' is one which cannot be commandeered and in fact is impeded when willed. To take place it requires specific conditions, another central thread to this book.

Note

1 Love in infant or mother or both increases rather than decreases the obstruction partly because love is inseparable from envy of the object so loved, partly because it is felt to arouse envy and jealousy in a third object that is excluded. The part played by love may escape notice because envy, rivalry and hate obscure it, although hate would not exist if love were not present.

(Bion, 1962, p. 10)

1

SETTING THE SCENE

Once the stage is set, psychoanalysis 'gets to work', inevitably, immediately and as of its own accord. Transference, repetition, regressive modes of thinking are set in motion. The scene includes an analysand who is suffering and making a demand, a psychoanalyst who is offering help, is receptive and unhurried, sessions at an intensive frequency and at regular times in the same place, and with the analysand in the reclining position. Bion (1979b, p. 247) writes:

> In analysis, the patient comes into contact with the analyst by coming to the consulting room and engaging in what he thinks is a conversation which he hopes to benefit by in some way. Likewise the analyst probably expects some benefit to occur – to both parties. The patient or the analyst says something. It is curious that this has an effect – it disturbs the relationship between the two people. This would be true if nothing was said, if they remained silent.

But the 'scene' is above all a reference to the scenarios which will, from the first moment, be created by the patient with the participation of the analyst, with whose own scenes they will interlock. There will be a constant process of locking and interlocking, which it is the task of the analyst to monitor and reflect upon. A feature of the scene is the implied 'other', be it another mental space, another realm, another time, another object, in short a fantasy scenario, even while the 'here and now' of the two people in the room is clambering. Whether we call it 'psychic reality', 'unconscious', 'illusion', 'phantasy', 'transference', this element is a defining feature of psychoanalysis. The stage is set in order to facilitate maximal

11

observation of this other scene, if the analyst is able to weather the 'emotional storm' (Bion, 1979b, p. 247). From this encounter develops a 'language', one which gives meaning to experience. The psychoanalytic interpretation is made within this context, "a context whose co-ordinates are fixed by the patient's demand, the analyst's expectations and the contract defining the analytic situation" (Baranger, 1993, p. 15). This is the frame without which there is no stage.

Like classical theatre it has a unity of space and time. It has rules, what Freud called 'the fundamental rule' or the rule of free association, a rule which is broken due to the fear of recognising unconscious anxieties (Green, 2000), and this is meaningful in terms of where and when it is broken. The analytic space has a 'curtain up' and 'curtain down' on the inner world and a particular way of talking which can appear strange to the outsider, which is why the record of a session can seem meaningless. On this stage, the internal world is played out, with a strict beginning and a predetermined end. The scenes become familiar as they repeat themselves with variations of cast, set and historical period, revealing desires and defensive movements. Within this frame, memories, scenes, dream images interweave and join up to construct a 'story', a story reminiscent of the past like Plato's shadows on the cave walls. How close or how far is it to what actually happened? How much is reconstruction and how much is a new construction? In any case, as Laplanche writes, "Historical reconstruction in psychoanalysis cannot be understood except as a reinterpretation of more archaic scenarios" (1974, p. 468).

The physical setting is sometimes 'silent', just a background which becomes assumed, as Momigliano (1988) put it, "like the darkness in a cinema, like the silence in a concert hall" (p. 608). For other patients the physical setting becomes the object of deep attachment or, on the contrary, persecution. The couch can be experienced as the lap or womb of the analyst, which offers the hope of a new beginning, a return to an idealised past or to good moments from the past. It can be connected to the sensation of the body moulding into the mother's body, an 'embodied memory' (Leuzinger-Bohleber, 2008) or it can be an 'embodied phantasy' (Bronstein, 2015). On the contrary, the couch can be experienced as dangerous and the out-of-view analyst intolerable. The reclining position and the necessary 'passivation' (Green, 1986) arouses fears connected with femininity (with its refusal as 'bedrock'), castration, homosexuality, seduction (Perelberg, 2003) and loss of control. There is a counterpart to this in the psychoanalyst's necessary 'passivity' which Scarfone refers to as 'passibilité',[1] a reference to the capacity to receive the transference, to being "disposed to being touched"[2] (2014, p. 8). It is not unlike Bion's notion of containment, but it emphasises the preparedness to be taken over, or I would say a preparedness to 'giving oneself over' in order to emphasise the aspect of this being in the service of the patient.

It may also be said that the psychoanalytic setting is a 'participant' if we take 'setting' in the widest sense to include its symbolic meaning. Psychoanalysis is never just a two-person affair, in spite of appearances. There is always a triumvirate of which 'the setting' is one important party: patient-psychoanalyst-setting, each of equal importance. The setting is the guardian of the analysis, a silent participant. There are two people in the room, but the shadow of a third is present. This presence/absence is significant and essential in defining the setting in its Oedipal configuration; the configuration comes in different forms, with the paternal as unspoken 'absent other' imposing a rule on the analytic pair, or in the form of the analyst as distinct from the analysis, as when Winnicott says to his patient at the end of the session: "I am coming in between you and analysis and sending you off" (1986).[3] This calls for the analyst's own bisexual functioning.

The setting marks the 'rules', both spatial and temporal. It marks the prohibition on incest and defines difference within the triangular situation. Steiner, introducing Segal's ideas, suggests that the attack on structure is the hallmark of the death instinct: "Anything that emphasises difference is an expression of structure and the ultimate goal of the death instinct is the achievement of randomness, of chaos, and of a structure-less state in which nothing exists which can give rise to envy" (Steiner, 1997, p. 7).

By restricting physical action, talking takes a central role, not only in the content of what is communicated but also as an 'action'. The pair talking/listening become libidinised as the central mode of exchange. Words are exploited in their ambiguity and double meanings. Freud made use of the "imagic aspect of words – the phonetic similarities of homophones, puns and alliterations" (Litowitz, 2013). Language may be used to communicate or to obfuscate. Language is also a vehicle which comes from outside the dyad

13

and disturbances are reflected in how language is used. French authors note the "transference on to speech" (Donnet, 2001, p. 136) in the analytic situation. Language is also imbued with pre-verbal elements, the sound and musical quality, for example, of certain words, something which conveys meaning in itself, and with phantasy elements connected with the relation to objects. The latter is observed clearly with patients who speak more than one language learned in different circumstances and times, and who prefer defensively, for instance, the more 'neutral' language acquired later in life for their analysis rather than the 'maternal' one. When I pointed out to a supervisee that it seemed 'mad' that she and her patient spoke in English when they had a shared mother tongue, she was taken aback at the idea, saying it seemed 'incestuous'.

Bleger (1967) considers the psychoanalytic situation to be the patient's most primitive 'family institution'. He describes the 'meta-ego' as being that institution which exists silently in the background and which is necessary for the formation of the ego. The frame often goes unnoticed but it contains the first stages of the organisation of the personality, specifically that of symbiosis. Hence the frame is the receiver of the psychotic part of the personality. He compares it with the body image and the phenomenon of the ghost member:

> we must accept that institutions and the frame always make up a 'ghost world' ... for Melanie Klein, transference repeats the primitive object relationships, but I think that what is still most primitive (the non-differentiation) repeats itself in the frame. . . . The frame is the most primitive part of the personality, it is the fusion ego–body–world, on whose immobility depends the formation, existence, and differentiation (of the ego, the object, the body image, the body, the mind).
>
> (Bleger, 1967, pp. 514–515)

He adds that it is the most regressive, psychotic part of the patient, "*for every type of patient*" (p. 516, italics added).

The frame gets noticed only when it is broken, creating disturbance in the patient (for instance, if the analyst has to cancel unexpectedly or relocates). Faimberg (2014) suggests that Bleger resolved the paradox that it is necessary to overcome the ritualisation of the frame while maintaining the analytic frame by positing that there are two frames, the one maintained by the psychoanalyst and consciously accepted by the patient, the other the frame of the fantasy world, the 'ghost world' on to which the patient projects. Donnet (2001) adds to this that the transference on to the setting goes unnoticed when the analyst similarly idealises the setting, and argues that this transference needs to be worked through and dissolved.

When we separate language, setting, mode, we do so artificially. In the clinical encounter one or the other may be more prominent but they form part of a whole. An interpretation will be made in a particular way. For instance, it can be 'saturated' or 'unsaturated' (Ferro, 1996), or ambiguous (De M'Uzan, 1983); it can be addressed to the secondary process of the patient, or it may aim to impact at the level of primary process. How the interpretation is phrased rests on important theoretical differences (Aisenstein, 2007). The patient will also hear it in a particular way. The interpretation may be experienced as expressing the love of the analyst or on the contrary may be felt as an act of aggression. The analyst's voice may unconsciously convey a message congruent or not with the words, or the patient may interpret it as if the analyst has become an internal object. The voice of the analyst itself with its sensorial and musical aspects may be cathected, and this also belongs to the setting.

Part of the setting is *also* the quality of the object's presence with its specific psychoanalytic mode of attentiveness, different from what is experienced outside sessions. I will come back to this in the section on the analytic attitude and go into it in greater depth in the latter chapters of this book.

While there is a large body of literature on the role of 'insight' or 'interpretation' versus 'experience', in my view this is another artificial division, since insight is part of the experience. The literature on therapeutic action and curative factors which addresses this division[4] is usually part of a larger theoretical debate; for instance, between relational analysts who emphasise the 'experience' and Freudian/Kleinian psychoanalysts who emphasise 'interpretation'.[5]

'Insight' is not a simple notion. It does not appear as a psychoanalytic concept in Laplanche and Pontalis. For me, 'insight' includes knowledge at different levels of consciousness and is mostly different from simple intellectual understanding (Grinberg, 1980). It is evidenced in a different way of experiencing external and internal reality. Insight is something which builds up during an analysis via the reintegration of aspects of the self and a change in the relationship to reality and objects, including the analyst. Changes bring further changes. Psychoanalytic insight is thus not monolithic and takes effect at various levels of consciousness. Insight given by the analyst in the form of interpretation is received in complex ways, which may or may not result in the patient acquiring insight. In my view, the psychoanalyst needs to convey her or his own understanding in a way which will be appropriate to the patient at a particular moment. This may or may not come in a form which describes or explains (see Chapter 11). Even when interpretations are given in a way which describe or explain, insight will in general not be remembered as such when the analysis is over (Segal, 1962). The analysand will usually just remember, besides the general experience, a few moments which stood out, for positive or negative reasons, and very often not those the analyst would consider important. What one hopes is that the patient will have developed, as Ferro puts it, "tools that allow the development and creation of thought, that is the mental apparatus for dreaming, feeling and thinking" (2006, p. 990).

Frequency

Derivatives of psychoanalysis use a lesser frequency of sessions. The goals are usually more specific and circumscribed. The psychoanalyst is not uninterested in the patient's symptoms, in their appearance, disappearance and replacement by other symptoms, but the removal of symptoms is not the primary aim, as in some more focused forms of therapy.

The psychoanalyst is addressing what I call a 'difficulty with living'. Cooper (2005) distinguishes psychotherapy and psychoanalysis as follows: psychotherapy is 'an event' while psychoanalysis is 'an experience'. It is 'psychoanalysis as an experience' which meets what I call the 'difficulty with living' and not 'psychotherapy as an event', which may nevertheless give short-term solutions.

Psychoanalysis is, by its nature, a very slow process, often painfully so for both parties. Freud uses the image of the battlefield to convey the strength of the conflicting forces which become played out with "the transference becoming the battlefield on which all the mutually struggling forces should meet one another" (1917, p. 454). He is here

16

referring to the forces of repression and "the tenacity or adhesiveness of the libido, which dislikes leaving objects that it has once cathected" (1917, p. 455). In his later work, Freud relates the difficulty in making changes to the conflict between the life and death drives and in particular to masochism and the sense of guilt (1923). The disagreement with Freud's latter formulation of the duality of Eros and the death drive is often on the grounds of its biological basis. Some see the origins of destructivity in environmental impingement. Others have wanted to retain the fundamental nature of the opposition but without recourse to biological substrate. Denis (2011), for instance, prefers to talk about principles of psychic functioning, which he calls 'principles of organisation and disorganisation'.[6] Segal writes that it is possible to formulate the conflict between the life and death instincts in purely psychological terms:

> Birth confronts us with the experience of needs. In relation to that experience there can be two reactions, and both, I think, are invariably present in all of us, though in varying proportions. One, to seek satisfaction for the needs: that is life-promoting and leads to object seeking, love, and eventually object concern. The other is the drive to annihilate the need, to annihilate the perceiving experiencing self, as well as anything that is perceived.
>
> (Segal, 1993, p. 55)

However we conceive of this, we cannot but be impressed in the clinical situation by the intensity of the struggle between positive and negative forces. While the destructive forces can be mitigated with time, the 'battle' cannot but take place. This is why psychoanalysis is never a quick and simple affair, and why development can never be simple and straightforward, and, most of all, but not only, for those individuals whose life experiences have come to weaken the life forces and strengthen the destructive ones.

The intensity of daily sessions concentrates psychic life into the analysis in such a way that important processes are heightened and psychoanalysis takes on a life of its own. It is in this sense that it becomes 'an experience' rather than just being 'an event'. Danielle Quinodoz (1992, p. 630) describes it thus:

> the frequency of sessions in psychoanalysis allows a very different process from that of psychotherapy, and ... this difference may

be likened to the difference between cinematography and still photography: if you project slides at a low frequency, you see the frames one after another, but once you exceed a certain threshold, movement appears, and you have transferred from still photography to the realm of cinematography. Both are processes in their own right, but they are different in nature.

Daily sessions give the analyst a greater possibility of being in touch with the unconscious themes in the patient's material and specifically in the transference (Sandler, 1993). Defences can loosen without immediately building up again. It is an observable clinical fact that increasing the frequency of weekly sessions has a significant impact on the depth of the affective experience. It also makes the weekend break more prominent, which in turn enables the analysis of the anxieties, phantasies and defensive positions aroused by it.

The level of involvement of the patient is not the same at the lesser frequency.

Freud already noted that while psychotherapy has its uses, the intensity of the passions ignited by 'undiluted' psychoanalysis is 'explosive' but necessary. He writes:

> The psycho-analyst knows that he is working with highly explosive forces and that he needs to proceed with as much caution and conscientiousness as a chemist ... I am certainly not in favour of giving up the harmless methods of treatment. For many cases they are sufficient, and, when all is said, human society has no more use for the *furor sanandi* than for any other fanaticism. But to believe that the psychoneuroses are to be conquered by operating with harmless little remedies is grossly to under-estimate those disorders both as to their origin and their practical importance. No; in medical practice there will always be room for the '*ferrum*' and the '*ignis*' side by side with the '*medicina*' and in the same way we shall never be able to do without a strictly regular, undiluted psycho-analysis which is not afraid to handle the most dangerous mental impulses and to obtain mastery over them for the benefit of the patient.
>
> (Freud, 1915, pp. 170–172)

The high frequency of sessions and the use of the couch with the psychoanalyst out of view, with as little interference from reality as possible, invites a regression to the world of the unconscious and the dream as well as a 'temporal regression'.

Traditionally, French psychoanalysts have been more concerned with topographic and formal regression and British psychoanalysts with temporal regression. It may be noted that the question of frequency in fact varies with different psychoanalytic cultures. Freud himself would see his patients six times a week, while the most usual frequency of psychoanalysis is now four or five times a week. Of course in Freud's days psychoanalysis lasted months rather than years, but even that could seem like a burden, especially as it often meant relocating to Vienna. Nevertheless, what Freud remarked then still holds true today:

> No one would expect a man to lift a heavy table with two fingers as if it were a light stool, or to build a large house in the time it would take to put up a wooden hut; but as soon as it becomes a question of the neuroses – which do not seem so far to have found a proper place in human thought – even intelligent people forget that a necessary proportion must be observed between time, work and success.
>
> (Freud, 1913, pp. 128–129)

While Freud noted that interruptions to the flow of sessions disrupted the work (the 'Monday crust'), surprisingly he never referred to the impact of his long summer breaks (De Urtubey, 1995). De Urtubey also noted how at the beginning of his career Freud announced to Fliess every September that he had no more clients and would soon be ruined, only to complain a month later of being overwhelmed by their numbers, which suggests that many of them ended at the summer break.

In France there has been a tradition of three-times-a-week psychoanalysis based on the idea that it is important for the analysand to have a time when he or she can take over the 'analysing function' and a time of 'working through' in the *après-coup* between sessions, the days without sessions also coming to represent the necessary 'third'.[7] This frequency is deemed suitable specifically for neurotic patients who can benefit from the 'cure type'.[8] The theoretical basis of French psychoanalysis has traditionally rested on the aim of freeing the associative process and encouraging the 'analysing function' of the patient, while the British approach is more concerned with the relationship itself at all times and the defensive processes associated with it. Traditionally, borderline patients in France would be offered a more 'psychotherapeutic approach', which may mean once or twice a week face to face, but may also mean more than three sessions a week due to the greater need for support and their lesser ability to do psychic work on their own. Psychoanalytic thinking in France developed after the 1960s under the influence of Winnicott and Bion, and, as in other parts of the world, with the preponderance of non–neurotic cases coming for psychoanalysis. While Lacan and many French psychoanalysts mainly used Freud's early model of the mind, Green and others saw Freud's structural model to be fundamental. Green (2010) describes the potential created clinically by this later model and by the conceptualisation of a death instinct, enabling understanding of non–neurotic structures dominated by acting out and repetition compulsion, by resistance to change, by masochism and a deep sense of guilt. Defences were understood to be no longer mainly those of repression but also those of splitting, disavowal and foreclosure which harm symbolic functioning. His debt here is to Bion's focus on the destruction of "the apparatus for thinking" (1962). Green insists on the difference between the two models, one model which has to do with conscience, namely *un*-conscious, *pre*-conscious, conscious, and the other model with Id-ego-super-ego, where the Id is not equivalent to the unconscious; the Id is closely linked to the body and made up of affects and drives rather than representations, as is the case in the notion of the unconscious (Green, 2010). What is in the unconscious is already represented; hence the importance of the dream, which in contemporary theory is seen as a form of thinking and transformation. The focus thus becomes the transformation of impulses which may be linked to very early trauma or transgenerational transmissions into unconscious thing presentations (Birksted-Breen *et al.*, 2010). From there they can be transformed into words in the analytic process.

In this line of thinking on the more severe pathologies the emphasis is on the lack of representation and the need to reach, through regressive processes, a 'figuration' (Botella and Botella, 2001), that is a representation where there was a blank. C. Botella (2014) talks about 'memory without recollection' and S. Botella (2010) of a 'memory of the Id', a memory that has no representations, no traces which can be remembered.[9] She notes that for the Freud of 1937, where the patient was not able to have a memory, patient and analyst could produce a construction with the help of regressive modes of thinking (S. Botella, 2010).

Frame and process

Freud did not use the word 'setting'. The setting *was* the method he developed. It grew naturally along with his discoveries and understanding from the 'rest-cures' of nineteenth-century Vienna prescribed by psychiatrists for 'nervous diseases', the cathartic treatment of Breuer and the hypnotherapy favoured by Charcot, finally emerging as 'the talking cure' so named by his patient Anna O, who also referred to it jokingly as 'chimney-sweeping'. A note by Strachey indicates that both of these expressions were in English in the original text (1910, p. 13).

There has been a tendency to separate aspects of the setting which are 'concrete' from aspects which have to do with what takes place within the situation. Green (2005) distinguishes what he calls 'the casing ... constituted by the number and duration of the sessions, the periodicity of the encounters, the modalities of payment, and so on' from 'the active matrix ... composed of the patient's free association, floating attention and listening, stamped with the analyst's benevolent neutrality, forming a *dialogical* couple in which the analysis is rooted' (p. 33). Donnet (2005) speaks of the 'analytic site' and the 'analysing situation'. The notion of 'analytic site' is one which allows for different modalities of treatment (including psychodrama) appropriate to different pathologies, making use nevertheless of a psychoanalytic process. What matters for him is the 'internal setting'. In the same vein, Parsons (2007, p. 1443) makes a distinction between external and internal setting:

> The internal analytic setting is a psychic arena in which reality is defined by such concepts as symbolism, fantasy, transference and unconscious meaning.... Just as the external setting defines and protects a spatiotemporal arena in which patient and analyst can conduct the work of analysis, so the internal setting defines and protects an area of the analyst's mind where whatever happens, including what happens to the external setting, can be considered from a psychoanalytic viewpoint.

21

compare Bleger 1967

Against using only extrinsic criteria, Donnet's notion of 'site' covers material aspects of the setting but also the analyst's position, including his or her countertransference, his theory and also the 'fundamental rule' of saying everything that comes to mind, with its inherent paradox that it is impossible to follow. Not all analysts announce the fundamental rule. Green (2005) advocates announcing it in its role of a law above the two parties and hence inscribing itself as a third. He adds that it is a complex injunction because the patient is asked to say everything 'but *to do nothing*', and hence it encourages a mode of waking *reverie*.

The setting is also often called 'the frame'. Milner (1952) was the first to use the notion of frame, comparing the analytic setting to the frame of a painting: the "temporal spatial frame [which] marks off the special kind of reality of the psycho-analytical session" (p. 183). 'Casing' and 'frame' speak immediately of an 'inside' and an 'outside', and of a hard, firm boundary between the two; they suggest a protected private space for inner thoughts and feelings. A constant and immutable frame which delineates between 'inside' the sessions and 'outside' enables resurrections of the past and allows what Green (1986) called a 'private madness'.

If one thinks of the frame as not only a spatial and temporal one but also as a 'mental frame', one can see that what seemed like a clear distinction is not so clear. Perhaps it is more appropriate to talk about conditions which delineate a situation in which different levels of meaning are generated. To take this the other way around, the significance of the frame is that within the frame words take on symbolic meanings, and nothing 'inside' said by either analyst or patient can be taken at face value because the 'inside' of the frame is in the realm of metaphor.

While the frame is a static metaphor, we speak of an analytic journey. Patients often dream of analysis as a voyage. Hilda Doolittle, poet, novelist, memoirist and analysand of Freud, described her psychoanalysis like this:

> We travel far in thought, in imagination or in the realm of memory. Events happened as they happened, not all of them of course but here and there a memory or a fragment of a dream-picture is actual, is real, is like a work of art or is a work of art … there are priceless broken fragments that are meaningless until we find the other broken bits to match them.
>
> (Doolittle, 1971 pp. 41–42)

Travel and place, movement and structure: the counterpoints. It is the stillness, firmness and constancy of the frame that enables travel to faraway times and unfamiliar mental lands. Two sides of a coin: stillness, repetition, fixity of the one; fluidity, capriciousness, discontinuity of the other. Without 'frame' there is no psychoanalysis. It is what gives rise to the process. The utterances of the psychoanalyst have meaning only within that setting, a meaning which is both about 'now' and about some other time or some other place. In psychoanalysis one often travels in time and space *without* knowing it. Patients repeat the past 'instead of remembering' (Freud, 1914), believing it to be the present, and this temporality which is neither past nor present, or more precisely at the same time past and present, is the psychoanalyst's main lens. Repeating is the psychoanalytic form of remembering. However, the role of phantasy, which continuously shapes mental content, adds complexity to any notion of simple remembering. In that sense, 'here and now' is at one and the same time 'there and then', of the past and of the 'other place' of unconscious thinking. There and then, understood in this way, are themselves in a state of complex interaction, making up a multifaceted 'now'.

The analytic process is characterised by repetition and at the same time movement following mutative moments; Pichon-Riviere, whose work has been very influential in Latin America, describes it as a 'spiral process' (1958):

> The superimposition of the spiral's curves illustrates this mixture of repetition and non-repetition which may be observed in the characteristic events in a person's fate, this combined movement of deepening into the past and constructing the future which characterizes the analytic process.
>
> (Baranger *et al.*, 1983, p. 9)

The analytic attitude, evenly suspended attention and neutrality

The analytic attitude, the basic attitude and position of the psychoanalyst, is part of the setting. Freud warned against therapeutic zeal which contrasts with an attitude of evenly suspended attention, the latter requiring on the contrary the suspension of attention to goals. Donnet (2001) compares the psychoanalytic situation with La

Fontaine's fable 'The Labourer and His Children', in which a rich farmer tells his children before he dies that there is treasure hidden on the land. After his death the children get to work on the land and, due to their efforts, the land becomes more productive. The moral of the fable is that the work *is* the treasure; there was no hidden money. Similarly with psychoanalysis, it is the journey itself which is to be valued.

The psychoanalytic journey takes us across the lands of one's memory, emotions and relationships to others. This in itself brings a certain freedom of thought, though not a freedom from the conflicts which are an inevitable part of the human condition. It is the importance of the journey itself, which demarcates psychoanalysis from some other forms of therapy and makes its comparison in terms of 'cost–effectiveness' or measurement of 'results' difficult, as these take place in a different realm, the one in the realm of values and meanings, the other in the realm of symptoms and behaviours. Nevertheless, there is an inherent tension between the wish to reduce suffering and the require-ment to be 'without memory and desire', as Bion put it. The paradox is that it is that latter attitude which enables suffering to be reduced.

The attitude of evenly suspended attention and more recent derivatives of it mark out psychoanalysis from other treatments and are in my view essential. As Donnet suggests, '[the analyst] returns to [evenly suspended attention] in the same way as the arm of a magnet keeps returning to the direction of the North Pole'[10] (2010, p. 707). A departure from evenly suspended attention is what indi-cates that an enactment is taking place and is cause for reflection. This is particularly likely with borderline patients whose predomi-nant tendency is to act out.

Freud characterised the attitude necessary for the analyst as one of 'neutrality'. This has been, and still is, a highly debated topic encom-passing such concepts as countertransference, *field* and enactment.

The aim of neutrality is to allow as much as possible to come from the patient. Segal writes that the psychoanalyst undertakes

> as part of the setting ... to provide that the analyst shall do nothing to blur the development of the transference, that he shall be there as a person whose sole function is to understand sympathetically and to communicate to the patient such relevant

knowledge as he has acquired at the moment when the analysand is most ready to understand it.

(Segal, 1962, p. 213)

Viderman (1979) took the view that "observance of the classical rules ... alone can give us some assurance against surreptitious adulteration through countertransference" (p. 290). Casement (1982) also describes how relaxation of the frame avoids analytic understanding. Many have argued against 'neutrality' on the grounds that the analyst can never be neutral, and can never not 'blur' the transference. It is an ambiguous concept "that silently garnered important operational meanings, first in relation to suggestion, then in relation to transference provocation, and finally in relation to id, superego, and ego analysis" (Makari, 1997, p. 1232). Freud referred to neutrality (in German, 'indifferenz') only once, in 1915, in his observations on transference love, and in relation to the positive transference. He noted:

In my opinion, therefore, we ought not to give up the neutrality towards the patient, which we have acquired through keeping the counter-transference in check. I have already let it be understood the analytic technique requires of the physician that he should deny to the patient who is craving for love the satisfaction she demands. The treatment must be carried out in abstinence. By this I do not mean physical abstinence alone, nor yet the deprivation of everything that the patient desires, for perhaps no sick person could tolerate this.

(Freud, 1915, pp. 164–165)

He was advocating neutrality so that the patient can feel

safe enough to allow all her preconditions for loving, all the phantasies springing from her sexual desires, all the detailed characteristics of her state of being in love, to come to light; and from these she will herself open the way to the infantile roots of her love.

(Freud, 1915, p. 166)

He went on to say, "the work then aims at uncovering the patient's infantile object-choice and the phantasies woven round it" (p. 167).

The idea of neutrality also comes with a warning against therapeutic zeal and educational purposes in his 'Recommendations to Physicians Practising Psycho–Analysis' (1912), although he does not use the word, and in this meaning it is closer to the notion of evenly suspended attention.

Interest in countertransference developed in the 1950s and brought with it a controversy as to whether it is best understood mainly as a result of the patient's projections, hence a useful source of information for the analyst, or as a result of the arousal of the analyst's own neurotic conflicts and transference to the patient. Freud himself considered the analyst's feelings to be a response due to the analyst's unconscious feelings, his 'transference' to the patient; hence the need for regular periods of analysis. Klein mainly endorsed Freud's view that countertransference comes from the analyst (Spillius, 1992).

Heimann, on the other hand, came to consider countertransference as one of the analyst's most important tools, "an instrument of research into the patient's unconscious" (1950, p. 81). She published her short paper in the *International Journal of Psychoanalysis* in 1950. Independently (Etchegoyen, 1991), Racker published his paper with similar ideas in the *International Journal of Psychoanalysis* in 1953, having already presented them to the Argentine Psychoanalytic Association in 1948. While Racker's studies are more systematic and complete (he discusses in particular how countertransference operates in three ways, as an obstacle, as an instrument and as a field, and distinguishes between concordant and complementary countertransference), Heimann only returned to the theme in passing. Etchegoyen describes how "when Racker presented his work to the Argentine Psychoanalytic Association in 1948, he caused unease, and an important analyst said haughtily that the best thing for an analyst to whom 'those things' happen was for him to re–analyse himself" (p. 265). In London too, Heimann's ideas caused unease. Spillius *et al.* have described this: "According to Pearl King, Klein asked Heimann to withdraw her paper [on countertransference] in 1950 (King, 1983, p. 6). Heimann refused to retract her paper" (p. 354). In 1955 Heimann made a statement that she no longer wished to be considered as a member of the Klein group. Within the British Independent group, Heimann's paper is considered to be seminal.

The idea that countertransference is a response to the patient that should be distinguished from the intrusion of the analyst's own neurosis or transference was rejected by Klein (Spillius *et al.*, 2011). However, Hinshelwood (2008) points to some archival notes which indicate that Klein did acknowledge that projective processes could lead to countertransference reactions and concluded that "countertransference for Klein is more than Freud's judgement that it is the analyst's complexes and internal resistances" (p. 101). Nevertheless, this is still far from considering that countertransference can be a useful tool.

In France, a line of thinking posits countertransference as necessary. In a classic book, Neyrault (1974) argues that the countertransference *precedes* the transference. Laplanche, in line with the Lacanian importance attributed to the desire of the Other, conceives of the analytic situation as a necessary first seduction by the analyst, who makes an offer of psychoanalysis, just as the mother's seduction of the child by her own desire structures the psyche.

In the 1960s and 1970s, influenced by Racker's notion of the analyst as participant observer and the frame of phenomenology (de Bernardi, 2008), Madeleine and Willy Baranger developed their notion of a 'dynamic *field*' (1969), describing the psychoanalytic situation as "a couple field" (p. 809) which is based on an unconscious phantasy that belongs to both parties. This notion of 'field' became very influential in Latin America, less so in Europe, except for Italy where their papers were translated in the 1990s. Their influence was first seen in the work of Ferro (1999), who drew on the work of Bion and of Baranger, and claimed that the basic focus of the analytic relationship is the conscious and unconscious intersubjective processes between analyst and patient, which he refers to as the '*bi-personal field*'.

Intersubjectivity took hold in all parts of the world, for instance, in the USA with Ogden developing his notion of the 'analytic third' (1994) and Grotstein of 'projective transidentification' (2005). And in France, Widlocher (2004) developed his notion of 'co-thinking': "collaborative psychic work leading to interpretive elaboration" in which he describes a "model of two associative fields, two networks of thought that intersect to a greater or lesser extent, forming nodal points" (p. 204).

In the USA, a growing literature on the role of the analyst's subjectivity, more directly influenced by phenomenology and the work of Sullivan (1953), has led to a large literature on 'enactment' considered as unavoidable and constant. Some contemporary analytic trends have abandoned the notion that any kind of aim at neutrality is possible or even desirable.

Lines of influence would require a study in itself. For instance, Duparc (2001) has claimed that notions of the field were developed in France by Viderman in the 1960s, perhaps inspired by Lagache's borrowing from behaviourism in the 1950s. Here I want simply to note the complexity of the development of ideas because it throws a light on why apparently simple notions such as neutrality or enactment are understood very differently, often without this being recognised.

What is clear is that there has been a general move in the conceptualisation of the position of the analyst from a nineteenth-century notion of the objective observing scientist, removed from that which is under observation, towards a more intersubjective perspective which follows a philosophy of science taking account of the observer as part of the field. Gabbard (1995, p. 475) writes of the "growing recognition in all quarters that the analyst is 'sucked in' to the patient's world through an ongoing series of enactments that dislodge the analyst from the traditional position of the objective blank screen". There remains nevertheless a wide variation between how psychoanalysts conceptualise this and work with it clinically. In a review paper on countertransference, Jacobs (1999, p. 575) writes:

> Looking back on the final decades of the twentieth century … future historians of psychoanalysis may well designate this period the countertransference years; for in this time few concepts in our field have gained as much attention, have been as widely explored and written about, and have been the subject of as much controversy as has the question of countertransference and its role in the analytic process. Certainly in America, but also, to a considerable extent worldwide, countertransference and the closely related issues of inter-subjectivity, enactments, self-analysis and the question of neutrality have taken centre stage as matters with which contemporary analysts are much preoccupied.

Those who reject the necessity of neutrality often describe a 'straw man': a cold, unempathic 'blank screen' analyst. In my view neutrality does not mean blank screen. Freud himself never used the notion of a blank screen and, as has been pointed out, accounts of the analyses he conducted show him to be far from this. Neutrality also does not mean that the analyst is not emotionally engaged with the patient. Indeed, the motor of analysis is a live engagement and it is important that the psychoanalyst is able to 'receive' the projected emotions. Neutrality comes from the concurrent maintenance of a 'third position', or at least a striving for it.

The ubiquity of enactment and the recognition that a field is created to which both participants contribute does not mean that the notion and importance of neutrality is to be abandoned in favour of some practices which might seem to encourage enactments. It is the responsibility of the psychoanalyst to monitor countertransference, to avoid gross enactments, and to keep alert to 'chronic enactments' (Cassorla, 2005), some of which may not become apparent for a long time, in particular when situations of impasse predominate. While complete objectivity is never possible and there is always a 'field', the aim is nevertheless to hold or return to a 'third position'. Neutrality of this kind requires constant work and monitoring, and what Baranger *et al.* call a 'second look' (1983). It includes distinguishing, as far as possible, that which has been projected by the patient from that which is coming from the analyst. Insofar as one is never completely independent of the other, the notion of field is a useful one to keep in mind even when the interpretative activity is focused on the patient and even though one's perception of the field can only ever be very partial.

In my view, neutrality is connected to the idea that the analyst refrains from actively taking on the role of a good object or, on the contrary, privileging the interpretation of negative transference. Klein mentions the countertransference reactions which result from the analyst trying to reinforce positive transference through reassurance when the patient is being hostile, or, on the other hand, dealing with anxieties by excessively tackling the hostile feelings in the patient (Hinshelwood, 2008). Neutrality is also connected to a receptivity which is in the service of the patient and in that sense is related to Bion's notion of 'without memory and desire', which aims at a basic position free from goals. Winnicott also writes: "In this kind of work we know that we are always starting again, and the less we expect the better" (1971, p. 37). Thinking about goals can have its place, but this would be when long–term considerations, such as termination, are being looked at, and these goals would be 'arrived at' rather than set out in advance.

In spite of extending Neyrault's idea that countertransference comes first insofar as the offer of analysis comes from the analyst, with his notion of 'generalised seduction' in which the mother is the seducer who addresses messages pregnant with unconscious signification ('enigmatic messages') that the child tries to decipher (1992), Laplanche is attempting to preserve the notion of neutrality when he writes: "We offer the analysand a 'hollow', our own interior *benevolent neutrality*, a benevolent neutrality concerning our own enigma" (2009, p. 246, italics added). The fact that it is impossible for the analyst to be completely neutral in all the senses described above, or that much of the time the analyst may only "bask in the illusion of more or less complete neutrality" (Fajrajzen, 2014, p. 989) does not invalidate the notion of neutrality, or at least of a neutral position as the mental attitude for which the analyst should aim. The fact that it is never attained in pure form does not invalidate it as a position characteristic of the analytic attitude. Making use of the structural model, Anna Freud's recommendation is still central in my view, whether we conceptualise it in terms of instances or in more object–relational terms. She writes:

> It is the task of the analyst to bring into consciousness that which is unconscious, no matter to which psychic institution it belongs. He directs his attention equally and objectively to the unconscious elements in all three institutions. To put it in another way, when he sets about the work of enlightenment, he takes his stand at a point equidistant from the id, the ego, and the superego.
>
> (A. Freud, 1937, p. 28)

The analyst is always being pulled in one direction or another, to join up with the super-ego in particular. Neutrality is the position from which deviations may be explored with a view to returning to it (Tuckett, 2011). Indeed, Fajrajzen has pointed out that the meaning of 'neutral' is 'not taking sides' (2014).

From my perspective, neutrality goes together with 'containment' and evenly suspended attention, which makes it a phenomenon that is far from 'blank'. A blank screen is something which brings nothing of its own (very different from that which is necessary for containment). Neutrality aims to create a space which

30

maximises the expression of the patient's internal world but also 'receives' it, whatever it may be. It does not try to circumvent the expression of hate or to prevent the inevitably disillusioning and frustrating aspects of the relation to the primary objects, and in particular hostility towards the mother, now relived in the transference relationship. That the analyst may have strong emotions at times, due to neurotic or non-neurotic countertransference, or may or not be able to understand these or make use of them, or may enact with or without becoming aware of this, does not invalidate the notions of neutrality and containment as a basic and necessary expression of the receptive attitude. The fact the analyst is 'a subject' and not an 'empty receptacle' (which would not be 'containing' in the psychoanalytic meaning of the term) and that there is no one-to-one correspondence between the mental states of the analyst and that of the patient, does not go against this, as seems at times to be assumed (Eagle, 2000).

Freud used the metaphor of the 'mirror' and not of the screen in his writings (1912). This should be understood within the context of his criticism of Ferenczi's experiments, Freud arguing against the analyst giving "intimate information about his own life" (p. 117). When he writes, "The doctor should be opaque to his patients and, like a mirror, should show them nothing but what is shown to him" (p. 118), he is not referring to detachment as such but to the importance of reflecting to the patient that which is coming from the patient, and not consciously introducing his own issues.

The notion of the mirror has gone on to inspire important writings. Lacan writes of the mirror stage being foundational to the development of the I (1977) in which a 'mirror' can be real or metaphorical (Barzilai, 1995). Winnicott goes on to consider the mother's face to be the mirror which enables the child in healthy development to know himself. He writes: "I am suggesting that ordinarily, what the baby sees is himself or herself. In other words the mother is looking at the baby and what she looks like is related to what she sees there" (1971, p. 112). This will be impeded, he writes, by a mother who is depressed or has rigid defences, then what the baby sees is not himself but the mother's face. One could say that the mother needs to be able to take on a receptive position, one which is neutral insofar as she gives herself over to the infant's experience. This does not imply that she has no feelings for her

31

infant nor a personality of her own. Bion's model puts more emphasis on the mother's psyche as a container for the infant's unbearable experiences which she then processes for the infant and gives back in a manageable form. In this model there is also a mirror but one which is conceived of as transforming, a transformation which will be coloured by the mother's own psyche. The difference is a theoretical one. The Bionian baby has an early sense of an 'other' into which he can project while the Winnicottian baby does not have a notion of a separate object, the experience of separateness coming too soon acting as a detrimental impingement (Caldwell and Joyce, 2011).[11]

If we consider the Winnicottian mirror or the Bionian container, we see a 'neutrality' which is not blank but an attitude of openness and responsivity to what the patient brings, and furthermore aims to contribute to the development of the patient's sense of self (what Winnicott calls the 'Real Self'). The position of neutrality is therefore one in which the psyche of the analyst is fundamentally involved in processing what is received, in transforming it and making judgements about what can be returned and how. It is neutral in that it aims to be in the service of the patient.

Laplanche and Pontalis (1973) mention another aspect of neutrality: the analyst "must not, a priori, lend a special ear to particular parts of this discourse, or read particular meanings into it, according to his theoretical preconceptions". This is also an aspect of Bion's notion of 'without memory or desire'. This stance can only be striven for, since perception itself is inevitably coloured by one's ideas and, as noted by Sandler, analysts have not only official theories but also "implicit private clinical formulations" (1983). Evenly suspended attention and neutrality have to be constantly 'won' in the practice of psychoanalysis.

This does not mean that a psychoanalyst should be without a theory. On the contrary, I believe a theory is the basic and essential frame within which the psychoanalytic interchange takes place. Without a theory, it is not psychoanalysis (Birksted-Breen, 2008) and within the analytic situation it has a paternal function. In the consulting room however there should be a state of 'free-floating theorisation' or 'evenly suspended theorisation', as Aulagnier reportedly called it. Bion advocates that a session should "not be obscured by an already over-plentiful fund of pre- and misconception". He adds:

the analyst needs all the knowledge of the patient and the discoveries and work of his predecessor in the field that he can muster.
This reinforces the need for a firm structure, a theoretical framework of psycho-analysis, which is yet capable of flexibility in
action. If the rigidity of the theoretical structure is weakened by
departure from theory such departures become easier to detect.

(Bion, 1962a, pp. 39–40)

My own clinical theory prioritises the notion of containment,
which I take to include both maternal and paternal dimensions, and
the backbone of the necessary structure. Containment is far from
just a passive and non-interpretative attitude, as is sometimes
described. It involves a basic attitude and particular receptive presence in the service of the patient, and a transformation of that
which is received which may or may not result in an interpretation.
Neutrality, evenly suspended attention/*reverie*, and containment/
receptivity/structure, go together and are the basic triumvirate of
the psychoanalytic attitude which the psychoanalyst needs to strive
for, deviations being an integral part of the analytic situation, which
provide essential psychoanalytic data. It is intersubjective if intersubjectivity is understood in the widest sense of the term rather than
as a theory belonging to a particular school of analysis and implying
certain techniques such as self-disclosure (Levine and Friedman,
2000), and is understood as being concerned with the phenomena
of the analytic pair.

Orientation of listening

One overarching frame impacting upon analytic listening is the
conception of the past in relation to the material of the session.
Psychoanalysis began with an exploration of the impact of the past
on the present, and questions concerning the meaning of history,
the role of memory, of 'historical truth' versus 'narrative truth'
never leave the field. Chianese (2007) writes of being tormented by
these questions: "The problem of reality, events, origins, the
meaning and the arbitrariness of our constructions and reconstructions continues to fascinate and at times torment us" (p. 17).

Freud early on abandoned notions of linear determinism and
temporality, and of a clear demarcation between reality and phantasy. As early as 1896, he writes to Wilhelm Fliess:

33

I am working on the assumption that our psychical mechanism has come into being by a process of stratification: the material present in the form of memory-traces being subjected from time to time to a *re-arrangement* in accordance with fresh circumstances – to a *re-transcription*.

(Freud, 1896, p. 233)

The year after this he writes to Fliess: "there are no indications of reality in the unconscious, so that one cannot distinguish between the truth and fiction that is cathected with affect" and "phantasies can operate with all the force of real experiences" (1897, p. 260). To Abraham he writes, "these impressions later exercise more powerful effects as a retrospective reaction [nachträglich] and as memories than they did when they were real impressions" (1907, p. 3).

In general, with decreased reliance on the topographic model, greater reliance on the structural model and a focus on object relations, there has been a move away from an idea that the aim of psychoanalysis should be to recover lost or repressed memories, which was Freud's first project. Fonagy (1999, p. 220) writes:

If we are serious about object–relations theory, and consider these relations as psychic structures organising behaviour, then it is these structures, and not the events that might have contributed to them, that need to be the focus of psychoanalytic work.... Therapies focusing on the recovery of memory pursue a false god. Psychoanalysts should carefully and consistently avoid the archaeological metaphor.

If the pursuit of lost memories has generally receded, considering the reconstruction or construction of the past to be a central aim of psychoanalysis has certainly not gone away, and there are still marked divisions among psychoanalysts when it comes both to a theoretical and a technical stance in relation to 'the past'. Blum (2005, p. 309) writes:

It is difficult to understand how analytic experience without the insights enriched by reconstruction would significantly alter unconscious, unrealistic self and object representations, as proposed by inter-subjective theorists. An emphasis on the mutative

34

effect of the here and now analytic experience takes account of the influence and effect of the analyst's counter-transference and subjectivity, but with loss of balanced focus on childhood, and patient's infantile neurotic fantasies and features. The analyst also engages in reciprocal self-examination and counter-transference analysis. The value of reconstruction is exemplified in the clinical material in which the past so prominently influences the present and impinges on the future. Without reconstruction, psycho-analysis tends to become a-historic, dissociated from the infantile unconscious, and the context and shaping of life experience. Reconstruction restores the continuity and cohesion of personal history, correcting personal myths while simultaneously fostering greater and more realistic self-awareness, knowledge, and insight. Spanning life experience, reconstruction integrates past and present, fantasy and reality, cause and effect.

Blum even considers reconstruction to be what distinguishes psychoanalysis from psychotherapy: "reconstruction is not neces-sarily a part of psychotherapy as it is in psychoanalysis" (2005, p. 308). However, Blum also makes a distinction between recon-struction and the recovery of memory:

The past is not only rediscovered but is recreated in clinical psychoanalysis. Memory is remodelled. The past has taken on elaborate new meanings, which did not exist in childhood. Moreover, developmental transformations may not be retrievable in their pristine form. The "second look" (Novey, 1968)[12] at childhood is through analytic eyes with the refraction of an adult lens.

(Blum, 2005, pp. 309–310)

It is in relation to trauma that questions of the past, reconstruction and construction always return. In a recent paper by Bohleber (2007), the subtitle of which is 'The Battle for Memory in Psycho-analysis', referring in particular to severe and social trauma, he writes:

when the transference-countertransference is analysed in the therapy only in the here-and-now of the analytic situation, and meaningful narratives then emerge without any reconstruction of the causative traumatic reality, these narratives run the risk of failing to distinguish between phantasy and reality and, in the worst case, of retraumatizing the patient.

(Bohleber, 2007, p. 343)

Hinze, in discussing the concept of construction, reports on those experiences which don't come as a memory as such but in the form of a hallucination of the patient which erupts in the analysis in a direct link to something that cannot be verbalised; he writes, "one can indeed observe phenomena with a connection to the past of the patient which is very concrete, that had hardly been processed and therefore had hardly been transformed or exposed to re-transcription" (Hinze, 2012, p. 1281).

Faimberg aptly points out that construction does not necessarily mean recollection but nevertheless "depends on an 'already there', on the psychic trace left by an event in the past, even if it is not recoverable as a recollection" (Haydée Faimberg, reported in Corel and Good, 2010, p. 1223). That which has happened to the trace is the result of the psyche's work which finds its expression in the analytic situation but which may be expressed in different ways. Bohleber, leaning on the work of another German psychoanalyst Argelander, draws attention to:

a misunderstanding common in transference discussions, namely equating the current situation with the infantile scene. Instead, he emphasizes the change in Gestalt that an unconscious con-flictive constellation undergoes if it is fitted into a new situ-ation. In this process, unconscious expressions of a specific kind are produced, whose significance is marked by both the latent conflict and also by the patient's current relationship with the analyst. What is manifested in the scene is never a single infan-tile experience but an infantile configuration constituted by many scenes with the help of screen memories. The infantile constellation is a creation of the psychic apparatus and no mere repetition of the infantile reality. Fitting it into the present situ-ation is a specific ability which Argelander calls the 'scenic function of the ego': a preconscious process based on general Gestalt principles. The analyst's equivalent response is scenic understanding.

(Bohleber, 2002, p. 11)

36

We can see that the whole question of 'the past' is highly complex. The notion of 'reconstruction' itself has to be nuanced. Hock (2014) points out that even in Freud's early work there is no real division between construction and reconstruction.

Generally speaking, with a growing interest in patients at the more borderline and psychotic end of the spectrum, and the most primitive layers of the psyche, there has been a focus within various theoretical orientations on an area of the mind beyond language and to a past which could not be thought. In the Kleinian model, that 'archaic' is to some extent organised in the form of unconscious phantasies, since there is "no impulse, no instinctual urge or response which is not experienced as unconscious phantasy" (Isaacs, 1948, p. 81). This point of view differs from Francophone psycho-analysts such as Green for whom there are id impulses lacking in representation, and for whom notions of 'unsymbolised' and 'unrepresented' form the psychotic core. This is not unconnected with what Lacan calls *the real*. Bion's notion of beta elements offers a bridge.

The notion of the analyst's needed regression in the sessions in order to capture those 'memories without recollection' and do the psychic work of 'figuration' is discussed by Botella and Botella (2001). De M'uzan (1994) also considers the analyst's regression to be neces-sary in order to capture experiences of the patient that are otherwise unavailable. There is growing interest in traces which may be found in visual, tactile or acoustic images, in the semiotic (Bronstein, 2015). These can find their way into dreams (Green, 2012; S. Botella, 2010) or in hallucinosis (Civitarese, 2015). Mancia (2006) has also written about the importance of capturing those very early experiences which make up the 'unrepressed unconscious'. In his view this unrepressed unconscious stores experiences, phantasies and defences which cannot be remembered because they belong to a presymbolic preverbal stage of development. "Nevertheless, they can condition the affective, emotional, cognitive and sexual life even of the adult. This unre-pressed unconscious can reveal itself in the transference and in dreams" (p. 89). Mancia attaches specific importance to the 'musical dimension' of the transference, that which is embodied in "the rhythm, tone, timbre and musicality of a sentence, as well as the syntax and tempi of speech" (p. 91).

My own clinical interest, as seen in a number of later chapters, rests in this area of work with patients who suffer from a deficit in the capacity to represent, and the technical implications of this. Dream elements, sensory fragments, the role of the analyst's presence and particular mode of attentiveness come to the fore, and the need for what I describe as 'taking time' (see Chapter 10). It requires bearing 'not knowing' and a willingness to be 'taken over' without a premature 'giving back'.

Just as the body never leaves the field of psychoanalysis, in spite of attempts to divorce the biological from the psychical, as Lacan proposed, the 'past' in psychoanalytic discourse refuses to go away. It never leaves the field of concern because temporality is at the heart of psychoanalysis, with questions such as: What do we mean by 'here and now' or 'then and there' within the analytic situation? We cannot do away with the past just as we cannot do away with subjectivity. All lenses will be partial and there is no precise one-to-one correspondence between the transference, countertransference and early experiences. When temporality is apparently collapsed into a 'now' it does not mean that the past is absent but, on the contrary, that the past is actively present. The notion of repetition however is complexified by the equally important notions of *Nachträglichkeit*, the continual resignification of events, of phantasy and of projection, making 'the past' much more than its literal meaning. Yet clearly psychically meaningful events impact, and some notion of the past is never absent from our thinking about a patient. The psychoanalyst is all the time making constructions in her own mind.

Cavell (2000, p. 213) writes:

'Narrativity' theorists … sometimes overlook the fact that who we are now is in part a consequence of this unchangeable past. They are joined by post-modernists who assume that we cannot both acknowledge, on the one hand, our debt to a real, objective world, and on the other, hold on to the idea that what happens in that world is always interpreted by us. But we do not have to choose between external reality and psychic reality. In fact, without the first idea, the second makes no sense.

Gibeault (2010) puts it that describing psychoanalysis as 'a retroactive processing of past history within a new relationship' helps to go beyond the alternative of historical truth or narrative truth. "It is this that may make the past appear in a different light or perhaps as a potentially new dimension" (p. 150).

Freud's own use of the notion of 'historical truth' is not unambiguous. In the *Introductory Lectures* (1917) he writes, "these scenes from infancy are not always true. Indeed, they are not true in the majority of cases, and in a few of them they are the direct opposite of the historical truth" (p. 367). However, in *Moses and Monotheism* Freud contrasts historical truth with material truth. After suggesting that 'historical truth' is closer to what Spence calls 'narrative truth', Morris (1993, p. 44) concludes that:

> It is Freud's strength as a theorist that he never quite lets these questions be settled. Having intertwined his concept of 'historical truth' with the persuasive and distorting powers of narration, he does not cease to search for some deeper and more definitive truth, something of which 'historical truth' would be a kind of narrative representation.

The question of 'reality' is equally complex. In *The Interpretation of Dreams* (1900, p. 613) Freud writes,

> The unconscious is the true psychical reality; in its innermost nature it is as much unknown to us as the reality of the external world, and it is as incompletely presented by the data of consciousness as is the external world by the communications of our sense organs.

Laplanche and Pontalis (1968, p. 3) comment,

> If Freud, again and again, finds and then loses the notion of psychical reality, this is not due to any inadequacy of his conceptual apparatus: the difficulty and ambiguity lie in the very nature of its relationship to the real and to the imaginary, as is shown in the central domain of fantasy.

They also add in a footnote that 'The successive reformulations of this principle in the various editions of the *Traumdeutung* show both Freud's concern to define accurately the concept of psychical reality, and the difficulties he experienced in so doing'.

It is important that we remain with these uncertainties. Non-resolution, ambiguity, 'overdetermination' are the very essence of psychoanalysis.

39

Screen memories

Freud's notion of the screen memory (1899) is particularly interesting in respect of the relationship between the real and the imaginary. Screen memories are vivid childhood memories which Freud recognised as concealing repressed experiences and fantasies pertaining to a time before or after the scene remembered. They are a construction, a compromise formation, combining reality, fantasy and defence. Freud ends his paper on 'Screen Memories' by saying:

> It may indeed be questioned whether we have any memories at all from our childhood: memories relating to our childhood may be all that we possess. Our childhood memories show us our earliest years not as they were but as they appeared at the later periods when the memories were aroused. In these periods of arousal, the childhood memories did not, as people are accustomed to say, emerge; they were formed at that time.
>
> (Freud, 1899, p. 322)

With Melanie Klein, the search for the recovery of the past moved to nonverbal experience. Klein writes about screen memories, or, as she calls them, 'cover memories' (1961, p. 318):

> We can see here that in the course of the analysis not only were early memories revived, but the emotions and anxieties which influenced his whole development had also come to the fore. In particular I am referring to memories in feelings which went back to earliest infancy and which often underlie a cover memory. Such cover memories are of importance if we are able in the analysis to discover the deeper and earlier emotional situations which are condensed in them.

Although Laplanche and Pontalis write: "Inasmuch as screen memories condense a large number of real and phantasy childhood elements, psycho-analysis ascribes a great deal of importance to them" (1974, p. 411), psychoanalysts have on the whole lost interest in them as specific phenomena. This is probably because of the tendency to treat all memories similarly and to consider their meaning in connection with the transference situation rather than concentrating on their origin and ramifications, which reflects, as LaFarge suggests, their "private, one-person mode of thinking" (2012). Although he questioned whether we have 'any memories at all of childhood', Freud later makes it clear that:

> Not only some but all of what is essential from childhood has been retained in these memories. It is simply a question of knowing how to extract it out of them by analysis. They represent the forgotten years of childhood as adequately as the manifest content of a dream represents the dream-thoughts.
>
> (Freud, 1914, p. 148)

The very notion of screen memory, even if little used, is emblematic of how past and present, phantasy and reality, inevitably intertwine, making the pursuit of one meaningless without the other. Where the main divergence lies is in how memories are interpreted depending on whether the primary aim is one of construction or focusing on the internal object relationships lived in the here and now. In the latter case, interest in memories shifts to the use made of their recollection at a particular moment and they are treated much as other material might be, or used as significant metaphors.

The vividness and persistence of screen memories as opposed to other memories has to do with how they condense a host of experiences and psychic situations. Mahon and Battin described them as "the early scenes that introduce the gist of plot and character" (2003) which eventually lose their significance as screens, to become souvenirs of the analytic journey (Mahon and Battin, 1981). They believe their decathexis indicates a structural change and may be used as a criterion for termination of analysis. What changes over time is the strength of the effects associated with the screen memory rather than the screen memory itself.

Screen memories reflect significant internal configurations and in that way they are important in the clinical setting. They capture in condensed form a central dynamic and grouping of phantasies and affects linking past and present, describing a central structuring of the patient's psyche often connected to the primal scene. For instance, a patient has the following screen memory: she thinks she is around four years old, and is watching her father and a female family friend playing chess. Now and again they put pieces to the side of the board. She is desperate to take the knight but this piece never seems to get placed aside. She waits and waits, and finally feels she can no longer wait and takes the coveted piece from the board. Her father and the woman react strongly, saying she cannot do that. She is overcome with shame. The primal scene underlying this screen memory is obvious and the effect it highlights may be followed as a central theme. Another patient has the following screen memory: she is on holiday with her parents, it is night-time and they have locked the door to their bedroom. She cannot find the toilet and becomes very distressed. Here again we see the underlying primal scene, this time with the experience of a lack of containment for the patient's emotional state.

With screen memories we are not in the domain of recovering the past in its 'material reality' so much as identifying a central phantasy and its associated dynamics which gives a picture of the internal world with its infantile elements, creating a continuity between past and present. Identifying its ramifications and articulation with other material is an entry into psychic reality, *then* and *now*.

Here and now

In developing the psychoanalytic method and creating the conditions in which the 'there and then' could fully come into view in the 'here and now' of the clinical encounter, Freud (1910) writes: "psycho-analysis does not create [the transference], but merely reveals it to consciousness and gains control of it in order to guide psychical processes towards the desired goal" (p. 51). In a later work, linking this to repetition, he adds, "the patient does not remember anything of what he has forgotten and repressed, but acts it out" (1914).

When we speak of the 'here and now' we are often speaking of a specific technical approach. In the post-Kleinian 'here and now', interpretations are focused on infantile parts of the self, and affective and defensive relations to objects in the now of the analytic situation. It is neither construction nor pure narrative, and yet these are not absent either in that it is the infantile phantasy world being addressed. It usually implies the exclusive use of interpretations which address what is happening between patient and analyst in the session. Insofar as the analytic situation is seen as "total situations transferred from the past into the present as well as emotion defences and object relations", as proposed by Klein (1952) and elaborated by Joseph (1985), interpreting the past can only be seen as having a meaning in itself, as being an avoidance, an 'excursion' (O'Shaughnessy, 1992) or a defensive intellectualisation (Joseph, 1985). On the whole it is left to the patient to make connections to the past. Feldman (2007, p. 623) explains this:

> The diminution in such force [projections and distortions] enables the patient to make connections which he was previously unable to tolerate – initially, and perhaps most importantly, in the present, as well as in relation to the past. This can allow the patient to achieve a greater sense of the presence of an organic history with meanings and connections. I suggest this process comes about through the analytical process modifying the internal forces that have interfered, and continue to interfere, with the patient's own capacity to make connections, to discover and tolerate the meaning of what emerges.

Klein herself did attribute importance to precise reconstruction. In her unpublished notes, researched by Spillius, she writes: "We must be aware that analysing the relations of the patient to the analyst both from conscious and unconscious material does not serve its purpose if we are not able, step by step, to link it with the earliest emotions and relations" (1945, quoted in Spillius, 2004). Klein also writes the following about a patient:

> the analysis brought up with great vividness the early experiences in babyhood, even to the extent that in some hours physical sensations in the throat or digestive organs occurred. The patient had been suddenly weaned at four months of age because his mother fell ill. In addition, he did not see his mother for four weeks.
>
> (Klein, 1946, p. 105)

Klein also uses the notion of reconstruction when she writes:

> All this is felt by the infant in much more primitive ways than language can express. When these pre-verbal emotions and phantasies are revived in the transference situation, they appear as 'memories in feelings' ... and are reconstructed and put into words with the help of the analyst. In the same way, words have

43

to be used when we are reconstructing and describing other phenomena belonging to the early stages of development. In fact, we cannot translate the language of the unconscious into consciousness without lending it words from our conscious realm.

(Klein, 1975, p. 180)

Segal also draws a direct relationship between the infantile situation and the patient on the couch when she describes the head movements of two patients as being remarkably like the head movements of babies turning away from the bottle or the nipple. However, she adds:

But what goes on in this infantile part at those moments has to be found out from the context and from more explicit material. For instance, in one situation when I drew my patient's attention to his movement he reported that he dreamt about a poisoned stream. His turning away from the analytical feed was due to a phantasy of a poisonous breast and was linked with a deeply suspicious attitude towards me of which, at that point, he wasn't conscious.

(Klein, 1982, p. 16)

"Mostly," she writes, "we base our growing conviction on the accumulated analytical experience, its correspondence with life histories and infant and child observations, which enable us to form an idea of infantile development and its vicissitudes" (p. 21).

The post-Kleinian 'here and now' technical approach is concerned with maximising affective impact. Freud himself stressed the affective aspect:

there are hints of repetitions of the affects belonging to the repressed material to be found in actions performed by the patient, some fairly important, some trivial, both inside and outside the analytic situation. Our experience has shown that the relation of transference, which becomes established towards the analyst, is particularly calculated to favour the return of these *emotional connections*.

(Freud, 1937, p. 258, emphasis added)

Blass (2011, p. 1138) argues that:

44

While Freud does not use the term 'here and now' in a technical analytic way, it may be seen that a concern with *immediacy*, that becomes central to all later views of the 'here and now' is essential to his thinking. This is already very noticeable in his *Papers on Technique*. Throughout these writings a dominant theme is that the analytic process requires that the patient's psyche find immediate and live expression within the analytic situation.

Psychoanalysts of different orientations ascribe to the importance of working in the 'here and now' but they give different meanings to this (Blass, 2011), in particular the extent to which it involves unconscious aspects and relates to a notion of psychic truth. Spence (1982, pp. 49–50),[13] for example, coming from a radical 'narrative' position, writes:

> In what way does narrative truth differ from historical truth? Consider a specific interpretation about how the patient might conceivably have felt at a certain time in his life. Proof that he actually had these feelings is probably out of reach because feelings and attitudes leave few traces – thus the historical truth is always in doubt. But to the extent that the interpretation explains many subsequent aspects of the patient's behavior and to the extent that it completes the unfinished clinical picture in just the right way, it acquires its own truth value and no further checking is necessary. To the extent that an explanation is persuasive and compelling, it acquires features of what might be called narrative truth ... psychic reality may, at any one time, contain elements of both historical and narrative truth, and its power to persuade is apparently independent of which truth is represented.

On the contrary, the notion of unconscious truth is central to the Kleinian conceptualisation, but even within the Kleinian group there are important differences as discussed by Blass (2011), Joseph's 'here and now' having to do with "what the patient is doing in the analytic relationship with his contents, the way he is holding on to them, causing the analyst to collude in this by eliciting various kinds of interpretations or avoiding receiving the analyst's help in understanding", in contrast with Segal, for whom the unconscious phantasy is what is:

most alive and immediate. It is what is feeding and giving meaning to all our thoughts and actions. The latter perspective would consider, for example, an omnipotent phantasy of controlling the loved object to be immediately present within the analytic relationship, whereas in terms of Betty Joseph the relevant level of immediacy would be in the details of how and when the patient brings about the enactment of this phantasy.

(Blass, 2011, p. 1152)

There is certainly no general agreement about whether or how to bring the past and constructions into the analysis, although there tends to be agreement (across theoretical groups) that making some connection to the past helps develop or consolidate a sense of the self and promote a temporal dimension of the self; but for some, the connections are left to the patient to make.

References to 'the past' and to 'history' may in fact mean a variety of things, in particular in terms of whether one is referring to preverbal history, post-verbal history, known history, discovered history, etc. With her notion of "memories in feelings" (1975, p. 234), Klein points to the lack of linguistic or visual representation of the 'past' and of the location of these presymbolic, preverbal aspects as affective repetition in the transference. In that sense, some of the modern developments mentioned earlier, concerned with areas of non-representation, are dealing with similar things, although the technique is quite different. At the most general level one could say that the task is still – using Freud's terminology – to link thing-presentations with word-presentations.

Generally, following Bion's groundbreaking development of Freud and Klein's work, interest has shifted from the content of the mind to the workings of the mind, the importance of the capacity to make links and the destruction of links, the search for knowledge and the destruction of knowledge, the oscillations between paranoid–schizoid and depressive functioning, the function of dreaming and what happens when it is lacking, the notion of containment and of uncontained sense impressions, to name a few. With this comes a shift away from an interest and distinction between past and present, and a movement towards an interest in the distinction between neurotic and psychotic functioning.

Both clinically and theoretically, the issues concerning the relationship of past and present and construction, of what is recollected and in what way in the analysis, will always be debated.

There is no one-to-one relationship between past and present, and the issues of past and present, construction and reconstruction, cannot simply be dichotomised, just as we cannot simply dichotomise the body and mind, or the role of the object and the role of the drives. A dichotomy between the 'here and now' and 'there and then' is artificial. The traumas of the past are relived in the *après coup* of the analysis, its traces leaving room for speculation. Central to psychoanalysis, both in theory and practice, is the complex interrelation of past and present. The function of the analyst is to enable 'a' past to truly become 'then'. Therefore the psychoanalytic 'here and now' is far from devoid of temporality and plays on the essential temporal basis on which psychoanalysis is constructed by creating the optimal conditions for the 'there and then' to come fully into view in the 'here and now'. More precisely it is the continually resignified past which we call the internal world that comes into view. I believe that ambiguity needs to be maintained in the clinical situation itself. The play of the various 'times' and 'locations' which make up the play of conscious and unconscious fosters symbolisation. Forgetting this is a source of impasse. In the consulting room everything has meaning in the here and now but none of it is simply here and now; nor is it simply you and me. Or, put another way, the 'here and now' always refers to that which is not apparently there, the unconscious, the lost connection to the past, the non-remembered, the non-represented. This is developed in Chapter 11.

In addition to the remarks in the Introduction to this book, these themes are the backdrop to the book, throwing a light on my own perspective on psychoanalysis. Often silent, in the background, some themes are more specifically developed and anchored in clinical situations in the following chapters.

Notes

1 A term he borrows from Lyotard.
2 The translation is mine, from 'La passibilité, la disponibilité à se laisser atteindre.'
3 This is picked up by Faimberg (2014) in her paper showing the importance of the paternal function for Winnicott.
4 Chused points out in 2007 that "the therapeutic power of interpretation and insight versus that of the analytic relationship continues to be questioned" (Chused, 2007, p. 777).

5 For an exposition of the historical debates around the role of interpretation, see Sirois (2012).

6 See also the section on the death instinct in *IJP*, 2015, Number 2.

7 There are also historical reasons for the three-times-a-week analysis (Birksted–Breen *et al.*, 2010).

8 'Cure type' refers to classical treatment using the couch as opposed to any variations. The word 'cure' in French refers to the treatment and not to the outcome.

9 Hock (2014) disputes making a clear distinction: " 'memory in the form of recollection' as well as 'memory without recollection' are … different forms of recollecting within one and the same Freudian theory of memory."

10 My translation.

11 For a full review of 'mirroring' we would need to discuss Kohut and his notion of 'mirror transferences' (1968), and the work of infant researchers who took the notion of 'mirroring' from Winnicott to describe the way in which mothers and babies interact, creating a characteristic 'dialogue' in which the exchange is bi-directional (Beebee *et al.*, 1997).

12 See Novey (1968).

13 Blass also discusses other uses of the term 'here and now', for instance, by American interpersonalists.

2

MODALITIES OF THOUGHT AND
SEXUAL IDENTITY

The construction of sexual identity is far from straightforward, as
Freud has already pointed out:

> observation shows that in human beings pure masculinity or fem-
> ininity is not to be found either in a psychological or a biological
> sense. Every individual on the contrary displays a mixture of the
> character-traits belonging to his own and to the opposite sex; and
> he shows a combination of activity and passivity whether or not
> these last character-traits tally with his biological ones.
> (Freud, 1905, p. 219; footnote added to *Three Essays* in 1915)

The construction of sexual identity can only however be understood within the more general context of the construction of identity. As McDougall put it: "The inherent difficulty facing the infant
in his task of becoming an individual is of a more global, more
'psychosomatic' nature than the problems encountered in coming
to terms with sexual realities" (McDougall, 1974, p. 436).

Identity and the construction of the self

Psychoanalytically speaking, the individual is fundamentally divided,
whether it is between conscious and unconscious, between id, ego
and super-ego, between internal objects and conflicting identifications, between true and false self. "The poor ego," writes Freud,
"serves three severe masters and does what it can to bring their
claims and demands into harmony with one another" (Freud, 1933,

49

p. 77). Psychoanalysis addresses the more pathological ways in which the attempt at harmony is established, and is concerned with limiting the disharmony by increasing knowledge and, in Freud's terminology, modifying the 'economy'. Insofar as, from a psycho-analytic perspective, the individual is fundamentally split and mis-representing himself due to processes of repression, denial, disavowal and projection, the notion of identity itself can fall outside the domain of psychoanalysis and, indeed, has no meta-psychological status. Identity has some connections with other more specifically psychoanalytic notions such as identification, internalisation, narcis-sism, integration, ego.[1] It relates to what is termed 'the self', although even that term is used differently within different theories, sometimes purely phenomenologically and at other times as having a theoretical status.[2] Identity falls into the domain of psychology when identity is taken as a given, but is of psychoanalytic interest when it is considered from the point of view of its construction, its defensive uses and its instability.

The individual is forever looking to achieve non-recognition of aspects of himself through splitting, denial, disavowal, repression and projection, while also looking to achieve coherence. That coherence may be more or less stable, will fragment during a break-down, will come to reconfigure more or less successfully at times of psychobiological changes such as puberty or the menopause, or of major life events such as illness or bereavement.

Psychoanalysis requires the disruption of the existing coherence in order to bring about change. Conscious self-representation is dis-rupted by being confronted with that which was unconscious or disowned requiring a never simple process of reconfiguration. De M'Uzan (2007) even suggests that moments of depersonalisation and derealisation in psychoanalysis are necessary for change to ensue.

This construction of identity is rooted in the vicissitudes of bodily preverbal phenomena, the relation to primary objects and later lin-guistic phenomena, in interaction with each other and contributing to the sense of an 'I'.

Lacan's proposal was radical. For him the infant and toddler con-structs the sense of an I via the image in the mirror (the 'specular image') which contrasts with the infant's experience of fragmenta-tion and of being out of control of his own body. According to Lacan, the infant's identification with this image gives him a sense of control and wholeness. As a result, however, there is a profound 'misrecognition' insofar as the image in the mirror does not match the experience. Hence for Lacan the self is permanently alienated from itself. Lacan calls the narcissistic identification of the mirror stage "the imaginary". Winnicott, inspired by Lacan's idea of the mirror, makes use of it to introduce the role and importance of the mother in reflecting the infant's experience, giving 'the mirror' a completely other meaning. He distinguishes between a reflection which is accurate and can help to develop the true self and a reflection which is coloured by the mother's pathology and will contribute to a false self. This is a very different and more metaphorical use of the notion of mirror, since the mirror is no longer the physical mirror but the mother whose way of being present is fundamental to the process of unification with all the complexity that goes with it.

For Lacan, the entrance into the symbolic order via language is necessary for the constitution of the subject, a subject which is always divided. For Klein on the other hand, the ego exists at birth and there is a natural tendency towards integration which is a dominant feature of mental life, as is also the tendency towards splitting. It is the internalisation of the good breast which helps to strengthen the ego and counteracts splitting. She writes:

> The feeling of containing an unharmed nipple and breast – although co-existing with phantasies of a breast devoured and therefore in bits – has the effect that splitting and projecting are not predominantly related to fragmented parts of the personality but to more coherent parts of the self. This implies that the ego is not exposed to a fatal weakening by dispersal and for this reason is more capable of repeatedly undoing splitting and achieving integration and synthesis in its relation to objects. Conversely, the breast taken in with hatred, and therefore felt to be destructive, becomes the prototype of all bad internal objects, drives the ego to further splitting and becomes the representative of the death–instinct within.
>
> (Klein, 1975, pp. 144–145)

Klein's description points to the complexity of the achievement of integration, even if there is a natural tendency towards it.

In my view Klein and Lacan point to two different processes, one which is more 'internal' by which I mean based on introjections

51

and the integration of splits, and the other which describes a construction of the I which is essentially narcissistic, has relevance to
the body image specifically (physical integration of the image in the
mirror) and of a subject shaped by the unconscious and 'desire' of
relevant others, and by structures vehicled by those others. In fact it
would be hard to completely separate all these aspects, especially
insofar as the image in the mirror does not exist independently, free
from introjections, projections and splits, and insofar as projections
also infuse 'the word', and insofar as the body image is a mixture of
what comes from 'outside' and what comes from 'inside'; that is, of
sensations. Imitation is also an important part of development,
which has some connection with 'the image' and the 'mirror',
attesting to the intricate connection between self and other.

This is further complicated by the defensive uses made of the
'image in the mirror' and of imitation, for instance, the taking on of
an identity in order to deal with fragmentation (see Chapter 6). Bick
coined the term "adhesive identification" (1968) to refer to a mode of
functioning which wipes out awareness of separateness. Donnet
(1995) speaks of *"identification d'emprun"* (borrowed identification).
The whole notion of 'projective identification' (Klein, 1946) makes
the issues of identification and of identity far from straightforward,
since the phantasy is that 'you are me' ('attributive identification') or
'I am you' ('acquisitive identification') (Britton, 2003). Sohn's concept
of 'identificate' refers to the outcome of the latter which aims to
maintain a narcissistic organisation in which there is no needed object,
such that "the identificate", resulting from mimicry, "believes itself to
be the whole ego" (1985b, p. 205).

Coming from a Lacanian position but, unlike Lacan, positing an
unconscious closer to the body and to affect and looking at the very
earliest preverbal experiences, Aulagnier (1975) describes the earliest
development of an I as embedded in an indistinguishable psyche-
soma and the role of somato–psychic experiences of pleasure in particular in facilitating the future representation of a unified body.
Even prior to the encounter with an other, for Aulagnier, it is the
somatic experience ('vécu somatique') which anticipates an I. For
her, in the beginning, the object only exists psychically by its power
to modify the somatic. Where Klein describes the good experience
or the internalisation of a good breast experienced as separate as
unifying, Aulagnier stresses the role of pleasure *before* an experience
of separateness. She writes:

The I (*Je*) can only exist by becoming its own biographer, and in its biography it will have to give a place to the discourses through which it speaks and makes its own body speak. These discourses on its singular body will give expression to the only inscriptions and modifications that the subject will be able to read and decode as the visible marks of a libidinal history, which, for its part, has been inscribed and continues to etch itself on this invisible side that is the psyche: it is as much a libidinal history as an identificatory history.

(Aulagnier, 1975, p. 1378)

She adds that the "necessary permanence of certain identificatory reference points would disappear if the I did not retain the certitude of inhabiting one and the same body irrespective of its modification". Aulagnier, in a Lacanian tradition, also describes, in a later stage, the importance of a first version of an I constructed in the mother's psyche: "The image of the body of the child that the mother was expecting always forms part of this 'anticipated I' to which the maternal discourse is addressed" (p. 1380). In this way she brings together the more internal bodily source of unification with the external source of unification, after which processes of identificatory positions come into play.[3,4]

Others have looked at defensive developments in later stages of life. Kris (1956) introduced the idea of a 'personal myth', a well-knit structure which acts as 'an autobiographical screen', a method of defence which can operate as a form of resistance in the analysis. It is defensive in that, he writes, it prevents certain painful experiences and groups of impulses from reaching consciousness; at the same time, "the autobiographical self-image has taken the place of a repressed fantasy" which represents variations on the theme of the "family romance" (p. 674). Sirois (2014) identifies different forms of personal myth, one which puts together the facts of life and one which invents a biographical fact, both of which are aimed at explaining one's origins, and the personal myth which underlines a character structure and is based on a type of child one was as forming the self-representation of the adult (for example, 'the exception' or 'the abandoned child'). He describes how this becomes actualised in transference and countertransference where it can be understood and dismantled.

An area of non-differentiation of self and other is considered to be a space of creativity by Winnicott. With his notion of the 'transitional space', he describes a 'not me' and 'not you' space which is potentially creative, the opposite of the internal impingement from the object. De M'Uzan in a similar vein with his concept 'spectrum of identity' (*spectre d'identité*) calls into question the boundaries between subject and object, and he also considers this fluidity to be fostering of creativity. He describes the need for the analyst to be able to tolerate some degree of regression, especially with difficult patients, facilitating the creation of a 'chimera', a product of both unconscious (De M'Uzan, 1978). Winnicott's notion of 'being' addresses a state in which there isn't a differentiation of self and other. He calls this the 'pure female element' which belongs to both male and female infants, and interestingly he introduces this in his chapter on 'Creativity and its origins'. Here he also discusses 'split off' male and female elements, due to the response of the object and the effect on the sense of a gendered self (1971).

The construction of sexual identity

The construction of the self invariably includes a positioning in relation to masculinity and femininity, or rather it is the most basic division. Sexual identity forms an intrinsic part of identity and is also constructed more or less precariously and in a more or less unified and stable way. The role of the 'image' and that of the mirror, both in the sense of the actual mirror and in the sense of what is reflected by the primary objects, may be seen to be centrally involved in this development. The concept of sexual identity has been described as the extrinsic designation of the self as opposed to gender identity which is the internal experience of the self as gendered and an integral part of one's self-identity (Meissner, 2005). Some follow Stoller in thinking of 'gender identity' as something non-conflictual and assigned through a sort of imprinting (Stoller, 1966). Others attribute its origin primarily to labelling (Lerner, 1976; Kleeman, 1976), while for others primary genital awareness is central (Galenson and Roiphe, 1976; Kestenberg, 1980). For others still, sexual identity is something that is acquired later and in a more conflictual way. Pines, for instance, writes: "Gender identity is established in early childhood and sexual identity largely resolved by the end of adolescence" (Pines, 1982, p. 311). Others use "sexual identity" and "gender identity" synonymously (Lester, 1976). McDougall links sexual identity with the Oedipal crisis. She stresses that neither gender identity nor sexual identity are identical to biology:

> we can assuredly propose that the attainment of our gender iden-
> tity and our sexual identity is in no way transmitted by biological
> inheritance but by the psychic representations transmitted, first of
> all by the discourse of our parents along with the important trans-
> mission stemming from the bi-parental unconscious, to which,
> later, is added the input of the socio-cultural discourse of which
> the parents are themselves an emanation.
>
> (McDougall, 2000, p. 158)

Laplanche sees the notion of gender as reflecting the process of assignment from the Other which fits into his "theory of general-ized seduction" but he writes: "unlike Person and Ovesey, who say that gender precedes sex and organizes it, I'll say 'Yes, gender pre-cedes sex. But far from organizing it, it is organized by it" (2007, p. 215). For Laplanche, "there are preconscious-conscious messages, and (...) the parental unconscious is like the 'noise' – in the sense of communications theory – that comes to disturb and compromise the preconscious-conscious message." It is what is mainly "le sexual *in the parents* that makes noise in the assignment" (p. 215, italics added). Laplanche uses "le sexual", a neologism, to refer to infantile sexuality. It is the infantile sexuality of the parents which is the origin of sexuality rather than a biologically given sexuality. In rela-tion to gender/sex/sexuel he writes:

> The conceptual distinctions are valid not in themselves but for
> the conflictual potentialities they conceal. Although they are
> binary, they are often the sign of negation and hence of repres-
> sion. Displacements may hide repressions, hence, the displace-
> ment of the question of sexual identity onto the question of
> gender identity. This displacement onto the question of gender
> identity may hide the fact that the fundamental Freudian dis-
> covery does not lie there but, alongside gender and alongside sex
> or the sexuated, in the question of le sexual or le sexuel.
>
> (LaPlanche, 2007, p. 202)

The fact that there is no agreement about even the terminology and definition of gender identity and sexual identity attests to the complexity, uncertainty and even disquiet surrounding these issues. Freud was careful in his later writings not to equate masculinity with activity and femininity with passivity. When Freud writes about the concepts of feminine and masculine he uses the words *Verblassen* and *Verflüchtigen* which convey that as one tries to grasp their nature it fades away. The important point for me (Birksted-Breen, 1993, p. 4) is that this ungraspability has to do with the overlap but disjunction between body and mind making the connection hard to grasp, creating an out-of-focus feeling. Furthermore, the body is itself not a simple notion. There is the real body but also the body as represented, consciously and unconsciously. There is no one-to-one relationship between actual body and psychic construction, and Lacan was instrumental in stressing that psychoanalysis is about unconscious desire and not in direct relationship to 'nature'. However, as Andrew Parker puts it, "the body never stops haunting the presumed autonomy of the unconscious, never stops littering the field of psychoanalysis.... Anatomy, then, is neither fully destiny nor lack of destiny in its psychoanalytic conceptuality" (Parker, 1986, p. 102), and it does "set some limits to the subject's phantasy" (Giuffrida, 2008, p. 111). The notion of castration, for instance, makes it clear that one is talking about a phantasy and not a reality, but at the same time 'castration' will be lived differently by the boy and the girl.

Bodily reality always involves a reference to a lack insofar as we are inevitably born male or female, and also infant and child rather than adult. The body comes to represent a reality which cannot be escaped from and which can lead to hatred and attack or extreme procedures to change that reality (see Lemma, 2009). A woman who once consulted me told me that she had had extensive facial cosmetic surgery and she was very pleased when her mother said to her that she could no longer recognise her. It seems that she had now given birth to her own body, and no longer had to 'face' her mother when she looked at herself.

Body image

The neuro-scientific and the neuro-psychoanalytic literature, following Head (1920), use the notion of body schema to refer to the frame of reference which allows us to regulate our posture and spacial orientation. Schilder introduced the notion of 'body image' which he defines as:

the picture of our own body as we perceive it and as we imagine it. It does not merely consist of perception in the common sense but it comprises elements of representations and thoughts. It is an immediate experience like the experience of any other object.... It has a particular importance and vividness and carries with it a very great amount of memories of specific life situations.

(Schilder, 1942, p. 113)

He adds, importantly, that it undergoes continuous change. Greenacre (1953), who was particularly interested in body image in connection to gender issues, describes the body image as developing from endogenous sensations, from contacts with the outer world and from seeing our own bodies.

In the psychoanalytic literature generally however, there has been a tendency at times to use the terms *body image, body schema* and *body representation* interchangeably. For instance, Sandler and Rosenblatt (1962) write: "Schilder's 'body image' corresponds to Head's 'body schema' and our 'body representation'" (p. 128). The term 'body image' is often used in contemporary literature to refer to the conscious representation of the body only. However, conscious and unconscious aspects are closely connected and I will use the term to include unconscious aspects. Laufer posits that developmental breakdown in adolescence occurs when the ego is unable to integrate the physical changes of puberty, "leading to a break in the relationship to reality when the body image could not be allowed to become integrated as the basis for gender identity". In such cases, Laufer writes, sexual development "becomes distorted and used defensively to maintain the *unconscious body image*" (M. Laufer, 2009, p. 283, emphasis added).

Body image and body experience feed into each other. Certain organs are particularly involved in the sense of unification, and in varying degrees for different patients: bone, skeleton, skin, musculature. The body image is itself an internal object in relation to the ego and to other internal objects. The body as internal object is imbued with conscious and unconscious phantasy and will fluctuate. It is important to distinguish internal objects as symbols and internal objects as symbolic equation. Internal objects are symbols when they are experienced as representing the object, 'the mother in my mind'. They are 'symbolic equation' when they are felt to be the actual object inside of the self. The baby according to Klein feels his mother to be a live person inside his body. The experience of the body operates at different levels of symbolisation. There is a difference between someone who thinks their body is *like* that of a hungry monster and someone who thinks their body *is* a hungry monster or that a hungry monster is gnawing from the inside. Torras De Beà (1987) adds that "the sensory body, as the non-symbolic form or bodily ego, coexists with representations corresponding to symbolic equation and with others which fall into the category of symbols" (pp. 176–177).

What we see in the clinical situation is how different levels of symbolisation are intricately linked but can show a preponderance of one over the other (temporarily or typically). Levels of anxiety will influence the balance and preponderance of one mode over the other at any one time, as indeed levels of anxiety affect the capacity to symbolise generally. This will also be reflected in relation to the gendered body. Thus, for instance, a woman using a mode of thinking which predominantly uses symbolic equation thinks that when she is wearing trousers she is a man. Concrete thinking in relation to the body can lead to concrete action. A patient, at the end of his analysis and under the sway of intense anxiety about how he would manage without the insight of his analyst, resorted to the concrete action of having laser treatment to correct a myopia. There are gradations between symbol and symbolic equation and they intermingle. A patient who washes her hair after a difficult session to 'get her analyst out of her hair' is aware that it is a symbolic action even if the action is experienced as literally freeing. On the other hand, a patient who believes that the cosmetic operation to her face will get her mother out of her body is acting at a psychotic level using symbolic equation thinking. The experience of the body, of body parts, and specifically of sexual parts of the body is imbued with phantasies, of 'infantile sexuality', the outcome of which is a complex interaction between impulses, sensations and relationships to objects, to part objects, and to other parts of the body, but also connected to defensive bodily expression such as one which uses the musculature, and which will influence and be influenced by sexual self-representation.

Language affect and the body

Language itself is imbued with bodily experience and is used at different levels of symbolisation. A patient speaks of his staying away from his sessions because "it is the only way of not being in the vehicle as it crashes into a wall" and that it is "getting closer to the prospect of scraping down to the bone of what it really means". For him the bodily experience is very real, literal and present, and his speech transmits the experienced catastrophe directly. At the other extreme, the speech of patients who use 'operational thinking' as described by the French psychosomatic school "has no ties to fantasy activity or symbolization. In reality, it is a matter of non-thinking since there are no connections to the drive source. It is a way of describing facts that does not implicate mental representations of these same facts" (Aisenstein and Smadja, 2010, p. 628). In between are the rich metaphors of speech, grounded in a bodily experience and used to convey meaning.

Green points out that the requirements of the psychoanalytic setting alter its ordinary conditions and that "psychoanalytic discourse is the result of the transformation of the psychical apparatus into a language apparatus", so that it achieves a "true conversion of everything it expresses in language (thing-presentations, affects, one's own bodily states, compulsive manifestations, attempts at acting out, and even desire itself". The voice is the mode of transmitting affect. He refers to Jakobson, who defined the first of six functions of language as the emotional function, and to Ivan Fonagy, who was concerned with the instinctual bases of phonation. In this he disagrees with Lacan who ignored affect, affect being the "condensed form of a complex ensemble comprising emotion, sensation, sensoriality" (Green, 2005, pp. 205–210).

This affective aspect has been present in British psychoanalysis when Lacan dominated the French scene. In 1940 Ella Sharpe wrote: "Individual metaphors used in analysis reveal ... the experiences of forgotten years", and that "no word is metaphysical without its first having been physical, so our search when we listen to patients must be for the physical basis and experience from which metaphorical speech springs" (1940, p. 202). She links speech in particular with sphincter control: "The activity of speaking is substituted for the physical activity now restricted at other openings of the body, while words themselves become the very substitutes for the bodily substances."[5] Rycroft also writes that speech is used at times as a symbolic substitute for infantile sexual activities, using speech "to discharge oral, anal, or phallic drives, or to gain exhibitionist or narcissistic pleasure" and furthermore will also endow the analyst's speech with identical or complementary meanings. In other words, he will react to the analyst's speech with pregenital meanings (Rycroft, 1958, p. 413). The patient's demeanour and speech and mode of relating will be imbued with conscious and unconscious sexual identifications and positions.

One can study the levels of symbolisation dominant at any particular time. For instance, does the patient believe he is actually soiling the consulting room when he speaks, is his fear of soiling only revealed by his figures of speech or by his inhibitions, or is he able to speak about his fear of messing?

Making use of Kristeva's work, Bronstein, in a recent paper and in this line of thinking, describes a 'semiotic form of communication' based on presymbolic phantasies which are intimately connected to the body and to unprocessed emotion which produce a powerful resonance in the analyst. She writes: "the different symbolic forms that unconscious phantasies can adopt and the important role played by sensory experiences, semiotic dispositions and their articulation with symbolic forms in the analytic situation and ... their coexistence can propel and enrich each other" (Bronstein, 2015). To this we need to add that the psychoanalyst will also emit a semiotic form of communication related to his or her primitive relationship to words. The form of the communication (tone, pitch, etc.) may also differentiate when the analyst can take a 'third position' from when the analyst is involved in an enactment. Carpy suggests that conjunction of signs that the analyst is being affected, while at the same time tolerating the projection, is in itself therapeutic when this capacity is introjected by the patient (Carpy, 1989). How the patient hears the analyst, whether affected or not affected, however, is also imbued with projection and unconscious phantasy.

The role of vision

Concreteness uses visual elements. In phallic monism, in Freud's account, the child's first theory of the difference between men and women is based on his or her most readily available visual evidence and 'seeing' that something is 'missing'. In this account the visual is central and there is a relationship to reality, even if it is only an apparent reality, since the girl has nothing missing in reality. The lack of visualisation of the female internal genital organs adds to the difficulty in the construction of femininity as other than lacking. What is important is that it is based on a binary mode of thinking. And certainly, for the child, most things in his or her world revolve around having and not having – whether it is the breast, the food, the toy, the mother or the penis. The experiential world is central in this binary mode of thinking. While sensation is central to the pleasure–unpleasure distinction, vision is central to the distinction of having and not having when it comes to sexual attributes. In the original debate on female sexuality of the 1920s and 1930s which centred around the question of whether or not the vagina was known to the child, Ernest Jones made the point that recognising the existence of the vagina meant acknowledging parental intercourse. The role of vision and the reassurance offered the boy by vision concerning the intactness of his sexual organs which the girl cannot rely on is often mentioned in the literature. The whole debate in psychoanalysis about whether the vagina and womb are known to the child or not and whether the girl is 'a little man' in her early development, as Freud suggested, I think has something to do with the fact that representing the non–visual of internal space requires some symbolic thinking. Perhaps little girls' love of pink is the concrete flag, the 'something' rather than 'the absence of', the equivalent of the penis which marks maleness, making use of a metonymic connection.

The development of a feminine identification which is more than the absence of the penis (see Chapter 3) or the presence of a visible attribute, seen in this way, involves a capacity for symbolic thinking and necessitates tolerating absence and loss. One could wonder if this is more problematic for the girl than for the boy because she has to twice give up the desired parent: first the mother, then the father. It is the experienced Oedipal rejection by the father, in the wake of an early disappointment in relation to the mother which often turns the girl towards adopting a phallic attitude when that disappointment cannot be worked through. On the other hand it has also been recognised in more recent literature that the boy's love for the father is also foundational to masculinity and involves the negotiation of loss.

Segal (2007) discusses the role of vision which "of all the senses … directly presents the infant with the fact of the mother's separateness and it is that vision which is attacked, using the same sensory channel for projective identification" (p. 68). Thus eyes may be used to destroy reality, to project and to create a world of madness.

61

It is through an understanding of the positioning in relation to the primal scene in particular, combined with the mode of thinking, that we can look at individual development. When concrete thinking predominates, working through the Oedipus complex is impossible because resolution is felt to involve actual murder and incest. It is also particularly difficult to resolve the question "what is femininity" if femininity is more than the absence of the penis, because concrete thinking relies on vision as its primary tool and the visual element is "penis or no penis".

I am suggesting in this chapter that the representation of the self in terms of masculinity and femininity will reflect levels of symbolisation, which vary within an individual in relation to specific issues linked with sexuality (in the widest meaning of the word to refer to the drives and their objects). For instance, a patient whose life is severely impaired by psychotic thinking believes that having body hair means she is male and that because she can feel aroused by a female naked figure she is 'a lesbian'. It would require a greater capacity for symbolic thinking and hence detachment from sensory reality to think that she is a woman with body hair or that having homoerotic feelings doesn't necessarily mean she is a lesbian.

Sexual identity is the result of a complex interplay of defences, projections and introjections, and is also separate from object choice and behaviour. Sexual identity can be used defensively to shore up a sense of lack of identity, and Rey (1994) describes borderline individuals as being neither male nor female, on the border, unable to decide. From a psychoanalytic perspective, speaking of sexual identity involves addressing the relationship between congruent (ego syntonic) and non-congruent aspects. Different levels of experiences, different modes of thinking and different representations of the self and the object, conscious and unconscious, coexist.

The construction of the self, as mentioned earlier, is rooted in the vicissitudes of somatic and relational experiences, and comprise identifications and internal objects. The internal object itself is a "precipitate" (Sandler, 2003) of perception and phantasy. 'Identification' differs from 'internal object', phenomenologically in that the internal object is experienced as separate from the ego, although this is not completely clear-cut since there is also an identification with the internal object, as when Klein (1952) writes that "auto erotism and narcissism include the love for and relation with the internalized good object which in phantasy forms part of the loved body

62

and self" (p. 435). The notion of identification is itself complex. I am focusing here in particular on the distinction between a form of identification which is based on symbolic thinking and a form of identification which is primarily the result of concrete thinking. While both may use visual elements, the latter makes more 'whole-sale' use of visual aspects. I called the latter 'concrete identification' (Birksted-Breen, 1999) to use a narrower term than projective iden-tification of which it is a form, because it emphasises the aspect of mimicry, or of the image in the sense Lacan described in the mirror stage.

I discovered that Money-Kyrle used the term 'concrete identifi-cation' in his paper on 'Cognition' (1968). Interestingly he gives the father's penis as an example when he writes:

> given an object, say father's penis, of which a thought has to be formed if conceptual maturity ... is to be achieved, I am suggest-ing that the development of this thought normally goes through three stages: concrete identification, unconscious ideographic representation, conscious, predominantly verbal representation.
>
> (Money-Kyrle, 1968, p. 694)

Money-Kyrle also writes about 'recognition' being the basic act in cognitive development, and he came to believe that the roots of pathology were in 'misconceptions' (see Segal, 1994).

An identification with psychological attributes, with a function rather than physical attributes, requires a detachment from a reliance on the visual aspect and the capacity to separate symbol and object. When thinking, on the other hand, is of a concrete nature, vision and visualisation have a central place, since what is manipulated is the thing in itself. The thing in itself however is also imbued with conscious or unconscious phantasy. For instance, the patient who, in anger with her analyst, cuts her own hair because she is wanting to 'cut her analyst out of her hair' is manipulating a concrete object but one which is based on a phantasy, an analyst tangled up with her and wanting to penetrate into her 'head' for instance.

We can see that from a psychoanalytic perspective the notion of identification is complex since it uses different modalities of thought and includes 'projective identification', a notion which itself is used in opposite ways, either to refer to a self-representation 'in projective identification with', such as 'the identificate' or, on the

63

contrary, to describe the ridding of an aspect of the self so that it is no longer part of the self-representation (as discussed in Chapter 1). Imitation is the earliest form of identification and part of normal development, as Gaddini has stressed (1969), and imitation and object cathexis go hand in hand in development. The various forms of identification can coexist and we can only speak of the preponderance of one mode or another. Hence 'sexual identity' is the end result of complex phenomena; it may be stable or unstable, it may be congruent or not with the actual body and it is permeated with unconscious phantasy. It is made up of various components related to the body, object choice, labelling, in an attempt at coherence through repression or splitting.

Psychoanalysis disrupts a rigid coherence, uncovers other-gendered aspects and the shifting of phantasy positions. Hypergenderized positions and an either-or way of thinking defend against persecutory anxiety or a fragile identity. Riviere discussed the use by women of "womanliness as a masquerade" as a device for avoiding anxiety (1929, p. 306). Psychoanalysis uncovers the personal meaning of 'masculine' and 'feminine' and 'homosexual' and the anxieties related to these aspects, leading to owning of previously hated, feared or disowned same- and other-gender aspects.

Mr L. is tortured by the fear that he is homosexual, although he has a satisfying sexual life with a woman. The fear stems from a pervading feeling of inadequacy in relation to his father and the feeling that he cannot become 'a man'. He desperately wishes to acquire his father's potency. His insufficient symbolic functioning means that he cannot identify with certain qualities of his father, and a paternal function, and incorporate them in fantasy because he believes it would only be through a literal incorporation of a powerful man's penis that he could become a man. His unconscious phantasy is of being penetrated by the powerful penis which would fit him like a glove and enable him to penetrate the woman with the potency he wishes for, a kind of primal scene phantasy in which he is between the parents. He feels drawn to act on the homosexual desire in order to shore up his self-esteem and more primarily to give himself a sense of unification in a (concrete) identification with an 'image', that of the strong penis. This aims to keep anxieties of unintegration, or of liquification or disintegration at bay. However, this brings further anxieties. Olmos de Paz (2012) suggests that this is a normative part of development, that a central fantasy of the boy is to be penetrated by a man in order to acquire potency, and she suggests that *intromission fears* are deeper than castration fears. She writes:

> In order to become a man, the boy is confronted with the contradiction of incorporating the object, symbol of potency, bestowed on him by another man, whilst also rejecting the homosexual desire reactivated by the processes introjection and identification.[6]

Freud, we know, saw the bedrock for a man as his passivity in relation to another man (1937). The 'refusal of femininity' he describes (1937) is a fear of the receptive position (which involves dependency and 'passivation'[7]) and this in turn interferes with introjection. Development necessitates introjection as a basic aspect both in relation to the mother and to the father and we can understand in this way Freud's conclusion that the fear of femininity is the bedrock for both sexes. It is a psychological bedrock rather than biological and has to do with the anxieties surrounding 'taking in'. It also requires the possibility of distinguishing phantasy from action and thus also being able to have a third position in relation to phantasy. Gaddini (1969) describes how identification evolves from an integration of imitations based on perception and introjections based on oral incorporation. If we take Klein's view that there is a greater propensity for introjective processes in girls, we can understand that the lack of visual substrata coupled with the blocking of introjective processes due to persecutory anxieties will create specific impediments to a feminine identification in women, and may explain also the preponderance of eating disorders in women. Femininity may also be problematic due to a difficulty with the "unconscious ideographic representation" (Money-Kyrle, 1968) of the female genital organs consequent to persecutory fears, and coupled with the absence of a conscious representation (see Chapter 3). Conflicts over the receptive position however are not specific to one sex or the other and impacts upon both. If the fantasy underlying the receptive position is one of 'femininity' or of 'homosexual' it brings specific issues of its own for boys, as described above. When concrete thinking predominates, taking in is felt to mean taking actual parts of the analyst, the breast itself, or the penis or babies, leading in turn to persecutory anxieties. Conversely it may also lead to the feeling that thoughts and words are literally invading and harming the analyst, and lead to guilt, shame or fear. Symbolic thinking on the contrary supports introjections of functions and enables a better bisexual mental functioning.

Defensive positions and integration

Identity suggests a unification, and has been described by the notion of 'self' and processes of 'subjectification', a notion proposed in France by R. Cahn, distinguishing 'self' from 'ego'. Green describes it thus:

> Although this notion has not acquired as much clarity as one would like, it can be assumed that the process of subjectivation is a new perspective making it possible to think about psychic evolution from the standpoint of a *subjective appropriation*. This does not simply transcend past stages, but integrates them in the name of a subjectivity in process, encountering many perils which compromise its acquisitions, and navigating at the risk of running into inclement weather of psychotic nature, especially in adolescence.
>
> (Green, 2005, pp. 115–116)

While this notion can become phenomenological rather than psychoanalytic, which is also the case when discussing the notion of identity, the issue of how the ego represents itself and how this changes over time or with psychoanalysis is of interest in its very tension with the conflicting and defended-against aspects. Identity reflects a certain capacity for integration and is in the nature of a compromise formation, or it can be a desperate attempt at some sort of cohesion in the wake of a fear of fragmentation. Laufer describes how the disturbed adolescent attempts "to control, attack, or repudiate the body while struggling to achieve an acceptable masculine or feminine identity" (M. Laufer, 1996, p. 351). The construction of identity may be part of a defensive organisation, and in particular the narcissistic organisation creates a subjectivity which is aimed at defending against primitive anxieties which will need to be dismantled in order for those anxieties to be faced (see Chapter 6). Similarly with gendered identity, which can be seen to change in psychoanalysis. While for Klein there is an assumption of gendered

66

ego from the start insofar as masculine and feminine will develop in gender-appropriate ways if defensive attitudes do not intervene to counteract this,[8] the Winnicottian child has to construct an identity from an initial non-differentiation which is 'female' (being). Winnicott writes: "when the girl element in the boy or girl baby or patient finds the breast it is the self that has been found" (1971, p. 83). In that context, Winnicott uses the notion of dissociation which he distinguishes from repression and describes a dissociated girl element in his male patient. One could say that the construction of the self is an end product or compromise, and it is in its tension with that which is repressed, dissociated, split off that it is of interest to the psychoanalyst. In the realm of sexual identity we are in a realm which is difficult to grasp because it involves paradox: being the object, loving the object, fusion and fear of fusion, dissociation, projection (of otherness), identification, relationship to internal object and also a relationship to the reality of the body. Lemma (2013), in her discussion of a transsexual patient, writes that "transsexual experience may be in some cases approached not simply as a matter of gender and sexuality but as a disruption in identity coherence" and that "marked and contingent mirroring of the self's bodily experience is most likely, for all of us, a vitally important feature of the development of a coherent sense of self firmly rooted in the body" (p. 290). One could also say that sexual identity is what contains and sometimes resolves the incongruities leading sometimes to repression, sometimes to projection or dissociation, and that sometimes resolution seems only possible by transformation of the body and of the other's perception of the body of the self. For Winnicott's patient the sexual identity was not in question even if, to be maintained, it had been necessary to dissociate an aspect of the self and of the object which was felt to be mad, while for Lemma's patient the sexual identity was also not put in question but was non-congruent with the reality of the body. In other situations it is the sexual identity itself and identity in general that are felt to be poorly delineated.

Freud spoke about the 'great riddle of sex'. The feminine mystery, 'the dark continent', is linked to the unknowable, the unconscious itself (André, 1995). Psychoanalytically there is no 'answer' but only a study of conjunctions and disjunctions between body and mind, and a study of the constructions in all their complexities. It is within this context that sexual behaviour, identifications and choices may be considered rather than in or of themselves. Of interest to the psychoanalyst are the movements in position observed in the transference relationship. The psychoanalyst's task is limited to looking at an individual's psychic positions and phantasies, and at unravelling the anxieties which generate rigid defences as these are played out in the consulting room.

Notes

1 The notion of ego is used in different ways by Freud and also by others. At times it is used descriptively or to include the whole person, similarly to 'the self', at others to describe a group of functions, or a structure of the mind.

2 Green, for instance, writes that he prefers to speak about 'the subject' rather than 'the self' because "The self has already too many psychoanalytic connotations – Hartmann, Jacobson, Kohut and others come readily to mind. In my terminology, the other refers more to a subject than to a self" (Green, 2000, p. 61).

3 For a further discussion of Aulagnier, see Flanders (2015).

4 For a further discussion of psychoanalysis in France, see *Reading French Psychoanalysis* (Birksted-Breen *et al.*, 2010).

5 The use of speech is discussed in relation to eating disorders in Chapter 5.

6 Translation taken from the paper given at the EPF conference and transcribed in the EPF bulletin. The paper was subsequently published in Spanish in 2012.

7 French psychoanalysts speak of fears of 'passivation' to refer to an erotic position in relation to the object. Green (1980) distinguishes it from passivity and to connote the active seeking of 'being done to' which could connote the 'feminine' drive activity in both sexes (Penot, 2005: 'Psychoanalytical Teamwork in a Day Hospital'. *International Journal of Psycho-Analysis*, 86: 503–515).

8 Klein only discusses a femininity phase for boys in 'Early Stages of the Oedipus Conflict'. *International Journal of Psycho-Analysis*, (1928), 9: 167–180.

THE FEMININE AND UNCONSCIOUS REPRESENTATION OF FEMININITY, A DUALITY AT THE HEART OF FEMININITY

Both inside and outside the psychoanalytic community, Freud's ideas about female sexuality and femininity have attracted criticisms ever since he first wrote "Some Psychical Consequences of the Anatomical Distinction Between the Sexes" (1925b).

It is often assumed that these ideas have been discredited, particularly in regard to the central place Freud gives to penis envy in initiating femininity. If we take an international perspective the situation is not so simple, and the debate is still alive, certainly implicitly if not always explicitly. What the passage of time has highlighted is complexity rather than resolution.

The issue of whether femininity is biologically determined or whether it is constructed independently from biology still polarises perspectives, as it did at the time of the original Freud–Jones debate, as it came to be known. The importance of this issue goes beyond the topic of femininity to the conceptualisation of psychoanalytic theory in general, and of sexuality in particular.

Very roughly (though schemas cannot do justice to the complexity of ideas) the approaches divide geographically. British psychoanalysts have, on the whole, not been very interested in the topic since the original debate. Notable exceptions have been Gillespie (1969), Balint (1973), Burgner and Edgcumbe, (1975), Mitchell and Rose (1982), Laufer (1982, 1986) and Pines (1993), all of whom are outside the Kleinian group. Apart from the latter, implicitly they

have tended in the main to follow Klein's original position according to which there is always an unconscious knowledge of the
vagina and internal space, and a natural heterosexuality.

Freud stressed the relative independence of the development of
masculinity and femininity from biological sex. He disputed the
naturalness of the heterosexual drive. This is clearest in the case of
the girl whose heterosexuality he describes as developing, following
a long homosexual phase in which the mother is the love object
and in the wake of a disappointment. For Melanie Klein, on the
other hand, there is an assumption of a natural femininity with its
primary wish to receive and be fertilised by the father's penis. For
the boy one could say that Klein departs from the more biological
by describing a 'femininity phase' in which the boy wishes to rob
the mother of her babies and penis inside her in order to possess her
riches, as does the girl (Klein, 1928, p. 172).[1] However, she also
writes: "the degree of *constitutional genitality* also plays an important
part as regards a favourable issue, i.e. the attainment of the genital
level" (p. 173, italics added).

In France, Lacan and his followers question, as Freud did before
them, the assumption of a natural heterosexual drive. They take it
further in asserting that there is no such thing as a pregiven male or
female subject, and that the human subject is constructed within the
terms of language – that is, from a logic that comes from outside the
individual. Lacan's emphasis on the aspect of Freud's work which
wants to keep psychoanalysis separate from biology and within the
area of mental representation, and which gives a central place to the
castration complex in the unconscious and in promoting development along masculine or feminine lines, has been very influential in
France even among those who are not followers of Lacan. Within
this perspective, Freud's notion of phallic monism, and the foundation of feminine development on the discovery of lack, still hold an
important place today.

Positions have become increasingly complex if we consider the
more recent view of those French non-Lacanian psychoanalysts for
whom the body is considered outside the realm of psychoanalysis
and for whom phallic monism is accepted and central, but who
nevertheless make reference to a feminine outside the opposition
phallic–castrated (Cournut-Janin and Cournut, 1993). Some French
Lacanian female psychoanalysts (e.g. Irigaray, 1985), while retaining
Lacan's model, assert that there is a feminine sexuality which is

beyond the phallic definition. There are of course also other perspectives in France, notably that of Chasseguet-Smirgel (1964) who was influenced by Klein's work and who considers penis envy to be essentially defensive rather than primary, and the knowledge of the vagina repressed because of 'incorporation guilt'.

In the United States, great interest in the topic has led to many and varied papers. On the whole, biological influences are deemed important in shaping femininity. The role of female anatomy and physiology for the development of ego functions (Erikson, 1964; Bassin, 1982) and in the elaboration of specific female genital anxieties (Bernstein, 1990) have been described. Penis envy tends to be considered either as defensive (Lerner, 1976), or as a metaphor for other, more general narcissistic injuries (Grossman and Stewart, 1976). When it is considered to occur 'naturally' as part of development, it is seen as an impediment to femininity (Blum, 1976; Parens *et al.*, 1976) rather than initiating femininity as in the classical theory. Some even consider that penis envy and the castration complex exert crucial influences on feminine development, but this comes on top of an early feminine phase involving the genital zone and does not initiate femininity (Galenson and Roiphe, 1976).

Specific to the American perspective is the concept of gender identity first put forward by Stoller (1964) and later refined by Tyson (1982), who proposes a developmental line divisible into core gender identity, gender role and sexual partner orientation. Core gender identity is the most primitive sense of belonging to one sex and not to the other. It is understood in this perspective to be a conflict-free source of femininity prior to the perception of sexual difference. This notion of a non-conflictual 'primary femininity' (Stoller, 1976) contrasts with the view of both British and French psychoanalysts for whom there is no area of cognition free of ambiguity, conflict and unconscious phantasy. While Klein also describes an early femininity, hers is a view of feminine development as continuously challenged by unconscious phantasy, anxieties, and projective and introjective mechanisms, and not in direct relationship to biological and social reality. Both Freud and Klein rely on a notion of primal phantasy. For Klein, unconscious phantasies colour the child's relationship to her own body from the start, and to the mother's body as the seat of both male and female part objects, and these will colour development along masculine or feminine lines. For Freud, it is not the perception of sexual difference

71

in itself that is meaningful, but the primal phantasy of castration which gives meaning to the perception and propels development along masculine or feminine lines.

The concept of primary femininity put forward by Stoller entails the notion that the girl develops a mental representation of genital femaleness at an early age. This view has led to the description of anxieties about the body which are comparable to but different from the boys' experience of castration anxiety (Bernstein, 1990) and to a 'female castration anxiety' as a fear of the loss of the female genitals (Mayer, 1985). Melanie Klein also writes about a feminine form of castration anxiety but, while for Mayer the anxiety stems from the girl's early perceptions of the male being without her kind of genitalia and the fear of losing that which is specific to her sex, for Klein the anxiety is more rooted in phantasy than in perception and has to do with the girl's fears of retaliation (to the inside of her body and her female organs) for her own wish to invade, spoil and rob her mother's body and its contents (the babies and penis imagined to be inside the mother). For both authors, castration anxiety can be associated with fears of punishment for Oedipal wishes. Klein's view on femininity is perhaps more in agreement, at least in part, with those American psychoanalysts who stress the anxieties connected with the 'inner genital' sensations of the 'early genital phase' (Roiphe and Galenson, 1981; Kestenberg, 1980), although for Klein there is no non–defensive phallic stage. As well as referring to the variety of female genital anxieties, current literature discusses the aspect of disappointment and loss in relation to the parental objects beyond the impossibility marked by generational differences (Elise, 1998).

In spite of these theoretical differences, the need has been felt, on both sides of the Atlantic, to understand and conceptualise a feminine 'before' language, or 'outside' language, or 'early' or 'primary', or before penis envy. Another recent meeting point may be found in thinking about the psychical representation of the body as a body of drives that are felt rather than a body that is objective and located according to anatomical space (see Chapter 2) so that the role of vision, which was central in Freud's thinking about the development of masculinity and femininity from the organisation of the castration complex, is now considered by some to be secondary (e.g. Gibeault (1988) in France, and Bernstein (1990) in the USA).

These are some *rapprochements*, but there still remains an important difference in a basic tenet of an influential French approach that adheres to the notion that from a psychoanalytic point of view the (real) body does not count. This marks the radical difference between an approach that anchors itself in biological difference and an approach that considers 'the feminine' and 'the masculine' within a phantasy system that lies outside the sexed reality of the individual. The complexity of Freud's own position on the relationship of mind and body is reflected in the fact that his theory has been seen by some as ascribing an inescapable biological destiny to man and woman – 'anatomy is destiny' – while others have understood him to uphold the revolutionary belief that, psychologically speaking, we are not born man or woman and that masculinity and femininity are constructed over a period of time and are relatively independent *of* biological sex. I have suggested (Birksted-Breen, 1993) that this opposition is there not because Freud was inconsistent or changed his mind, but because this opposition is at the heart of the matter. For Freud, the ego is foremost a bodily ego and psychic phenomena are rooted in the drives, while at the same time psychical events do not simply parallel biological determinants.

This duality is at the heart of femininity in the contradiction between what I call *negative femininity*, which is based on the experience of lack as described by Freud, and *positive femininity*, which refers to the wealth of experiences connected to having a female body (Birksted-Breen, 1993). By 'positive' I do not mean that this will necessarily be experienced in a positive way, and the experience itself may be steeped in negative feelings. I refer to positive as opposed to negative simply to mean femininity in its reference to more than absence (of the penis), a reference to the experiences, anxieties, and conflicts relating to the internal female organs and to specific female experiences and phantasies. This includes the fears described as fear of penetration and of damage to her inside body (Horney, 1926; Klein, 1932c; Bernstein, 1990; Schaeffer, 1997), fear of lack of control (Bernstein, 1990; Richards, 1994), fears of loss of the pleasure–giving function (Jones, 1935; Richards, 1994), fears of loss of reproductive function, and fears of fusion and annihilation (Chasseguet-Smirgel, 1984). I follow Klein in understanding these fears as resulting from anxieties and projective mechanisms in relation to the mother and also to the father. It is important to note that both positive and negative femininity take their meaning within the relationship to the parents. Even Freud's description of penis envy is rooted in the girl's relationship with her mother and her dissatisfaction and jealousy. Giuffrida (2008) makes use of Green's notion of 'negative hallucination' to describe the girl's own knowledge or misrecognition of the vagina: "Negative hallucination ... can be taken as a cross-roads of sources which, depending upon the development of primary relations, can lead either to representation or to the 'negativization' of representation" (p. 115).

It is worth noting that there may not be as clear a distinction between 'envy' and 'desire' as is sometimes implied in the English language. Laplanche and Pontalis in their *Language of Psychoanalysis* write: "Two variants of the term are in fact to be met with in certain passages of Freud's writings: *'envy'* (*Neid*) and *'desire'* (*Wunsch*) for the *penis*; there are no grounds for inferring, however, that any distinction is intended." (cf. e.g. the *New Introductory Lectures on Psycho-Analysis* 5b.) In French also in fact, 'envie' can have the meaning of 'envy' but also of 'desire for', which indicates the close link between the two.

It is in relation to women that the issue of the place of the body came to the forefront since it is for the girl that Freud postulated a construction of her femininity that did not parallel her biological sex, whereas the boy's development follows in Freud's account a biologically syntonic path. Freud speaks of the "repudiation of femininity" in both men and women as bedrock (1937). For the woman it is her own biological sex that she is rejecting. With the advent of feminism and greater equality between men and women in the Western world, women can celebrate their femininity, and yet analyses still often reveal a denigrated image of the feminine. Freud wrote that this repudiation is a biological fact, and Lacan understood it as transmitted through language ("the symbolic order"). This rejection of the feminine may also be understood as an envious denigration of the mother with all her riches (Klein, 1932c), and a desire to triumph over the omnipotent primal mother (Chasseguet-Smirgel, 1976), and also as a way of dealing with anxieties in relation to the inside of the body and the fear of attack. It leads to a denigration of the receptive position. It has been suggested that depressive feelings are considered to belong to a feminine part of the personality because they have developed in identification with the mother and her function as a container of the infant's anxieties and depression, and therefore the refusal of femininity is a fear of depression (Bégoin, 1994). It will frequently be observed how a phallic attitude is used as a defence against

74

depressive and also psychotic anxieties. It also defends against the fear of passivity when passivity is linked with distress rather than with pleasure (Green, 1998), with regression, with lack of control. The phallus refers to a state of wholeness and completion (and conversely incompleteness). It is represented by a penis in never-ending erection. Penis envy is often phallus envy, the wish to have or be the phallus which, it is believed, will keep at bay feelings of inadequacy, lack and vulnerability (see Chapter 6). The characteristics of the female genitals, open to invasion, make them an easy representative of vulnerability, while lack belongs to the 'phallic logic' along the lines of having and not having, being and not being (Gibeault, 1988). Lack may also be understood in terms of the denial of the vagina.

Schneider notes a duality in Freud's own writing; while his texts on femininity centre on the phallic logic of lack, in the texts which touch on mythology and literary works it is possible to see how the woman is characterised by her interiority: 'the casket', a hollow space which can receive, a place of birth and death where the forces of destiny are played out (Schneider, 2002, pp. 598–599).

This dual aspect of femininity, in its reference to lack and in its more immediate bodily reality, is what I will illustrate and explore clinically with the analysis of Charlotte, a vivacious, irascible, at times violent woman in her thirties. Her parents emigrated from overseas not long before her birth, and there is evidence that this had a disturbing effect on her mother such that she was unable at times to respond sensitively to her baby. Charlotte's actual experience of her mother is of a moody, 'exciting' and sometimes cruel person. She, in turn, tormented her younger brother upon whom she felt were bestowed all natural gifts and successes. She was rejecting of her father although she admitted to a close relationship with him prior to puberty.

Crippled by severe anxieties and emotional problems, Charlotte never achieved her academic potential at school but eventually, developing her drawing skills and using her imaginative abilities, she obtained a responsible job in a design company for which she still works.

The picture that unfolded in her analysis was of deep-seated anxieties revolving around a terror of death and of disintegration. Charlotte had dealt with her anxiety, among other ways, by attempting to control her body with anorexia nervosa and compulsive exercising. The female body represented death to her because of its monthly reminders of the passage of time and finite reproductive possibilities. Menstruation itself was linked with death and decay, as the following dream during a menstrual period revealed:

> I was in my old flat and there was a dead woman on the floor. I told the police but they didn't come and said I'd have to live with it for a few days. I thought I couldn't possibly live with this dead, decaying woman stinking up the place and told my mother, but she didn't seem to care either.

Putting on weight was frightening because it is a literal expansion of boundaries and thus entails the threat of falling apart. Charlotte believed that, in contrast, the male body showed unity and timelessness. Therefore not only did she envy the male body, but she liked to imagine herself as having the body of a young man. As a child she had been a tomboy, carrying a gun on a belt around her waist and refusing to wear dresses. Once, when she indicated that she thought her vagina and rectum were linked, and I interpreted her dislike of the little girl she thought of as ugly and smelly, she became upset and shouted, "I've got a great body you know, I could have a harem and fuck them all", but then she calmed down and said she did not want to make links with the past, with the smelly, ugly little girl. "I didn't like myself except when I had the gun," she said, and then turned away from the little girl altogether by adding, "I've always thought of myself as a boy, ever since I can remember." This fantasy also allowed her to feel in charge. When she played with her brother she would make him be the mother while she would be the father. As a young woman Charlotte's sexual passions had been for women, although she also had sexual experiences with men. We could see in her analysis how this experience of herself as a young man made her feel more unified, less vulnerable and more in control. It also gave her a sense of identity to make up for the little sense of who she was. At times, Charlotte also liked to think that she could be whoever she wanted to be, that she was really neither man nor woman, which meant that she was everything. I understand this refusal of the very basis of the human condition of belonging to one sex and not the other as encompassing both her terror of death and her hatred of any limitations. Mortality itself was a limitation that she could not accept.

In the early years of her analysis, Charlotte fantasised being a young man in a sexual relationship with her female analyst. This phallic stance enabled her to feel tough and kept at bay all the feelings she associated with the feminine position, in particular feeling small, helpless, lacking or ashamed. She feared the regressive pull to infantile experiences which she linked with the feminine. The feminine position also meant leaving herself open to attack and invasion, and she protected herself from that. "I'm afraid you'll force things into me ... you'll fill me up and there will be nothing left of me.... You will tear out my insides and my brains." She experienced me, at this point, as forcing her into a submissive and hated feminine position while extracting her potency (both masculine and feminine). So instead she wanted to be the man. She engaged in relationships in which she felt herself to be the man and thus strong, while her female partners were meant to be vulnerable and needy.

After a comment I made about a little girl in her who felt abandoned (which I thought, on this rare occasion, she had given me a glimpse of), she exploded in rage: "That's balls, I'm he-man, Tarzan, and you're wancky Jane." She kept depression at bay by becoming omnipotent when she felt threatened by internal collapse. Charlotte also felt that as a man she could be more separate from me, have 'contours'; otherwise, she complained, she would be 'smudged' and there would be nothing left of her. Being the man with me was also a retreat from Oedipal rivalry. She wanted to be my husband, my 'number one' as she once put it, because that would mean neither rivalry for me nor rivalry with me. Once, when she had meant to speak of herself as a man trapped inside a woman's body, she made a slip and said a woman trapped inside a man's body. What she kept trapped was the vulnerable, mortal, desirous woman.

When, after some time, Charlotte made moves in a feminine direction, she expected a maternal, envious, retaliatory attack. She believed that the gynaecological problems she developed were proof that I was destroying her internal organs, ruining her life – that I wanted to stop her being a woman like myself. Nevertheless, over the years of the analysis, Charlotte's relationship with me and to her body began to change. She began to think of herself more often as a woman. The change first occurred in her relationship to a female partner. She seemed to be searching for a mother who would cherish the little girl in her, while she had always thought this girl was 'ugly and smelly'. But still she struggled against the vulnerable position and the fear of invasion which she thought the feminine position placed her in. Her partner became a phallic mother whom she could not get 'out of her hair' (she dreamed of her as a "witch with a broomstick putting glue in my hair"). This paralleled her feeling of being bewitched and trapped by her analyst. With another partner, she became frightened at the loss of boundaries between them when they were 'the same'. Sometime later Charlotte had the following dream:

> I was going to a Freudian clinic. It became a brothel and I was waiting to choose a woman, wondering what a woman does with a woman prostitute. Then this group of men came and I was terrified of them, that they would rape me. Then I was going up the hill to the clinic again; there was this mad girl being brought there by her parents.

I thought the 'mad girl' whom she brought to psychoanalysis was her terror of the feminine, receptive position, now for the first time expressed directly in relation to men. In her analysis it was possible to see very clearly how, when she had been able to be more receptive to my interpretations, she suddenly became suspicious and secretive. This dream in fact followed a session when she had been more open to hearing what I had to say, and now she feared invasion of her mind represented by male rape.

When her fear of the feminine position abated, Charlotte wished to be a woman in relation to a man. This started in a concrete way. She imagined and hoped that the gynaecological operation she had to have would turn her into a woman. She dreamed that she had to make a journey in which she had to be a black stallion and he would be cut open. In the dream a friend said it would be all right because the horse would die but she would not. She did not want to die, but thought she had to make that part of the journey.

The surgeon and I were seen as her hope of transformation by cutting out her maleness, the stallion. When in hospital, she dreamed that her surgeon was in love with her and, as his wife was infertile, he wanted to marry her. On waking up she felt her 'insides' were like a flower opening up, and she cried about her father whom she had always despised. A few months later she again dreamed about the surgeon, that he was in love with her and would leave his wife. She then told me that in the dream she wanted him inside her, though normally she was not interested in a man's penis.

As Charlotte began to feel more feminine, this brought problems: "Life was much easier when I felt I was one of the men." She had a terrifying dream that she had a stake driven through her head for being herself, like being a heretic. It was only days later that she could explain to me more fully that by 'being herself' she had meant being a girl and pleased about it, and the stake driven through her head was a punishment for this. I understood that she had been a heretic to a part of herself that forbade her to be a woman because this brought huge dangers.

Becoming more aware of her feminine body was difficult. She had never known she had 'an inside' she said, until the surgeon/father had named her body parts (cervix, ovaries, etc.). She was pleased to discover this but was disturbed by the surgeon's words after the operation: "You now have a perfect cavity", she reported him saying. She added that she would rather have fibroids than a cavity. The thought of a cavity was terrifying; it made her think of Munch's painting *The Scream*, or coffins going in to be cremated. For her the female body was not only representative of the passage of time and death, it was the source of death and destruction (her own wish to cremate or swallow up the penis, and her fantasy of the primal scene).

In spite of this, Charlotte began to feel that her body was more a part of her. She stopped being so obsessed with it, and her compulsive exercising diminished. She said she felt herself to be a woman, that 'her gender' had changed and that she did not want to be a man any more. She could admit to me that "as a child I was always the prince. As a prince you didn't have to yearn for a prince." Now that she was yearning for a prince however, no ordinary man would do. Yearning still felt so humiliating to her that it spoiled any potential relationship.

One day Charlotte told me: "I don't think of myself as a boy any more, now I think of myself as a girl – even when I'm jogging." But then she went on to say that she still felt she had something missing, "I haven't got that special thing that you have ... all women have it, even ugly women." What was now missing was no longer the penis, but something feminine. The next session brought Charlotte talking about fears that her gynaecological problems were starting again and how she despised her sister-in-law.

Her envy of her pregnant sister-in-law was thinly disguised. She had wanted to ask her sister-in-law's advice about 'what to do', meaning how to meet a man. It seemed that the missing element was the feeling of having an attractive feminine body and the capacity to attract a man. When she was able to have a pleasurable and satisfying sexual experience with a man Charlotte felt relieved, but this was immediately followed by pains in her pelvis and the fear of something terrible happening inside her. When I took up the point that she thought she deserved to be punished for her pleasure, the pains went away and she said she thought she was all right inside after all.

What I aim to bring out with this clinical description is the bipolarity of femininity. Giving up the phallic position was not enough to make Charlotte feel feminine. Although without the fantasy penis she felt she was a girl, something was still missing when the 'cavity' she had been denying was felt to be a hole of death and destruction. Femininity would only be confirmed if she could feel that her internal sexual organs were intact and benign. Both her femininity and her masculinity were experienced as subject to envy: "If I'm feminine you'll be envious; if I'm masculine you'll feel threatened." She spoke of my scratching out her insides with my fingernails and making her stupid. She felt her 'insides' and her mind to be 'going wrong'. I was threatening both her masculine and her feminine attributes. While I understand this to relate to her own envious and jealous attacks on the mother, the father, and on their relationship (particularly at a part-object level), I do not think envy of the penis is simply a displacement for envy of the mother's breast, and of her womb and its contents. I think each exists in its own right, although of course the patient who cannot manage envy in relation to the breast will also find this problematic in relation to the penis, especially insofar as it represents the link of the parental relationship. Women who most envy men are those who, like Charlotte, are not able to value their femininity because it is closely tied up with oral or anal aggression. In the case of Charlotte the unconsciously damaged object (father) and her own damaging organs became a source of unconscious guilt and persecution and consequent hatred. They had been made non-existent. When she no longer felt herself to be a man, and could own her body, something was still missing of her sense of femininity as long as it remained a source of extreme anxiety.

I have found with other women, too, that during their analysis, giving up a masculine defensive stance did not automatically equal feeling feminine, although, as in the classical theory, it did initiate a movement towards femininity which then confronted them with rivalry and envy of the mother, something previously defended against. While for Freud there is a primary non–recognition of the vagina and womb, I found that my patients' 'missing' female organs, which they reported when they accepted the missing penis, were keeping at bay severe anxieties about the damaging potential of those organs. Charlotte felt she had an incinerating cavity, while another patient described feeling that there was a waste disposal in her abdomen that ground everything up into waste; this was said in the context of talking about a fear of having damaged her mother's womb and babies, and expressed a confusion between reproductive organs and intestines. Without the penis and without the frightening internal organs, these women feel they are left with nothing. As another woman put it: "I think of my mother and you and other women as having a shape even though my mother is old and bent, but I feel shapeless.... I could put up with having a masculine shape or a feminine shape, but the problem is having neither." The male body is more easily felt to have a shape due to the externality of the sexual organs while the female body is felt to be defined by that which is missing.

Masculinity can be an attempt to have 'a shape', as it was for Charlotte, but the feminine shape is more than just the absence of penis. Penis envy hides a fear of feminine lack and intense Oedipal anxieties and anxieties connected with aggression. The phallic attitude is an escape from lack, both masculine and feminine, and an escape from the frightening feminine.

The feminine which is felt lacking, which 'other women have', is an image of the mother able to find pleasure and value in her own body, and able to attract father. In the situations described above, the feminine body cannot be thought about and owned because it has in phantasy damaged the parental couple and the father's penis, and is feared to be in turn under attack. This is especially problematic when reality seems to confirm these fears.

The negotiation of these two dimensions, namely acceptance of lack (and difference) and acceptance of the feminine body (with the complex anxieties rooted in the relationship with the mother and father) and their interplay traces a woman's experience of her own body and her sexual position.

81

Note

1 This leads for Klein to a "femininity-complex" (1928) dominated by the fear of retaliation from both mother and father, the basis "of a super-ego which devours, dismembers and castrates and is formed from the image of father and mother alike".

4

SEXUALITY IN THE CONSULTING ROOM

Freud first viewed sexuality as disorganising, a threat to the individual and to society in that it took no account of reality and thus had to be repressed:

> The concept of 'sexuality', and at the same time of the sexual instinct, had ... to be extended so as to cover many things which could not be classed under the reproductive function; and this caused no little hubbub in an austere, respectable or merely hypocritical world.
>
> (Freud, 1920, p. 51)

He moved to a view of sexuality which was less anarchic when he put together sexual instincts and ego instincts. Sexuality, in his later theory, became Eros, "the preserver of all things" (1920, p. 52); it "seeks to force together and hold together the portions of living substance" (1920, p. 60 footnote) and "holds together everything in the world" (1921, p. 92). It cannot be thought of without its opposite, the death instinct, which aims at the dissolution of what is living; "Eros and the death instinct [are] the motivating powers whose interplay dominates all the riddles of life" (1922, p. 340).

French psychoanalysts tend to retain the centrality of sexuality, some putting an emphasis on the early view, others on the late view. Laplanche retained both, giving them different names. Brigitte Eoche-Duval (2009) writes: "Laplanche invokes sexuality in its full demoniacal power to 'unbind'; for this he uses the French neologism '*sexual*' (as distinct from "*sexual*'), contrasting it with the binding tendency of Eros."

For Laplanche it is the unconscious 'enigmatic' messages of the parents that introduce sexuality to the child. He uses the term 'sexual' to refer to infantile sexuality which he defines as "what is condemned by the adult" (2007, p. 204). He writes: "what is lacking in both Freud and Lacan is a consideration of the enigmatic dimension, otherness, on the part of the child's adult protagonists: the others of the primal scene" (1995, p. 667). This contrasts with Green for whom "the drive is the matrix of the subject" (1997, p. 347) while the "objectalising function" – that is, the power to create new objects – also has prime importance. Green also stresses that "Freud's theory of the drives has been unjustly opposed to object relations theory. Now these two conceptions are not opposing but complement each other, since the last theory of the drives that includes the life and love drives implies the existence of the object. It explains the force that animates us and drives us forward, whereas the retreat into the self, depression or schizoid decathexis show that it can be neutralised, more or less temporarily lost, or severely impaired in a definitive way. Let us remember Freud's terms: 'love or life' drives. Love of life is our most valuable good.

Echoing Winnicott's basic role for the analyst being of "keeping alive" and "keeping awake" (1965, p. 166), Green adds importantly in his last book, "It is from this side that the analyst delivers his struggle" (2012b, p. 193).[1]

Modern developments in other parts of the world have often moved away from the uncovering of sexual wishes as the primary aim of psychoanalysis or looking at sexuality as a binding element, and have turned to looking at how sexuality itself is often used for defensive purposes and to deal with narcissistic issues and psychotic anxieties. It is for this reason that Glasser (1985) suggests that "far from being 'weak' and 'unruly' man's sexuality is his most powerful and willing servant, or assistant" (p. 405).

The understanding of perversion as a solution to intrapsychic conflict has gone along with a changing definition of what is considered perverse. Fonagy (2006) writes: "The key indicators are not the fantasy nor the activity but, rather, the compulsive, restrictive, and anxiety-driven character" (p. 12). He adds: "Normality and perversion is thus an inappropriate dimension that could and should be replaced by our understanding of the degree to which a particular type of sexual activity serves functions other than erotic pleasure."

For some, developments in a direction away from the centrality of sexuality have gone too far; Green gives a paper in London entitled at least partly ironically "Has Sexuality Anything To Do With Psychoanalysis?" (1995) based on his observation that reference to sexuality has declined in clinical presentations and is restricted in psychoanalytic writings to papers specifically to do with sexuality. This was in 1985 and certainly this trend has not been reversed. His aim in the paper was to "[restore] the importance of genital sexuality and the Oedipus complex to their central place" (p. 871). He does this by pointing out that Freud makes a distinction between Eros and sexuality which is a function: "So we have a chain, the concept: Eros (love and life instincts) – its exponent (libido) – its function (sexuality)." Eros accounts for the binding to the object; this provides peace and security which are preconditions for pleasure. "The reference to sexuality underlines that [the relationship to] the love object is mainly a pleasurable one" (p. 882).

Already in 1974 Laplanche writes: "I would like to state my distrust of the desexualization of psychoanalysis, which can be clearly seen in much of the modern theorizing" (Laplanche, 1974, p. 467). Roussillon warns 15 years later that the central importance of the sexual is "under threat from certain developments in Anglophone psychoanalysis that, especially under the banner of narcissism and 'self analysis' are strangely diminishing its impact and scope of reference" (Roussillon, 2011, p. 528). Fonagy, in a somewhat Laplanchian turn, writes: "The enigmatic dimension of sexuality creates an invitation that calls out to be elaborated, normally by an other" (Fonagy, 2008, p. 23) and relates the disturbing aspect of sexuality and its subsequent organisation to how sexual feelings are ignored and left unmirrored by caregivers. For Laplanche however, what is important is the transmission of that which cannot be given meaning. For him the 'enigmatic messages' of the m/other are experienced by the infant as 'excess', and later also by the adult as something which is overwhelming and exceeds translation into meaning.

We can see that the understanding of 'sexuality' from a psychoanalytic point of view is far from resolved. I do not think it is a question of 'either/or'; sexuality may be considered as a force in its own right with its disturbing aspects and may also be looked at in terms of its defensive uses, and in particular in terms of its place in relationship to love and hate. Within the psychoanalytic situation it is necessary to study in each situation how sexuality is experienced, the use made of it, and how it connects with love, hate and pleasure. Notable is the frequency with which sexuality is repressed or split off in the patients who consult us, how often it is that these patients cannot integrate a bodily intimacy with a close, loving relationship, and also the extent to which sexuality can function as binding or ridding the self of unwanted affective states.

In this chapter my focus is more specifically on sexuality as it manifests in the consulting room, making a distinction between 'silent sexuality' and 'noisy sexuality'. I will argue that sexuality dominates the psychoanalytic encounter. It underlies the analysis at all times but manifests itself in many different ways. It is the driving force of the analysis, the 'life drive' necessary to both parties within the psychoanalytic pair, but it can also paralyse the analysis and thus requires different handling at different times. Sometimes it is explicit and sometimes it is implicit. Sometimes it needs to be addressed as such by the analyst and sometimes it forms a backdrop. I will suggest that it is the silent sexuality which needs to be given a voice, while the clambering of noisy sexuality needs to be further explored to find its purposes.

My own perspective takes as a given the two main axes of the centrality of the Oedipal configuration, and of a basic duality of life and death forces, enhanced or mitigated by that which comes from the encounter with the object. The form and manifestations of sexuality in a wide sense of the word will be shaped by each individual's negotiation of these two axes and positioning in relation to the primal scene.

Silent sexuality underlies the psychoanalytic relationship. It belongs to Eros, the life force embodied in the libidinal attachment of the patient towards the analyst and the analyst towards the patient. Eros is not only the cause of symptoms but also an agent of cure (Roland Gori in De Mijolla, 2002, p. 536), or at least it offers and supports that potential. It opens up to the potential for something new, it promotes the drive to relate, and to symbolise. It incorporates the sexual instincts but is wider than that. It includes the instinct for knowledge (Blass, 2006). It is the ally of the analysis. It thrusts the analysis forward, promotes links between one association and another, between yesterday and today, today and tomorrow; it underpins productive work and enables productive work to grow. It is also 'the stuff as dreams are made of' since it drives to represent. And dreams are the stuff of analysis. When an analysis is developing, it is because an area of quiet illusion is operating which is neither delusional in intensity and destructive of reality, nor so hated by the self that any emotional connection with the analyst is denied. Such a state of affairs rests on a capacity to symbolise which itself rests on the possibility of making links. Noisy sexuality, by which I mean sexuality which is explicitly and insistently displayed in the consulting room, has a more mixed origin as will be discussed below. Silent sexuality is also to be found in mental mechanisms. Projective and introjective mechanisms have as their accompanying phantasy penetrating and receiving, which in turn form the basic dimension of the differentiation between masculine and feminine. Even projection, if not too massive, will aim to communicate and link with the object; patients on the autistic spectrum who fail to project pose difficulties for the analyst. The phantasy of penetrative or receptive activity will attach to any number of organs, so that the eye, for instance, can be either feminine/receptive or masculine/penetrative, but the opposition is always there. When Susan Isaacs (1948) says that every instinct has a phantasy, I would add masculine or feminine. When Bion gave the female symbol to his notion of the container and the male symbol to the contained, he was pointing to an underlying phantasy. In fact I would say that even that could be reversed if one thinks of the phallus as container to a fragmented self. Bion's emphasis on the importance of 'linking' and the 'attack on linking' as having a fundamental impact on the development of the psyche I understand as related to the libidinal wish to unite or, on the contrary, to destroy contact with the accompanying phantasy of penetrative and receptive linking versus the breaking of all contact. When Klein described a feminine phase in both girls and boys, it was to do with the nipple–mouth primary connection. The bisexual functioning necessary to psychic health which develops from the identification with both positions is this silent sexuality at the centre of psychic functioning which combines with gendered bodily reality in various ways. An instance of the 'sexed' reality of mental structure is my own use of the term 'penis-as-link'. Developing Britton's idea (1987) that the missing link of the Oedipal triangle is the parental relationship, and exploring the structuring aspect of the masculine element, I have used the term 'penis-as-link' to refer to the position of the child which recognises and internalises the triangular configuration. I made a distinction between penis–as–link which recognises the parental relationship and hence both sexual difference and generational difference with its implications for mental functioning, and the phallus which does not recognise it. Although it has some connections with Freud's distinction between a phallic stage and a genital stage, the distinction is not identical because penis–as–link refers specifically to the parental relationship and is based on the premise that there is from early on an awareness of the parental sexual relationship. It is based on a model of positions rather than stages. Penis–as–link implies an awareness of difference between the parents and of the position of the child outside that relationship. It is the recognition of that primal relationship and its consequence, the exclusion of the child from it. On the contrary, the phallus organises along narcissistic lines in a rigid way. It does not recognise difference, it is and it has, or by reversal, it isn't and hasn't. It is based on concrete thinking. It is quite other than the organisation of the penis–as–link. This will be further developed in Chapter 6.

Sublimation, or in an object–relational model, symbolisation, which is at the heart of the psychoanalytic process, has as its motor a silent sexuality in that the search for new forms and new objects stems from a libidinal movement. It is the libidinal tie to the object and its loss or renunciation and the search for substitution which promotes the movement towards symbolisation. The movement towards new objects is also promoted, as Klein writes, by the forward drive of the libido.

> It is, however, not only the search for new objects which dominates the infant's needs, but also the drive towards new aims: away from the breast towards the penis, i.e. from oral desires towards genital ones. Many factors contribute to these developments: the forward drive of the libido, the growing integration of the ego, physical and mental skills and progressive adaptation to the external world. These trends are bound up with the process of symbol formation, which enables the infant to transfer not only interest, but also emotions and phantasies, anxiety and guilt, from one object to another.
>
> (Klein, 1952, p. 434)

The classical notion of sublimation derives from a model relying on instinct theory, and therefore is a manifestation of sexuality but has much in common with notions arising from other models such as the capacity to symbolise, the capacity to repair the object, the capacity to play, the development of a transitional space, the development of an internal space. While in her earlier work Klein describes sublimation as the libidinal cathexis of ego-tendencies,[2] in her later work, when she becomes less committed to classical theory, the notion of reparation as central to maturational processes takes over with its stress on a complex process in which anxiety and guilt play a central part.[3] In both models the idea of renunciation is important, but in the Kleinian perspective it is the process of mourning the object involved in a successful renunciation that leads to sublimation via symbol formation.[4] I have been interested in a particular instance of sublimatory activity within psychoanalysis when a patient in the latter phases of the analysis, faced with the need to renounce the analyst, finds a creative way of verbally representing the analytic process to the analyst; I will return to this issue in Chapter 11.

Sexuality was little talked about directly in the analysis of my anorexic patient Marie. Certainly it did not help that Marie spoke very little altogether and therefore also offered me a limited range of interpretations. For the first two years of her five-times-a-week-analysis she was virtually mute. A lot of my interpretations addressed the struggle inside herself about a wish to talk and communicate with me, and the stronghold from the part of herself that would not allow this. I also addressed how humiliating she found it to need me. For a long time, the subject of food did not come up. I only obliquely mentioned the subject of eating, symbolically, in relation to what she took or did not take from me. From a transcript of the sessions it could look as if sexuality was not much part of this analysis. Yet I would say that the struggle between Eros and the death drive was what underpinned the whole analysis in an almost palpable way, and this is exactly how I thought about it at the time. I could 'feel' it in the room. My patient hung on to my every word and I hung on to her every — and very few — words. You could have heard a pin fall in this atmosphere of absolute breathless expectation on her part and on mine. The frustration, one could say, increased the libidinal pleasure in finally receiving. In fact she once told me how she could increase her own pleasure in eating by starving herself first. When I describe a transference atmosphere in which 'you could have heard a pin fall', I am really describing the shared fantasy that she and I would have been shocked by the – however imperceptible – suggestion of a third in this intensely libidinised atmosphere, of an infantile nature. But it was not just the oral activity of talking and the auditory one of receiving which were highly cathected in Marie's analysis. I was also obliged to look intently at her. In order to orientate myself in the silence, I had to be very alert to every and all non-verbal clues. I was acutely aware of imperceptible movements which gave me clues as to what she might be feeling. I could tell from her attitude if she was wishing for closeness, if, for instance, she stroked an item of clothing between her fingers, or on the contrary wanting to withdraw when she did not. Most of the time I felt she was struggling between the two. I never commented on the non-verbal cues but made use of them to guide my interpretations. Nevertheless, she was aware of and embarrassed about her bodily presence and in the early years she would always hide her face with her hand. She had an acute sense of her presence in my presence, and an embarrassment at my bringing to light her feelings. When she first started coming to the session in a skirt after some years she looked as if the clothes were just sitting on her rather than belonging to her, and she seemed very ill at ease and embarrassed. While the Oedipal drama was not much addressed directly, clearly Marie was afraid of being a woman in the presence of a woman and it is significant that she waited until she ended the analysis before having a baby. I would say that a lot of the work done on her refusal to 'take in' had some bearing on the acceptance of her femininity, on the connection of mouth and vagina, even if it was not spoken of in these terms. The difficulty in talking is common with anorexic patients because eating and talking are both libidinal activities, involving the mouth and throat (see also Denise, Chapter 5). The significance of speaking as a genital activity has been described by a number of authors (Abraham, 1924; Segal, 1923). With the anorexic there seems to be a genitalisation and confusion of oral and vaginal. There is a failure of symbolisation so that the oral sphere is equated with the genital sphere rather than coming to symbolise it. It accounts for the fear of impregnation in cases of anorexia, as mentioned by Freud.

Klein suggested that when too powerful genital impulses come too early they affect the oral relationship to the mother. It is an open question in each case as to why there is this failure of symbolisation, and a question about the relative importance in each case of the strength of impulses, parental handling and parental fantasy.

Braunschweig and Fain (1971a, p. 132) describe an atypical group of women who had a 'premature' recognition of the vagina as an erogenous zone. They find it within a particular configuration:

> To sum up, we could say that the mother's indifference to her daughter's sexual development, an indifference that has been manifest ever since her birth, and the father's inability to ensure his power, seem to play an important part in this premature recognition of the vagina as an erogenous zone.

They do not discuss this in relation to anorexia nervosa but I find their thinking of interest in connection with it. There does seem to be in the internal world of these patients a collapse of the Oedipal configuration in its structuring function which makes them feel that there is no protection from an engulfing mother. Their description would also fit in with what family therapists suggest is the father's weak role in the families of anorexics. The feeling of being intruded upon (by an engulfing or phallic mother), typical of anorexics, is in part the projection of the more unconscious wish to intrude. While she withholds her words, the anorexic intrudes with the disturbing feelings and worry she creates in others.

Talking can represent specifically a phallic activity. For instance, Klein writes about Grete, aged nine, that she looked upon speaking and singing as a male activity. "A single word stood for the penis and a sentence for the thrust of the penis in coitus and also for coitus as a whole" (Klein, 1932c, p. 101).

Not talking is also a defence against the pleasurable libidinal activity. In the latter part of the analysis Marie told me how much she enjoyed talking.

She also said to me, "To be able to speak, to make contact by talking, that is such a new experience for me, when it happens it's wonderful, like when a blind person starts to see." And she added, "I no longer need to deprive myself by fear of becoming dependent."

Marie started to talk about all sorts of things. She was at first excited and embarrassed to do so, and hid her blushing with her hands. I came to realise the extent to which shame had played a role, and of the significance of speech as a sexual activity, as described by Abraham (1924) and by Segal (1923). Freud, in a letter to Abraham in 1909, writes. "The aversion to talking is ultimately based on the other intended (sexual) uses of the mouth."

As she was getting ready to finally end her analysis, with all the sadness and trepidation that came with it, Marie could say to me with pleasure, "I want to eat you up". She could now use words to symbolise her wishes rather than fear the words to be the action. And she could allow herself the pleasure of articulating the wish and in using words to make a connection with me.

For the first time sexuality seemed more directly in evidence, not through what she talked about but in her evident pleasure and excitement, and her blushing. Talking was now a sublimation of her infantile sexuality which the analysis had helped release, and she could enjoy it and also make use of this to communicate her feelings.

Klein points out that speech not only assists "the formation of symbols and sublimation, but [is] itself the result of one of the earliest sublimations" (1926, p. 104).

Green (1974, p. 4181) describes the instinctualisation of language as taking place in psychoanalysis due to the particulars of the setting. He writes:

> It is important to note that the patient is not allowed to act but is asked to say everything which comes to his mind, thus transmitting the object relation by means of language; this entails that analytic treatment necessarily leads to an instinctualization of language. This results in language no longer being used for communication as it is in everyday life. Talking to the analyst involves entering into a very close relationship with him, which is both loving and destructive. There is no equivalent to this in everyday life because, besides language, there are other means of communication such as gestures, actions and face to face relations which vary with the reactions of the recipient.

Language is thus an important way in which the libido manifests itself and underpins psychoanalysis, a way essential to its development. It is language and also such things as the voice and sound of the analyst. Conversely it can be used in a destructive way, words becoming missiles which aim to invade, disturb, confuse or destroy the analyst's thinking. The latter can also hide the binding force of Eros which gives this activity its vitality and bond to the analyst, as in a sado–masochistic engagement.

The end of Marie's analysis opened her on to the integration of her genital sexuality. She spoke of taking her little nieces to the seaside.

She told me that she became fascinated with the seaweed uncovered by the spring tide, "like a lost primitive tribe now discovered". She described the seaweed with little creatures attached to it. The seasonal and cyclical reference, in combination with the primitive and the historic, depict the life cycle, and the integration of a psychic past now known. The imagery also lead us to curiosity, about sexuality and pregnancy, about her analyst's body, about her own fantasy life and primitive feelings, and to the spring of her own life which was soon to be possible. Infantile and adult sexuality could now be integrated.

I now turn to what I call noisy sexuality, the one which makes itself known with insistence in the consulting room. The noisiest of all is the erotised transference.

Like Charlotte in Chapter 3, Beatrice developed an erotised transference as a way of staving off severe anxieties of persecution and fragmentation. Beatrice keeps her love fuelled by romanticism. "Coming here is painful and exquisite," she says. "Suffering is love, if you don't suffer you don't love." Just as she turns pain into pleasure, Beatrice turns fear into excitement. Not far beneath the surface, I thought she had a terror of this analyst whose enthralling and tantalising qualities she wants to cannibalise and possess. Excitement is also used to wipe out need, emptiness and inadequacy. Even her anger is a source of excitement and idealisation, without which she would feel dead. Her ambivalence to me is clear when she speaks of 'the kiss of death'. After one holiday break she told me a dream in which "I looked in the mirror and my face was like one of those buildings that reflect, my face was like patchwork pieces of reflecting glass". She then said,

> I'm in little pieces, I'm different people. When I look in the mirror I don't see myself, it's distorted, I don't know who it is, I can't go out, I feel I have no skin, the air hurts; I have to go out otherwise I will die. I have to run to keep myself alive. I have to starve myself, at least I won't be poisoned.

This is my patient in a fragmented state from which she attempts to get out by an erotised phallic stance aiming to seduce me. It is this characteristic of binding together that can give sexuality an organising function, in the case of Beatrice along masculine lines. Beatrice uses sexuality to organise her fragmented self and in order to feel in control of her object.

What has particularly impressed me with the erotised transference is the patient's belief that her own insistent desire is the way of creating total attention in the analyst. Sexual desire has a single-minded quality and the patient is attempting to gain that single-minded attention from the analyst. The analyst is to mirror her absolute preoccupation. Everything else is to pale into insignificance. It aims to destroy the Oedipal structure and get rid of "the other of the object" (Green, 1986, p. 882) but I think it is more than that; it is something about the desperate search for total control of the object and to force the object to totally focus on the self as a matter of life and death. The patient does this by trying to appeal to the analyst's narcissism, seeking the creation of a mutual narcissistic entrancement. Dropping out of the mother's and the analyst's mind is experienced as terrifying annihilation. The 'noisy' sexuality is an attempt to be seen and heard, for fear of falling into a void. The desperate and insistent forcing of attention gives it its intrusive aspect. There is evidence that, due to a bereavement, Beatrice may well have fallen out of her mother's mind as an infant and it seems that she expected to fall out of her analyst's mind too if she did not force her presence there. Creating excitement in the session was aimed at preventing catastrophic anxiety. It also meant that it was hard for me to have the space to reflect rather than react since that space was experienced by her as an abyss. While the living out of Beatrice's erotised transference, used to control and demand, was her attempt to defend against psychotic fears of fragmentation and annihilation and against depression and emptiness, it was also the motor by which she could be involved in her analysis. However defensive, it had enabled her to form a powerful attachment which she could internalise and which gave her a sense of purpose. She could be furious, screaming and shouting at me. This was part of her strong connection. Her worst fear was that there would be no connection, just a void. The void is the absence of the object and the absence of involvement. Jones (1927) introduced the notion of aphanisis to describe the loss of sexual desire, and suggested that the fear of loss of sexual desire was the most profound fear for both sexes. The noisy sexuality was Beatrice's attempt of stave off the void, a state with no object and no libidinal investment. In fact I thought that the erotised defensive transference hid much of the time not so much a void as a more silent libidinal infantile desire, to touch and be touched through the various senses which the noisy sexuality aimed to squash because it felt shameful and humiliating.

In contrast, Carole attacks the link to the analyst. She consulted because of her difficulties with her husband. Carole's characteristic way of relating is to push her analyst away which I see as an attempt to protect a fragile sense of self from painful intrusion and in order to hold herself together. Psychoanalysis is experienced as something very hurtful whatever is said. The following dream took place following an argument with her husband in which she felt that he was being obtuse to what she was telling him, and in particular to the idea that most of what occurs in a relationship is not the reality of a relationship but goes on in fantasy; this condenses her experience of the analytic situation, but also reverses positions in that it is now the husband who refuses to take in a psychoanalytic perspective: "There is a man with a telescope and she knows he is a murderer and the telescope is what he uses to murder with."

For Carole, relating appears to be experienced as the attempt to force a point of view into the other so that a point of view becomes a dangerous phallic attack. The analytic lens is experienced as murderous. One can see here the potential murderous transference and countertransference emotions at the centre of the analytic exchange and investigation, whenever meaning is sought, and the 'chicken-and-egg' situation between her point of view not being understood and the murderousness it leads to, and the fear of intrusion which attacks the insight and thus prevents understanding. I could feel myself in the countertransference wanting to say triumphantly "you see" when at last I thought she won't be able to deny something obvious. This situation of one person forcing a point of view on to the other, of one mind annihilating or poisoning another mind as the template of interchange prevents the development of a good internal object that can transform rather than re-project, and of an internal 'skin' which can protect from the invasion of another mind. The situation in the dream describes a basic analytic situation in which my analytic mind – here seen as phallic – is felt to be dangerous. In the incident which she associates with the dream, she is the one with the analytic mind who is trying to force a point of view on to someone who is non-comprehending. In the analytic setting it is often difficult to distinguish between a real misunderstanding or not hearing on my part, from my simply having a different but valid perspective. The telescope in the dream condenses

95

many ideas: the phallic intrusive voyeuristic eye/I, the use of insight for destructive purposes, the sado-masochistic provocation enacted in the sessions around interpretations as phallic projectile, the 'keeping an eye on' certain distant situations from the past which means that the past becomes not something which is worked through and assimilated but a collection of grievances to be stored and kept awake, a weapon of recrimination, and the telescoping of situations so that they get reproduced *ad infinitum* from past to present and from generation to generation,[5] and indeed in her childhood she had been forced to 'see' disturbing situations between her parents which could not be made sense of. There is also evidence that they each tried to force a point of view on the other and on their children, leading to violent enactments and eventual divorce.

Carole starts another session by saying that I don't realise that she didn't have a mother. Her mother wasn't there. Her mother was always out at work (and indeed her mother had worked long hours including night shifts during Carole's childhood). There was her grandma, she said, but she was only there twice a week. The twice a week rang a bell for me but it was only after the session that I realised that this connected with the fact that Carole had spoken of her wish to cut down her five sessions a week to two in order to have more time for herself. I now realised that she had taken something I had said the previous week as indicating that I would agree to this, and this was a sign that I was giving in but also more importantly that I was giving up on her.

She brought some dreams:

> She was in her parents' house and there were snakes, one of them in particular was frightening, it was huge, grotesque even. They became worms, "you know, like when people have worms sometimes, coming out of me (*sic*!)."

In the next dream:

> She is in a car with a new baby and her husband and his cousin Sam, they are going up a tower, driving around but it is very narrow and her husband keeps hitting the sides and then Sam is hanging over the edge to make him see the danger that they could fall all the way down. Then they are in a loft apartment and there is the feeling of things being all over the place. The last bit conveyed to me a sense of unintegration.

Carole had been complaining in the session that her husband spent too much time at the pub after work with a colleague, so I simply pointed out that there was a threesome in the car. She immediately retorted that there can be some very good threesomes, like the one made up of her (widowed) grandma, herself and her brother, and how that was an example of how a threesome can work, how it can be a very good thing. She implied that it was the only good threesome in the family. The brother she refers to is an older idealised stepbrother to whom she turned when her younger sibling was born. She thought she had a special connection with him and would get lost in imaginative play with him. Her studying literature and going on to be an academic was connected with this relationship. Thinking about the new baby in the dream, she says she would like a child but the problem is that she is not sexually attracted to her husband.

I thought the dream described the result of her poisonous hatred of me when she thought I was not upholding the full time analysis, for not being attentive to her. But I want to draw particular attention to how it is the sexual couple which is attacked while instead she idealises the sibling couple, brother and sister with their grandmother. This led to a state of mind, 'in the loft', where she feels scattered. And indeed, I myself found it extremely hard to think in the session and could only make connections and reconstruct what had been happening once the session was over. The huge grotesque snake in the dream I think reflects her hatred of that 'more important' relationship between the parents based on sexual desire, the sexual link which she has made grotesque and then turned into shitty little worms. The 'good threesome' is one in which there is no parental couple. In fact in that threesome the main relationships are between her and the grandma, and her and the stepbrother. A relationship between the stepbrother and the grandma doesn't figure. Even the relationship to the stepbrother is described as something which is not differentiated between two people, and more as a state of narcissistic entrancement. It has to do with an aspiration for a state close to what Freud describes with his notion of Nirvana (1940 [1938]), a seemingly pleasurable state but which Freud linked to the death drive and the undoing of connections. Sexuality has been silenced by the death drive whose aim is to undo connections (Freud, 1938), and what Green calls the 'disobjectalizing function'. Whether more innately or more environmentally determined – and I believe that Carole had had to deal with a large degree of psychic intrusion and that she did not have an object who could act as "a protective shield against stimuli" and container for her distress, in combination with her own hypersensitivity and intolerance[6] – the outcome was one in which the search for a nirvana-like state threatened the libidinal link to the object, the analyst and her husband for whom she felt no desire.

In all three of the cases discussed, the fear of intrusion, the central feminine anxiety, is notable. It manifested around the attitude to food in the first case and led in the analysis to a sense of my having to be extremely cautious and restrained in my interpretations; in the second case it was defended against by the patient's own phallic intrusiveness, and the danger was always of the enactment of the sado–masochistic interchange she tried to provoke. In both of these cases the libidinal wish, silent or explosive, tenuous or charged with aggression, was evident. In the third case, the wish to break all links predominated and endangered the libidinal connection to her objects, who risked giving up on her.

There has been disagreement as to how to understand what I call 'noisy sexuality'. Freud himself wrote that the transference neurosis should be kept "within the narrowest limits" and analysts since then seem divided as to how much of the erotic in the analysis is defensive, and how much needs to be allowed to develop (Bolognini, 1994). Sexualisation has also been described as having a protective function. It is a way of dealing with anxiety (McDougall, 1978, ch. IV) and a way of binding aggression and preserving the object (Stoller, 1975), of expressing conflicts by projecting what has been disavowed (Fonagy, 2008).

My patient Beatrice used erotisation to drown painful feelings in excitement and to provide a sense of bodily unity. Erotisation was also used to make herself feel 'big' rather than small and needy, a partner rather than a child. But at the same time it contained within it the attempt to satisfy infantile tactile, olfactive and other needs in an all-enveloping way to make up for experienced non-availability.

Often, both noisy and silent sexuality coexist and the task is to search for that which is silent, for the unconscious phantasy. One promiscuous man in analysis, Daniel, whose sexual fantasies, heterosexual and homosexual, invaded the sessions, eventually settled down and married. There was then a prolonged period in which his wife was presented as someone who was always wanting him to end his analysis or making him miss his sessions. My interpretations about the various permutations of this threesome, of the provocation or projection of jealousy, went on for a long time without modifying the situation. Eventually what emerged was that what was being enacted was a masturbation fantasy in which two women were fighting over him while he remained passive. It also became clear that the situation satisfied the masochistic wish to be bullied by his wife (and by me) as we both 'demanded' and desired his presence. Silently, this situation was very gratifying and risked provoking an interminable analysis.

Every analysis has a silent sexuality, the libidinal drive which keeps the treatment alive, keeps the patient coming. It is the motor of the transference. It can be used to *bind* destructive elements as described with Daniel.

The degree to which the analyst is seen as the real object rather than a representative of the object will colour the analysis. The *erotised* transference describes the former. It has been distinguished from the *erotic* transference which has a less psychotic flavour (Bolognini, 1994). In the erotised transference, what I refer to as 'noisy sexuality', the 'as if' quality can be virtually non-existent, 'as if' in the sense that Chasseguet-Smirgel (1992, p. 20), for instance, writes,

> The infant at play, the actor and the spectator, are all simultaneously aware and unaware that 'it is just a game.' The rules of the game are spelled out, the curtain rises, and we are transported into another space where things are 'as if' they were real. The analytic situation obeys this principle. When the session begins, the patient enters another universe, rather like the words 'once upon a time' indicate we are being led into the world of fairy tale.

For some patients, the problem will be that they cannot risk entering the analytic world as if it were real, while for others like Beatrice, on the contrary, there was little distinction between the space inside the analysis and outside the analysis. Fonagy and Target discuss related issues (1996). In fact in order to use a more symbolic mode of thinking in relation to her analyst, Beatrice had to tolerate a libidinal link of a more infantile nature, a more silent sexuality. The erotic as opposed to the erotised I thought was later expressed when she told me about a childhood play, imagining all sorts of things, exploring underground places and secret openings. *That* erotic has its roots in infantile sexuality, sensuality, penetration, exploration and curiosity. We could also see this in the 'silent sexuality' which would eventually emerge in the analysis of Marie.

In making a distinction between silent and noisy sexuality, I have wanted to take into account the many guises in which sexuality manifests in the consulting room, from the quiet primary libidinal link to the analyst, to the more obvious sexual manifestations, not forgetting situations where a silent phantasy keeps the patient in analysis but prevents the analysis from developing. As always in psychoanalysis, we should not be distracted by the noise; the silent is what we aim to bring out.

Notes

1 Translation taken from the book review of *La Clinique Contemporaine* (Green, 2012) by Mancini in *International Journal of Psycho-Analysis* (2014, pp. 1356–1360).
2 Early analysis (1923) in *Love, Guilt and Reparation* (1975).
3 For a discussion of 'The sublimation debate' between Anna Freud and Kleinians see Hinshelwood (1997).
4 Segal writes:

> One of Freud's greatest contributions to psychology was the discovery that sublimation is the outcome of a successful renunciation of an instinctual aim; I would like to suggest here that such a successful renunciation can happen only through a process of mourning, This giving up of an instinctual aim, or object, is a repetition and at the same time a reliving of the giving up of the breast. It can be successful, like this first situation, if the object to be given up can be assimilated in the ego, by the process of loss and internal restoration. I suggest that such an assimilated object becomes a symbol within the ego. Every aspect of the object, every situation that has to be given up in the process of growing, gives rise to symbol formation. In this view, symbol formation is the outcome of a loss; it is a creative act involving the pain and the whole work of mourning.
>
> (Segal, 1977, p. 196)

5 Haydee Faimberg (2005) uses the image of the telescope and the word 'telescoping' to describe how the traumas of one generation are relived in the next.
6 Britton discusses minus K in terms of an inadequacy on the maternal side to process accurately the infant's projection, and "on the infant's side, an inadequate tolerance of the mother's approximations to understanding. As, on the whole, we proceed by a series of approximations in analysis, if we have a patient who experiences approximation as traumatic or aggressive" (Britton, 2000, p. 64).

5

BULIMIA AND ANOREXIA NERVOSA
IN THE TRANSFERENCE

One can approach eating disorders and specific eating disorders from the point of view of what they have in common, and indeed there are certain typical features which may be found in the different eating disorders: the avoidance of dependency on the maternal object and the narcissistic preoccupation with the self, the anal control of the object, the control over instinctual desires, among others. There are similarities between anorexic and bulimic patients in relation to how shameful or humiliating they feel their needs to be, and in their preoccupation with their body image and with being seen.

One can also take an approach which cuts across the specific disorders and considers them more in terms of the level of disturbance of the particular patients presenting these disorders, which ranges from a life-threatening disorder to one which is almost within the normal range of preoccupation with food and body image.

Because the eating disorder is only the symptom and because it is multi-determined, there are many levels and ways of understanding it which also has to take account of the individual patient and his or her history. It is however a symptom which can be so pervasive that it becomes a way of life, or of near death. Often when we speak of anorexia nervosa we are also speaking of a character formation, of a patient whose life and psyche is permeated with that issue, and not of a patient who may as part of his or her problems have an eating disorder which is more or less prevalent at different times.

Unlike some other symptoms, an eating disorder attaches to the most basic and vital function of the body. For this reason it is

101

tempting to look at it in relation purely to orality, although it clearly interacts which issues of anality, and of genital sexuality, as we know from its typical development at puberty or adolescence. Often there is a confusion of zones, leading to shame. But it also has to be remembered that in normal development eating is linked to the earliest and most pleasurable experience of sucking at the breast, so that the vicissitudes of infantile sexuality and the relation to pleasure in conjunction with the relationship to the object needs to be considered.

Like all symptoms, the eating disorder at once expresses and avoids, and its specific meaning for a particular patient has to be sought. The issues around body weight, for instance, can express an intolerable 'too much': too much desire, too much need, too much sensation, too much intrusion; exerting control is an attempt to limit this and a means of survival. The fear of being fat can be a fear of being out of control but also a fear of abnormality, concentrating on a body part which comes to signify badness. The frequent issues around the 'too big bottom' point to a connection between mouth-vagina–anus, and to greed and aggression. The bulimic or over-weight patient who speaks of 'eating rubbish' is expressing anal spoiling and turning away from a potential good feed from the primary object. Greed which replaces need does not lead to satisfaction due to its aggressive and spoiling nature. Eating 'rubbish' compulsively, as a masochistic self-feed, is felt to be safer than depending on an unreliable object. Reducing the world to issues of food is a desperate attempt to find a way of controlling what is felt to be uncontrollable, while relying on a person is experienced as risky. Appetite itself is hated (Lucas, 2001) and sometimes disavowed. In fact, eating-disordered patients have very demanding and needy internal objects, and a 'greedy' super-ego which never lets up and makes huge demands both of themselves and of their objects, and this permeates through their attempts to need nothing. They seem to be constantly in the middle of an internal battlefield which can be hard to bear for themselves and for their objects. They are in a never-ending battle with their own body, experienced as a bad object. A sadistic super-ego leaves them with a characteristic low self-esteem. Tustin (1984) suggests in a paper on anorexia nervosa that these are patients who are extremely sensitive and for whom sensual pleasure feels 'too much' and too threatening. Williams (1997) considers that many of these patients have been projected into by their parents, while Lawrence (2002) describes an internal intrusive object which is often linked to intrusive aspects of these patients towards their parents.

Different theoretical orientations can account for how the main problem is located differently by different authors, in the oral symptom, or in preoccupation with death and anxieties about being annihilated, or in anxieties about feminine Oedipal wishes, or in the body image, or in issues of separation, or in disturbance of ego structure. There have also been attempts at classification of different types: melancholic, fetishistic, hysterical, obsessive-compulsive (Ripa di Meana, 1999, reviewed by Lawrence, 2001). Other distinctions have been made between individuals who are at the more neurotic and those at the more psychotic end of the spectrum, or in terms of the balance of strength between anorexic and non-anorexic part (Lucas, 2001). Sours (1974) makes a distinction between anorexics who refuse food in order to attain autonomy, the more disturbed of whom show structural ego defects related to a failure in early separation and individuation, and anorexics who deal with the resurgence of Oedipal feminine wishes in adolescence through regressive solutions to an oral aggressive position where cannibalistic fantasies arouse fears of destruction of the maternal object. There is also an extensive literature coming from the field of family therapy.

The choice of symptomatology within the range of eating disorders will depend on many factors and, in the literature, classifications vary. Sometimes anorexia includes all those who refuse to maintain a normal body weight whether by restricting intake or purging (Freedman and Lavender, 2002). For the purposes of this chapter the distinction I make is between bulimics who engage in cycles of gorging and vomiting, and anorexics who restrict their intake of food to a dangerous level.

While anorexia is, at least partly a defence against sexual oral-genital impulses, bulimia can enact an erotised phantasy. By making herself vomit the patient is re-enacting the scene of forced entry followed by evacuation, a sado-masochistic scene. The vomiting sometimes expresses a phantasy of the penis ejaculating over the breast in a contemptuous and soiling way, or an excited defecation. The primal scene is enacted in a defensive bisexual identification aimed at denying the humiliation of primal scene exclusion, as Schwartz (1986, p. 449) describes:

the stereotyped ritual of gorging on food and forcing one's finger down the throat to induce regurgitation represents in part a simultaneous identification with both parents in the primal scene with an acting out on one's own body the imagined role of the sadistic phallic father and castrated suffering mother.

I understand the phallic identification as a wish to avoid the experience of being needy, small and lacking both in relation to the mother and in relation to the primal scene in which is projected violent intrusive and hateful feelings.

Sometimes there has been exposure to a disturbing parental sexuality and it is this which is being re-enacted, and sometimes there has been boundary violation, and the vomiting is an attempt at managing that which feels unmanageable. The bulimic/vomiting symptom also relates to the experience of an early environment which did not offer a protective shield against impingements so that intrusion and expulsion become compulsively erotised and re-enacted as a way of managing and dealing with anxiety. Often these patients have been at the same time neglected and over-stimulated. A lack of containment describes their experience. In the limited context of private practice and supervision, I noted that the patients who make themselves vomit have, more often than patients who restrict their intake, been subjected to sexual intrusion and/or severe traumatic family histories. In the case of anorexic patients I have found at times a lack of differentiation of the self in relation to the parents of the primal scene and of the parents from each other with a consequent confusion and subsequent attempt at splitting.

Schwartz (1986) suggests that early and frequent exposure to primal-scene stimuli occur with great frequency in eating-disorder patients in general. Opinions however are divided as to whether there is more incidence of childhood sexual abuse in the group of eating-disordered patients than in the general population (see Lawrence, 2002). It needs to also be remembered that while we find 'indigestible' experiences in eating-disordered patients, patients who suffered trauma and intrusion can develop other symptomatologies.

The origin of the disturbance is no doubt always multifaceted. Categorisations and generalisations have the disadvantage of ignoring the specificity of individuals, their conflicts and their histories. From a psychoanalytic perspective we can only describe the complexity of the individual patient, her internal world and her defences, as these are relived in the psychoanalytic situation. At the most general level, one can say that for the eating-disordered patient there is a failure of symbolic function so that food is equated with experience or thought and is used as an attempt to control emotional experiences which are felt to be dangerous or overwhelming, by avoidance, forced entry or vomiting.

Psychoanalysis offers a stage on which the dramas of the internal world are re-enacted. The provision of the space and the use of words instead of action can in themselves create anxiety. When working psychoanalytically with an eating-disordered patient, what is central in my view is to consider in specific detail how the eating disorder manifests on the analytic stage and to pay close attention to the movements in the transference and countertransference, as I will describe. I have found with bulimic and anorexic patients with whom I have worked that at the forefront there is always a sort of 'struggle for life', as if they are only barely allowed to live and enjoy, and every small movement in that direction is hard won and easily destroyed.

Jacqueline is a single French woman in her thirties whose parents left a North African country in traumatic circumstances, losing relatives in the process. Her own move to London from a city in the South of France, leaving behind her parents and two siblings, although desired by herself due to a good work opportunity, reawakened severe anxieties around displacement, and she asked for help a year after she arrived, encouraged by a woman with whom she shared an apartment.

Jacqueline made herself vomit every day. I will describe a sequence a few years into the analysis when making herself vomit had become infrequent. In a session at the beginning of the week, Jacqueline tells me that she dreamt – and this is unusual – that her mother had come to help her and had made her apartment look nice. Jacqueline had in reality just moved to a new place, this time into an apartment of her own, and this had been a sign of her development, but she had subsequently felt overwhelmed by how much needed to be done following her move. In this particular session however she went on, after describing the dream, to express gratitude towards me for remembering things about her and towards her brother for his love and constancy. This felt very new, genuine and moving. In the next session however she described a dream which warned of an impending danger. In the dream a child was climbing up the glass shelves in the kitchen (shelves which in reality she had been putting up in her new apartment) and the child's brother was watching gleefully as the child was about to knock down all the glass shelves, fall down and hurt herself. The child's brother was also making fun of her for being frightened of what was about to happen. In the following session Jacqueline described a dream in which her mother had an evil look and her brother was masturbating. After this session Jacqueline made herself vomit.

In this sequence it seems that the grateful feelings expressed at the beginning of the week had been difficult to maintain, perhaps out of an envious feeling towards her own loving self and towards a mother and analyst who had been felt to be helping her, and perhaps because the good experience can lead to loss, a loss imagined as traumatic. The two things go together insofar as the good object is envied because it is thought to contain the goodness which would make one immune to traumatic loss. It is also the case that a good experience feels uncontrollable while destroying gives the illusion of control.

Importantly, Jacqueline is able to represent the inner struggle in the second dream, and she shows herself to be worried about what she knows unconsciously will inevitably happen psychically. She depicts the internal situation, in which she finds herself painfully struggling against a self-destructive urge in which she knows in the end that 'the child'/her gets hurt. Her concern about this situation is also mocked.[1] With the third dream the awareness of a conflict or of anxiety is no longer represented, and it seems that the battle against the self-destructive urge has now been lost. The internal mother has become a persecutor rather than someone who can help prevent the destructive urges, and her own concern has been wiped out. At this point Jacqueline feels she has something intolerable inside her, no longer thoughts and emotions but unbearable physical sensations in her abdomen which need to be evacuated. As the third dream also depicts, a masturbatory situation takes over. It is an attempt to feel in control of something too disturbing to be thought about. Both of us had been helpless in preventing this turnaround.

What precedes vomiting is at times more clearly depressive. Vomiting in that case is an attempt to get rid of a damaged object and of feelings of guilt. This was an aspect of the situation described above in which guilt becomes so intense and persecutory that it cannot be thought about and instead is evacuated.

It is also useful to look in detail at what follows the vomiting, whether it leads to relief, detachment, or to a depressive or guilty feeling leading to a new cycle of vomiting. When good and bad experiences can be better tolerated, a different development can slowly take place.

Bulimic patients in my experience often stop making themselves vomit fairly early on in their analysis which attests to the extent to which the symptom depicts something quite 'unmanageable' without someone there to help, but also suggests an ability to make use of a 'container' when it is available. Once the analysis is on the way and the vomiting is no longer used as a 'self-help' method, the bulimic situation becomes enacted in the session where it can be interpreted. For instance, there may be a subtle mutual enactment as when a patient fills the session with incoherent disturbing bits and pieces over a few sessions and then goads the analyst into making a 'harsh' interpretation which provokes an 'explosion' which unconsciously aims to relieve the patient, in the way that vomiting did, of an incomprehensible and uncomfortable state, a mixture of emotion and sensation. In this situation both parties have been subjected to something unbearable and pushed into 'bulimic action'.

In a different scenario, Barrows describes how her patient, Miss Y, often did not metabolise interpretations but regurgitated versions of them without allowing the content to affect her at a deeper level (Barrows, 1999). She connects her patient's fear of being emotionally touched to her patient's fear of her parents' internal objects experienced as vengeful ghosts, in the context of their unmourned losses. This resonates with my experience of a number of bulimic patients for whom the vehemence of their attacking super-ego links with parental traumas. In my view they are hypersensitive to being 'touched' so that contact is very disturbing and the experience needs to be evacuated in order to gain control and feel more separate. While the anorexic stops anything getting in, it is precisely the feeling of not being able to protect herself from something getting in which the bulimic patient is battling with, and she has to repeat the 'getting in' and 'throwing up'. Often this is with a background of actual sexual intrusion as well as intense parental projections. This fuels the erotised aspect of the bulimia as shown with Jacqueline.

I now turn to a different picture: anorexia nervosa. The protective barrier in this case is powerful. I focus here on a particular aspect of anorexia, namely the wish and fear of fusion with the mother. A number of authors have also been impressed by this aspect (Bene, 1973; Spillius, 1973; Bruch, 1974; Boris, 1984; Sprince, 1984; Hughes *et al.*, 1985). From this perspective, anorexia may be seen as a girl's attempt to have a body separate from her mother's body, and a sense of self separate from her mother, the pathological nature of this attempt arising from the very lack of achievement of such separateness prior to adolescence. The anorexic is caught between the 'terror of aloneness' (Sprince, 1984) and the terror of psychic annihilation. Whereas the wish and fear of fusion with the mother could lead in the boy to sexual perversion (Glasser, 1979), in the girl it could lead to finding a way of having a body different from the mother's body, as if maturing into adulthood is experienced as becoming the mother (Hughes *et al.*, 1985). In the extreme it would mean doing away with her body altogether. The wish to be fused, the refusal to take and the attack on the representation of the mother's body through self-starvation are given fuel by feelings of envy. As with perversions, 'normal' adulthood and, in this case, femininity, are denigrated in favour of a different way of life and body appearance (including masculine elements).

Boris (1984, p. 319) discusses fusion in terms of the lack of a 'not me' and 'not you' space. Making use of Winnicott's idea of the transitional space (1971), he says: "the transitional space is like a buffer, a neutral zone, between two bodies (as if a demilitarized zone) which makes room for the play of imagination and the apprehension of reality – both." The anorexic has failed to maintain those boundaries and hence that space.

I have also been struck by the experience in the transference and countertransference with anorexic patients, from a purely phenomenological point of view, of the lack of a space between patient and analyst. One might think of this as the lack of a third term – the father who disrupts the phantasy of fusion. I use the term 'father' here as one talks about 'the breast', not the actual organ or the person, but the father as representing the other, and the space between mother and infant, the space without which there will be no symbols, no words. I am suggesting, therefore, that there is in anorexia nervosa a disturbance in the area of symbolisation connected with this lack of space. In anorexia nervosa the food is felt actually to be the mother rather than representing her care, and the

108

maturation of her body is felt to be taking a piece of her mother's body away from her, rather than developing a body which symbolises adulthood and motherliness. In the sessions, the analyst's words do not symbolise care but are felt to be the milk, or nipple or penis which literally make her fat, pregnant, sleepy, poisoned, etc. Projection, envy, the lack of needs being met appropriately and the consequent need for total and omnipotent control of the object, can all contribute to this lack of transitional space and hence hinder the development of the capacity for true symbolisation.

If a person's identity is constructed in language (Lacan, 1977), then perhaps the refusal to talk, so characteristic of anorexics, is also a refusal to take on an identity (as female) and a refusal to be defined (as adult). The anorexic girl is continually attempting to achieve a separate identity in the face of this lack of differentiation, but not the one which is structured for her, and she maintains a state in which she is in phantasy both fused with Mother and not like her.

I wish to illustrate these points and some of the determinants of this state of affairs through the description of the first four years of the analysis of an anorexic patient, Denise. I have found the features I describe to be present in other anorexic patients. There are, of course, aspects of anorexia nervosa which I will not be discussing here, for example, the somatic delusions, the obsessional features or the sexual fears, all of which are important. My aim here is to illustrate what I feel to be a central type of object relationship of the anorexic patient to her analyst and hence to her primary objects.

I will divide the material from the first four years of psychoanalysis into three phases. A first phase was characterised by Denise's wish to be merged with me in order to deny need, slowly giving way to a second phase when she could accept greater separateness from me and begin to communicate more verbally but during which she was repeatedly trying to destroy her own wish and attempt to become an 'ordinary' adult woman. During the third phase, anxieties about loss and death which had been defended against by the anorexic state of mind were released. My exclusive attention to and interpretation of her mode of relating to me and of her states of mind, in an unhurried way, rather than any discussion of food or weight, enabled, in my view, this development.

Denise is in her twenties. She has been overtly anorexic since her early teens. Denise comes from a French-speaking country where she pursued architectural studies, the profession of her mother and

109

father. Denise had just come out of the anorexic unit of a hospital in her home town when her father took up a contract in London. Denise, who did not wish to go back to her studies, came to London with the family. She was under 6.5 stones when she went into hospital. Her weight increased in hospital but went rapidly down again when she came out. Denise had suffered from amenorrhoea for years. When she moved to London her doctor arranged for her to go for regular appointments at a hospital. A few months after this she started analysis with me, following the long-standing advice of this doctor. Denise was then 23 years old.

Denise arrived 15 minutes early for her initial consultation with me. She struck me as being tiny, like a child. She was wearing cord trousers, a shirt and running shoes, and I thought her gait was that of a boy. There seemed to be a disproportion between her head, which took up a lot of space because of a mass of reddish curly hair, and the rest of her, which seemed to shrivel away progressively. She had an enigmatic faint smile on her inscrutable face and she made me think of one of the Marx Brothers – Harpo; this was before I found out that she too was almost dumb. Interestingly, she once compared herself to another silent comedian, one from her own country, Marcel Marceau, when she described feeling in the previous session like his act in which he pretends to be wearing a mask with a permanent smile while his face is intermittently struggling to get through.

In this first consultation, I invited Denise to tell me something about herself and why she had come to see me. She was silent and tense, and eventually said, "this isn't going to work". She seemed to be struggling with herself about whether or not to get up and leave. I tried to encourage her to talk, but again she said, "there is no point in this". I took up how she was showing me the difficulty which had brought her here, that she wanted to be helped but then she felt in despair because she couldn't let another person try to give this help. She was silent and eventually said she found it humiliating. We struggled along like this until the end of the time I had allocated to her. I then said that I would like to help her find out what her difficulties were about and gave her the times of the vacancy I had. She said: "I think you'd better keep that vacancy for someone else." I said she felt she wasn't worth it. She looked tense and upset. As she walked out she said she did not think she wanted to come again. I said I thought she should at least come tomorrow

110

and we could discuss it further. Denise did continue, coming five times a week, though for a long time I would never take it for granted that she would keep coming. Months later she said to me: "You asked me why I wanted to come ... they think I'm coming because of anorexia, I'm coming because I don't like what I am, what I do, what I think."

In the first phase, lasting over 18 months, Denise hardly spoke. In a typical session she arrived early. She did not look up when I came to collect her from the waiting room. She lay very still on the couch with her hand covering her face. Her fingers are cyanosed. She could remain entirely silent for up to three sessions running. When she did talk she rarely made more than one to three statements. These would be very brief and usually highly ambiguous or even incomprehensible. The tone of her voice was also often ambiguous, so I couldn't be sure of her mood. Usually she did not respond to what I said. She left without looking at me or saying goodbye, banging the door when she was angry.

I felt that Denise wanted to be merged with me, that I should know things about her without her having to tell me, and, most of all, that I should get it absolutely right. To talk meant acknowledging that she needed something from me and that I had something she hadn't got. She said on one occasion: "I'm being very generous when I talk because that increases the difference" (between us, she meant). The very use of words meant acknowledging the presence of two separate people who have to use a common language to understand each other, and I sometimes had the fantasy that she and I were buried in a tomb of silence for eternity. Denise often used the pronoun 'you' to refer to something she was feeling or thinking, as if she and I were one person.[2]

There was a phase where she came closer to acknowledging some regressive wishes, holding the sleeve of a large woolly sweater against her face as a child might hold a blanket for comfort. She reacted by becoming severely anorexic. She told me that she wanted to have the strength not to eat anything. She felt hungry and the soles of her feet were cold and her head ached, but she had to prove that she was strong. She said that she can only eat if she has a reason to eat. If she tells herself that there is a reason for keeping to a certain weight, then she is justified to eat, but then she thinks it is just a trick so that she can eat, and then she cannot eat. I took up how much she hated needing someone or something outside herself

111

in order to keep alive, how she wanted to feel she depended on no one. She replied, "I could say to myself, in order to keep alive, you need something or someone, eat you silly fool – then I think I'm just giving myself an excuse and I can't eat."

In a later session, referring to her parents commenting on some food she was eating, she said, "they always point out that I'm not infallible and then I smash a cup". I know how tactful I must be in pointing out her progress if it is not to be totally smashed up. She once told me of her admiration for a friend of hers who was killed while on an expedition, her admiration for the fact that he could deny his own comfort and safety to the point of death, that not even death would make him renege his ideals. In fact, anything short of death means imperfection.

Denise never told me what she would be doing or had done during weekend or holiday breaks, but she did describe one holiday, two years later, which expressed the state of omnipotent self-sufficiency and of fusion with an ideal breast into which she withdrew:

> Two summers ago, when I was in Norway, the last week we went to this island with a hill in the middle. We were the only people there for one whole week. It was hard, pushing one's way through the forest, but it was great. The last night I went to sleep and I thought, I'm the only person who knows how to live, and in 24 hours I'll be back in London and I won't be able to do anything.

And, as after most holidays, she very nearly broke off treatment. In fact she broke off treatment with the doctor at the hospital with whom (I found out later when he wrote to me) she had been having 'psychotherapy' concurrently with her analysis. She had, he wrote, now reached a weight close to her target weight.

It was clear that Denise did not successfully block off her need but on the contrary that she felt only too painfully aware of them and that she found it extremely difficult to tolerate the frustration of these needs. On one of the very rare occasions on which she was late, she eventually described how she had been stuck in traffic. An ambulance had come and couldn't get by: she had got very wound up. She switched on the radio, and it was much too loud and about all the things on the news which made her feel wound up (I

112

presumed she was referring to tragedies and violence). She arrived 20 minutes late and thought ... (she stopped). She didn't tell me what she thought, but I imagined it was that now she was here she couldn't see why she had felt so desperate about getting here or what it was she was coming for. I thought she was telling me about a part of herself that feels a tremendous urgency and emergency to get to me, and the murderous feelings and rage this leads to when she is frustrated and how her only way of dealing with this is to want nothing. She left the session saying, "now I have to face the bogeyman". The situation she described also reminded me of an infant who gets so excited that she cannot feed. I thought it also described the way in which she stops herself getting to the 'breast'. "I want so much and I hate myself if I take", she said one day. And on another occasion she was able to let me know how, behind her wall of silence, she felt intensely: "I just have one basic feeling state which is a mixture of frustration and resentment and which is made up of hate, fear, horror, and makes me just want to crash about."

One important way in which Denise dealt with her feelings of need was by perceiving me to be the demanding and needy one whom she could then frustrate and control. I would be hanging on to her every word, straining to hear her very soft voice, being left dangling when she stopped in mid–sentence, or when after half an hour's silence she would finally say three words but I couldn't grasp them or they didn't make sense, and she would never repeat or elaborate upon what she had said, so that I was left feeling that I had missed something which would have made everything clear! She controlled my 'feed' with great strictness so that I was constantly kept in a state of undernourishment but also in this way she could control my response to her, increasing my pleasure and excitement when she finally said something, after being deprived, just as she once told me how she can increase her own pleasure in eating by starving herself first.

I was also struck by how there was a sense in which she and I had to compete for resources. There was a curious rhythm to the sessions: long silence ... I would say something fairly brief ... long silence ... she would say something fairly brief ... long silence ... I would speak again, etc. It was as if we had to take it in turns and it had to be equal shares. She wouldn't give me more than I had given her. There was a sort of rivalry as to which one of us was the more needy one or the more deserving of fulfilment. One day she was annoyed about her stomach rumbling and I took up that she didn't mention that my stomach had rumbled first (with hunger, I thought). She said: "I thought to myself 'I can beat you at that game'." On another occasion, when I pointed to the aspects of myself and of herself that she saw as never-satisfied infants, she replied, "I wonder which greedy baby deserves to be fed".

Denise also wanted to make out that talking was for my benefit only: "What if I never talked? I think that you would tell me that I have to talk." This was connected with the way, too, that Denise wanted to see me, as a voraciously demanding and never-satisfied parent. This was, of course, the sort of exacting internal parent inside her which really had the characteristics of a greedy, never-satisfied baby. She told me once that she was doing an impossible wallpapering job for a woman, impossible because there wasn't enough paper, but the woman told her that she had to manage nevertheless. Meanwhile, this woman's mother was dying and Denise was filled with hate, fear and horror. I thought that she was describing how she feared she could not survive in the face of such a cruel, exacting part of herself, as she felt I, too, would not survive.

I also felt that Denise wanted me to experience something of a sense of hope which then becomes crushed (disappointment is a common experience, it seems, in those who deal with anorexic patients). I had a particularly acute experience along those lines one day. I was talking to her when suddenly I looked up and noticed that she had her hands on her head with her arms covering her ears, and I experienced a moment of acute panic and disorientation when I realised that I thought she had been listening but now found she was 'deaf' and my words had fallen into a void. I wondered to what extent she was communicating to me her own experience of sudden and utter aloneness when she expected contact, and how this would make her wish for self-sufficiency, or else wish to be one with a loved person. But even aloneness suggests the existence of another, and in that moment I felt that it was my identity as an analyst, or even my very existence, which had been threatened, and perhaps it is that very sense of identity and self which Denise is searching for through an anorexic solution.

Although Denise wanted me to understand her perfectly without having to explain anything, and wanted to be merged with me, she also felt extremely intruded upon when I did understand, and it was with great reluctance that she would let me know that I had got it right. Once, when I commented on something she had said, she retorted: "Oh! I just said it to create confusion." I thought that Denise's great secretiveness was meant to humiliate me but also to protect her sense of separate identity. Denise could not find a way of taking in order to discover her own sense of self. To take, for her, meant to be taken over, and psychic annihilation.

The seeds of the second phase were sown gradually. Denise could begin to acknowledge her dependency on me as a separate person: "I used to be able not to care, but now it doesn't work anymore, that's what I meant yesterday when I said I wish people had left me alone."

Rather than using the 'you' to refer to her own thoughts, Denise now used 'I' and addressed me more directly. This suggested to me at once greater differentiation between us and greater intimacy. She could now let me know how much she did want to come. The whole rhythm of the sessions changed. In a typical session she now started talking after a short silence. She said a few things before waiting for me to speak, and carried on if I remained silent. My countertransference changed too. I began to feel less concerned that Denise would break off treatment, even though she would occasionally threaten to, and it was still a very real possibility after holiday breaks. I no longer felt that I had a fragile baby on my hands whose survival depended on my perfect handling and tuning into. Simultaneously I noticed that I became less patient with her silences, and less able (or willing) to tune in and read the non-verbal communications during these silences. I now expected more of her.

Denise never resumed her architectural studies, although she had done a few years already and she repeated many times her anguished complaint that she didn't know what to do. (Only years later did she tell me that during the early part of her analysis she had spent many hours every day running.) Then, about 18 months after starting analysis, unbeknown to me, Denise applied and was accepted for a postgraduate degree in education, with the idea of becoming a French teacher. She only told me about this some months later when a clash with the times of her sessions was approaching. She told me with great difficulty, convinced as she was that I would laugh at her for thinking she was capable of it.

Denise started her course and this proved extremely difficult for her. She faced the same sorts of problems which presumably led her to interrupt her original studies. From the very first day she wanted to give up and to end it, and it was touch and go whether she would continue. I felt, much as I had felt before with the analysis, that the burden was upon me to prevent her from destroying it, and it felt like an enormously tiresome, discouraging, repetitive burden. I told her she was giving me the option of either being like a mother who would get exasperated and tell her to get on and do something, and that would make her furious and she would want to stop doing anything, or like an over-indulgent mother who would say that it didn't matter if she didn't want to do anything, but then she would feel that I didn't care. This seemed to ease things temporarily.

Having managed to make it to the end of the course, the next problem was getting a job, or rather accepting a job, as Denise apparently had no problem being offered a job. She would say, with relief, that she did not get the job, but on closer inspection it turned out that when she was asked if she felt she could manage it, she would say no; or, when asked whether she would accept the job if she was offered it, she would say no (and was then told she would have been offered it). Partly, of course, it was difficult for Denise to acknowledge that she wanted something, but also no job was the right one.

She did eventually accept a job and again this proved enormously difficult for her. She was teaching difficult secondary school pupils. Denise saw in the pupils her hatred of being taught and helped. "I don't like teaching, at least if you're being taught you can kick the teacher. I don't want to teach people who don't want to be taught." She found it excruciating to stand in front of a class, and felt watched and criticised. Denise also hated being a beginner, making mistakes, not being an experienced teacher straight away. She was convinced that it came easily to the other teachers, and she felt there was no way of getting help. She found it difficult to deal with the rebellious pupils. She felt that she was not good enough for the work, but at the same time that this sort of work was not 'good' enough (that is, worthy enough to make up for how bad she felt herself to be).

This was a familiar theme, as we had often seen how Denise felt that only undoing the past would be tolerable and relieve her of her enormous guilt. She felt nothing was worth doing, because it could never be good enough to make up for her past spitefulness and recalcitrance, and also because there was no point doing something when she knew that she was bound to destroy it in the future.

Denise could not stand being defined as a teacher, or as anything for that matter. She wanted to feel that all roads were open to her.

116

She wanted to be different, special. I thought that her secretiveness during our sessions had to do with this too. If she was clear and told me her thoughts, then she would be an 'ordinary' patient and I would know that her thoughts were ordinary.

Although Denise hated doing nothing, it became clear that, now that she was 'doing something' both in her sessions with me and in her outside life, she felt herself to be in much more direct competition with me and with other people, and she found it intolerable not to be the best. She thought she did not have the authority and charisma she felt she needed to make the pupils listen and work, while she felt that I had that capacity to make her work. This is illustrated in the following episode.

During this session Denise spoke of the teachers having a meeting about safety. Everything is dangerous and she had felt in a panic. She spoke about how she does not like teaching (because it's 'dangerous', I thought) and then she said she could only cope by telling herself that she was not going in the next day (until the last minute). She thought that the pupils were laughing at her. I said that she was terrified by her wish to kill those children who were giving her such a hard time.

To my surprise she then told me about a dream (the first in three years of analysis).

There was this child who shrunk and I stepped on it and killed it. It was shouting and I trod on it. It was either shouting or it was dead. It was so hard when it was shouting and so easy to kill.

Later she replaced the idea of killing the child by saying it turned into nothing. She went on to say: "this morning I was teaching a first year, they were copying a text and I realised that there were still 50 minutes and I didn't know what to do. In those cases I start writing 'Oh my God', back to front so others can't read it." I thought that she was telling me about her hatred of the shouting child in her, and how easy it was for her to stifle it or put things in such a way that I could not 'read' her thoughts. She seemed also to be referring to a fear that, in her maturation, that needy first-year child was shrinking and would be totally forgotten, especially as she felt she was either all screaming infant or else she had to completely squash that infant in order to function as an adult.

117

What I really want to bring out is the strength of Denise's reaction to having told me a dream. She very nearly gave up her job (perhaps her analysis) because she felt so exposed (in front of the pupils). In fact, she did not go into work and was not sure she could ever go back again. After the weekend she came to her session in a rather manic mood and told me how she had taken part in a stunt race, wading through a river, and how she could really hold her own (in a group of men), even though she is small and that the only person in her group who had been faster was over six feet tall. She was nearly or totally silent for the next two sessions, and on the third she said, "I wonder, if nobody can make me go into work, which they can't, what will happen?" It was only then that I saw more clearly that she wanted to prove to me that I could not make her work and how surprised she had been when she had found herself 'working', telling me a dream. I said she hated teaching and wanted to give it up when she felt that I could make her work while she felt she could not make her pupils work, that she had felt elated with the stunt racing, not only because she had done well, but also because she felt that in that sphere she didn't have to compare herself with me.

She returned the following day saying that fortunately she had gone back to work today and it wasn't so bad. She then told me about classes she just could not control but that she had not told anyone. She said that she had not wanted just to dictate things to the pupils and had tried to use less conservative methods, but how some sixth formers had complained about this to the headteacher. I took up how she had wanted to be freer here with me, in particular in feeling able to tell me about a dream, but then how a part of herself had wanted to come and spoil this and reinstitute order and control. Perhaps it was relevant that she spoke of the sixth formers, the most 'grown up', the side of herself most potentially in competition with me. After this she became able to tell me, with great shame, that she felt that in doing the job she was 'dressing up', and that she could only be a 'pretend teacher', and how it must be obvious that she is just like a child. She also thought that the fact that she was French had made it possible for her to pretend to do the job but something was missing of being 'a real teacher'. I took up how she wanted to remain a child, and how she felt I would laugh at her for wanting to be like me. She said, "but that's it, how could that be possible, I'm miles away, it is laughable.... Anyway, I don't even want to be a teacher."

I should mention here that she once let me know that she changed her clothes in her car before coming to her sessions because she felt too ill at ease; that is, that she could not present herself to me as an adult woman and wearing a skirt. "I feel intimidated by the girls at school who are blatantly sexual ... but it does not mean I want to be like them", she could tell me, and now, for the first time, she told me that she was suffering from amenorrhoea. For the first time she also told me that she had a boyfriend, a relationship she had been having for "nearly as long as I've been coming here". But still it was a great struggle for her to let me see a more grown–up side of herself (the sixth formers want to be treated like children).

The destructive attack on her wish to be a grown woman, like her mother, and the concurrent scorn for her (and for me when I am seen as the mother), because she feels she is 'miles away', made me think of my very strong countertransference feeling every time she cuts her hair from lovely long, reddish curls to a very short, hard, boyish cut, which I experience as a direct, almost physical attack on myself.

It was only a couple of months after the episode I described above that Denise told me one day that, in her words,

> something strange has been happening in the last month or so, without my even realising it: I've put on more weight than I could have imagined possible, I don't know if you've noticed, and I wasn't even aware of it; when you're used to being preoc-cupied with it, it takes some getting used to. It's so different, I don't know how to take it.

She also told me that she can look forward to eating something, eat it and feel satisfied, that she can 'get it right'. She mentioned, too, how she had begun, for the first time, enjoying being with other people.

But still, Denise was struggling with her feelings of envy: "the difference between us makes me inadequate", she says. And she hates her job because she does not feel capable of being a teacher. It is very hard for Denise to accept that she may want to be an ordinary adult woman like me. "I want to hang on to an uncon-ventional idea of what matters", she said, referring, I thought, to her wish for omnipotent self-sufficiency and scorn for the adult world. "It still comes to me in a flash, I know it's not true, but it

119

still comes to me in a flash that if I don't eat, everything will be all right and that if I do it will be worse ... the worse thing is that I know it's going backwards." I thought she was also referring to an idea that if she didn't take and learn from me, then she wouldn't have to need me and compare herself with me.

The third phase which I will describe was ushered in by Denise's increasing ability to tolerate intense feelings of need and dependency on me, in the fourth year of analysis. She told me quite cogently one day that in order not to be disappointed, a solution was to not want anything, but that the problem with that was that it also did away with the possibility of feeling good when she did get what she wanted, and this was worth the risk. Of course she did not always feel like this, and her anorexia was very graphically expressed when, on another occasion, she said, "what I can't swallow is the idea that all I want is to be looked after and give up all responsibility". And yet Denise did make clear how much she wanted to be loved and nurtured, and I began to understand that her repeated statement that she could never do anything of value (in her working life) related to her fear that she could never be of value to me. This was another source of humiliation and envy in that she knew that I was of value to her.

Having been able to recognise how much she wanted from me, Denise could no longer avoid a new set of anxieties which were to form the main preoccupation of this third phase: "What do you do if you want something but it's not there?" she asked. To begin with, this came out in the form of her thinking about how she could manage without coming to see me anymore. She could not see the point of carrying on in the knowledge that, one day, she would have to stop coming. Weekends were different, she indicated, because then she could look forward to coming back. I say 'indicated' because still so much of the time it was up to me to decipher some fairly cryptic comments. However, very clearly, she said: "When I'm not coming any more, one day, then the feelings I have for you and you for me will die." Now we were coming closer to what emerged as a very frightening concern that I could die, a concern that she was trying not to think about. When I put this into words for her, she said she spent the whole evening hating me for touching on a raw nerve and leaving her with it. Finally she said: "If Jim wasn't there, I would die."

120

I thought that she was telling me something of a sense that without me she would be left to starve, and I took up how I thought her anorexia was a way of being the one to control starving or not starving. (I thought that the aim was not death, but to escape death through a phantasy of omnipotent self-sufficiency.) In the next session, Denise told me that she cannot cut herself off from her feelings as effectively as she used to, "but how do you feel those things, the potential disaster and deprivation, and still carry on?" This was not just a rhetorical question, because Denise does want to know how I deal with such questions; whether I 'carry on' by denying the possibility of death.

One way in which Denise was still dealing with this question herself was by engaging in a highly dangerous sport. "It's feeble to feel frightened", she said to me, trying once again to prove that she is not limited by her bodily needs or characteristics. As with not eating, I think that Denise was wanting to prove in this way that she can transcend her body and hence prove her immortality.

Around this time, Denise was to miss a week and a half of sessions because of a long weekend away with her boyfriend, followed by a school trip. During this time I found a message on my answering machine one day saying that she would like to come to her session next day, and could I telephone her if this was not all right. When she came the next day she said that she had been certain that I would phone to tell her she could not come, but when I had not she became convinced that something must have happened to me. After this session she went on the school trip, and a few sessions after her return she told me the following. Her boyfriend, who had been out for the evening, did not return when she expected him. Throughout the night she kept dozing off and waking up to find that he was still not there. She got very worried, knowing that he would telephone if he was not planning to come home. In the early hours of the morning she had the following dream:

This little girl was having a medical examination and the woman doctor, I'm not sure if she was a doctor or what, was making a running commentary. She was pointing to a mole on her body and then she pointed to two bumps on her head; it soon became clear that the two were related, that they were malignant tumours, and there was this sense of tension and inevitability. But suddenly the woman said there was nothing wrong with her. The feeling of tension and of relief felt like too much.

Denise found out the next day that her boyfriend had tried to ring to explain that he would not be coming home, but she had not answered the phone. I thought that in the dream Denise was depicting the malignant process which goes on inside her mind when she is not coming to her sessions, as when her boyfriend is away and she starts thinking that he has had a car crash, a process which cannot be interrupted by evidence to the contrary (my return, his phone call) and which is responsible for the extent of Denise's despair about the state of her internal objects and her feeling that nothing she can do is ever 'good' enough. The two bumps, I thought (but did not say), referred to her boyfriend and I, the two parents and the two breasts. The only way of retrieving such a hopeless situation in the dream is through a magical process of wish-fulfilment where all is well after all. In fact, the dream had not been reassuring in spite of this conclusion. I thought that in the dream there was also reference to a feeling that I cross-examine her about what she has been up to in her mind during our time apart in an attempt to reveal what is in her 'head': her destructive thoughts, the violent crash, her pervasive badness. "I wonder what it would be like not to have an imagination that gets carried away all the time?", she said a few sessions later, allowing me to know that behind her silence and the paucity of phantasmagorical elaborations there lies quite a different story.

It was becoming possible to talk with Denise about the difficulty in addressing directly the spoiling part of herself, a part of herself of which she, on the whole, is not conscious. This is an area in which I had always had to tread very carefully, as her sense of worth was already so bruised and she was so sensitive to any remark on my part which she felt was distancing and critical.

Now that Denise was more able to stand feeling envious and did not need quite so much to scorn what she coveted, and now that she was markedly progressing in her analysis and in her external life, something else emerged which threw some light on her need to keep herself as a prepubertal child.

After the summer break, Denise had been feeling very negative about her job, saying that if people knew how it made her feel, surely they would not make her do it. She did not fit the job, she said, and she must do something about finding something else. For a while she almost managed to convince me about this, but eventually I took up that she was telling me that surely I could not know how humiliating she finds it coming here, how inadequate it makes her feel, because if I did I would not force her to face those feelings.

She came to the next session in quite a different mood, saying that she had been preparing herself quite well for starting work and felt happier about it. The following session was after her first day back at work. She was wearing a skirt for the first time. She also said that to her great surprise the day had gone well. She had been able to be firm with the pupils and set the tone for what she expected of them. She said it was necessary to make them feel that the work was important. For the next week, Denise said that it was so different, that it made all the difference not to feel totally inadequate. But then Denise began to develop the delusional belief that she had harmed me and that I was displeased with her, and she became anxious, pleading with me to tell her what she had done wrong and that it was not worth it if it was harmful to me.

It seems that Denise felt that she can only mature by quite concretely taking a part of me for herself, and this led to persecutory anxieties and fears of loss of love. When, soon after this, Denise started menstruating for the first time in very many years, she developed a gynaecological problem which required investigation and which she was convinced would require major surgery and the removal of an organ. This was unfounded. It is as if only one of us can be an adult woman. In that sense, one can say that in stopping her physical maturation – in phantasy stopping time – she was protecting both her mother and herself from destruction and death. It was a few years later that Denise was able to end her analysis. She was now able to express directly the great sadness she felt about ending.

In my work with Denise and with other anorexic patients, I have been struck by how painful and intolerable they find the very limitations which make us human: the limitation of belonging to one sex and not the other, the limitation of a life which has a beginning and an inevitable end, the inevitable inequalities of life which is embodied in the relationship between the giver and the one who is given to, the fact that in order to survive the baby needs a breast to rely on. The anorexic tries to deny such limitations and believes she can omnipotently defy death, that she can eat nothing and still survive, that she does not need anyone and that she can stop her body getting old and dying. The anorexic patient wants to be superhuman, other worldly. I described how Denise's pathology aimed at avoiding comparisons – she attacked her own wish to be like the admired and idealised analyst, as a feminine and sexual parent or as an awe-inspiring teacher – while the denial of emotional and bodily needs was also an attempt at mastery over death and a phantasy of immortality. She wanted to be 'different', to avoid comparison, but more than this she wanted to find an identity 'outside' the conditions of human existence. In that sense it was an attack on reality.

In all these ways, anorexia nervosa is more than a disorder in the psychological meaning of body weight or a disorder in relation to food. It is an attempt to annihilate the very nature of human existence – inequality, progression through the life cycle, sexuality and death.

For both the anorexic and the bulimic patient, a central issue, as described, is in the area of a difficulty with symbolisation. The bulimic patient feels literally invaded by her primary objects' own disturbance and unmourned experiences. Sensations replace affect and thought, and she is compelled to evacuate bad and undifferentiated feelings, experienced as unpleasant and intolerable bodily sensations through vomiting, or in the transference through 'eruption'. Bion's description of a 'no-breast' situation describes vividly what the infant will be left with when containment is not available and how containment can reverse the situation:

> the infant, filled with painful lumps of faeces, guilt, fears of impending death, chunks of greed, meanness and urine, evacuates these bad objects into the breast that is not there. As it does so the good object turns the no-breast (mouth) into a breast, the faeces and urine into milk, the fears of impending death and anxiety into vitality and confidence, the greed and meanness into feelings of love and generosity and the infant sucks its bad property, now translated into goodness, back again.
>
> (Bion, 1963, p. 31)

The anorexic patient, on the other hand, tries to prevent bad feelings by refusing food. Williams (1997) speaks of "'no entry'

124

system of defences", while at the same time the anorexic enters her object with powerful projections. The bulimic patient feels she cannot prevent 'entry' and she gets overwhelmed and suffused with elements which cannot be transformed into something coherent, tolerable and manageable. A secondary sense of control is gained by violently throwing up and throwing out the bits and pieces. Erotisation of the process makes the activity take on a life of its own. The eating disorder invades the life of eating-disordered patients, reflecting the 'too much', overwhelming and invasive quality of their own experience or that of their objects.

In this chapter I have wanted to show my way of working with eating-disordered patients by addressing the manifestations of the symptom in the transference relationship rather than speaking of the symptom directly. This helps to explore the meaning of the problem and allows communication to take place in a different sphere, hence reducing the pressure to act out somatically and paving the way for more symbolic thinking. Towards the end of the analysis Denise put together eating and relating. She said that she could now look forward to eating something, eat it and feel satisfied, and that she had begun for the first time to enjoy being with people. It is noteworthy that she puts these two things together.

A forward and backward movement is a general feature of mental life, and Freud spoke about this as the fundamental life and death drives. I have found this to be expressed particularly starkly in eating-disorderd patients. Psychoanalysis can only aim to enable, painstakingly, over years, the balance of forces to change.

Transformation takes place when the capacity to face, distinguish and verbalise feelings becomes more possible, and, as I have wanted to show, this takes place very slowly and requires of the psychoanalyst to think with the patient about the micro-processes as they occur internally and in the analysis.

Notes

1 This is reminiscent of what Rosenfeld (1971) describes as 'the gang' whose role is to maintain the status quo.
2 In French, the language of the analysis, she used 'on', which makes it indiscriminant between self and other.

6

PHALLUS, PENIS AND MENTAL SPACE

In this chapter I look at the representation of the masculine element in the psyche.

In their dictionary of psychoanalysis, Laplanche and Pontalis (1973) write that in contemporary psychoanalytic literature the word phallus tends to be used to describe the symbolic aspect, while penis denotes the male organ in its bodily reality. I will argue that phallus refers to one specific symbolic aspect only and that there are other symbolic aspects for which the word phallus is not appropriate. In particular, I want to make a distinction between the phallus on the one hand and the penis as representing the mental function of linking and structuring on the other. I will call the latter 'penis-as-link' in order to distinguish it both from the penis in its purely bodily reality and from the phallus. I suggest that it is theoretically and clinically important to make a distinction between phallus and penis-as-link.

After discussing the difference between phallus and penis-as-link I will go on to show how each belongs to a different psychic organisation and, with the help of clinical material, I will discuss the relationship of each one to mental space, which will be the main focus of this chapter.

My interest in this distinction started with thinking about women who adopt a phallic way of being. I noticed that while wanting to be, or to have, the phallus, these women concomitantly attacked the function of the penis as representing a link between the parents and that this led to a lack of internalisation of that function. I then found that this was true of some men too.

The word phallus in psychoanalysis derives from Freud's notion of phallic monism whereby only one sexual organ is known in childhood. Freud himself used the word phallus only rarely but he did make extensive use of the adjective phallic as in 'phallic stage', 'phallic monism', 'the phallic mother' or 'the phallic woman'. It is the individual's psychic position in relation to phallic monism which for Freud determines masculine or feminine development both in boys and girls (1925). The phallus, therefore, as Laplanche and Pontalis write, "turns out to be the meaning – i.e. what *is symbolised* – behind the most diverse ideas just as often as (and perhaps more often than) it appears as a symbol in its own right (in the sense of a schematic, figurative representation of the male member)" (1973, p. 313). It is in a similar vein that I use the term penis-as-link – as having to do with what is symbolised.

With Lacan's work (1966), the word 'phallus' started to appear more frequently in the psychoanalytic literature. Lacan's theory goes beyond a simple reading of Freud because of its structural linguistic underpinning, but for the purposes of this discussion, what I think is useful is his emphasis on the concept of the phallus as a reference to the inherent lack and incompleteness of the human condition and the impossibility of total fulfilment. The phallus represents an illusory wholeness, a state free of desire.

Melanie Klein opposed the notion of phallic monism and of a normal non-defensive phallic stage of development, since for her there is always an unconscious knowledge of the vagina and womb. This theoretical difference, at the heart of the 'Freud–Jones debate' of the 1920s and 1930s, is by no means dead, although it has become more complex, as I discuss in Chapter 3.[1]

It is possible to go beyond the opposition of this debate if instead of thinking developmentally we think of different configurations, or positions, or 'logics' (Laplanche, 1980; Kohon, 1987; Gibeault, 1988) which coexist in the unconscious. The phallic position is based on the distinction between having and not having, being and not being. The phallus represents the state of completeness and of being without need – 'beyond' the human condition – and exists in the unconscious as a basic position. This does not exclude other configurations in which the vagina is known and involving the phantasies described by Klein in relation to the inside of the mother's body. From this perspective, it is neither a question of a phallic phase followed by a genital phase, nor is it sufficient to speak purely of the defensive nature of the phallus because of the ubiquitous nature of this configuration in the unconscious.

Boys and girls face different issues in the phallic position and the literature attests to the special difficulties encountered by the girl. While the phallus is the possession of neither sex,[2] the boy can more easily believe that his penis gives him possession of it and this becomes woven into his relationship to his objects.

I suggested in Chapter 3 that for women there is a duality and opposition in the unconscious of a femininity experienced as lack, and a femininity which is more closely connected to the body (see Birksted-Breen,1993). What I call penis-as-link is part of the position or configuration in which the vagina is known. It has to do with the tripartite world of the self in relation to the parents as different but linked to each other. It refers to the linking of two objects in the sense that Bion writes that "the prototype for all links ... is the primitive breast or penis" (1957a, p. 308). It involves the knowledge of difference and by the same token the recognition of incompleteness and need for the object.

A not dissimilar distinction is made by Braunschweig and Fain (1971b) when they write that there is often a confusion between the penis as object of phallic narcissism and the penis as object of Eros, and that narcissism and eroticism do not get on well together. What I call the penis-as-link is instrument of Eros whereas the phallus is instrument of the death drive insofar as it aims to destroy that link.[3]

Although Lacan writes that the phallus refers to the Oedipal structure through the breakup of the mother and child unit, it seems to me that it is the 'penis-as-link' and not the phallus that has a structuring role in mental functioning because it links mother and father, masculine and feminine, and marks the full Oedipal structure (Britton, 1989). I aim to show later on with some clinical examples how the shift from the phallic position to the position of the 'penis-as-link' has implications for mental functioning.

It has been suggested that my notion of 'penis-as-link' is giving a privileged place to the penis and why not call it vagina as link. Gyler (2010), for instance, mentions the criticism by Elise that, with this notion, the penis "still gets to do everything", and by Perelberg who thinks that it is a return to the biological penis. In my view this is to conflate unconscious representation and value, body and representation. Representations have a basis in the body, and at the same time are not the body. The paradox is that there is no one-to-one relationship between body and mind but nor can the body be

128

ignored in the construction of the psyche and of representations. Were one to be writing a paper on 'the breast' as a representation, one could also say that the breast gets to do everything, and indeed Chasseguet-Smirgel has suggested that the theory of phallic monism aims to eradicate the narcissistic wound created by the child's helplessness and total dependence on the mother (Chasseguet-Smirgel, 1976). In making a distinction between penis-as-link and phallus I was interested in considering specifically the male element and its structuring role in the unconscious and the role of the father as the other object of the mother. One might think of precursors of this structuring role in the form of the nipple around which the infant structures him- or herself but it is different in that penis-as-link refers to a three-person situation (which requires a notion of difference and of an 'other'), and it is this internal configuration which is structuring. We know how much the notion of the 'absent father', which is the absence of *the representation* of the father, recurs in different pathologies; it is a reference to the absence of that structuring function (not so much as father as such but as father in the mother's mind) whatever the reality of the presence or absence of an actual father. In my view unconscious representations are at least partly based on the body (see, for instance, the fantasy of the bulimic patient of being an ejaculating phallus); it is however in a loose connection with the body so that the receptive and the penetrative are not the prerogative of one sex or the other, whether in conscious or unconscious life. Equally, neither possesses 'the phallus' and both are confronted with their exclusion from the primal scene, a "narcissistic mortification" (McDougall, 1974, p. 437).

I think that some of the literature on female sexuality, in particular, has suffered from the lack of a distinction between the phallus as representative of omnipotence and completion, and the unconscious significance of the penis as linking (Gordon, 1993) and structuring (Kurth and Patterson, 1968). Phallic sexuality is based on the identification by man or woman with the phallus in order to deny lack and the panoply of feelings associated with it, including need, envy, fear, guilt and helplessness. In that sense it does give a structure but a defensive narcissistic one. It is this phantasy of the penis as phallus which confers on to masculinity its coveted position, and if we think of this phantasy as ubiquitous it goes some way towards explaining social phenomena which have given men greater power and status. Added to this, the 'refusal of femininity'

129

which Freud saw as bedrock stems in part from the characteristics of the female genital which represent the potential for invasion, hence vulnerability. Receptivity becomes confused with being broken into. The maternal 'container', a representation of the womb, also holds the frightening elements projected into the mother which makes woman a dangerous and 'dark continent'.

I am suggesting that Freud's concept of penis envy is often phallus envy, which is what gives that envy in some women the intensity of its illusory quality, like the pot of gold at the end of a rainbow. The ambiguity of '*Penisneid*' (in German: both the wish to possess as an attribute and the desire for) often refers to the phallus which will be acquired sexually to confer power as when a woman patient spoke of feeling 'cocky' after being praised for a piece of work by a man she thought was a close friend of her female analyst. This came in the context of wishing to be free of her dependence on her analyst.

I have often found a split in homosexual women, denigrating men while idealising masculinity. The idealised masculinity is a reference to the phallus that wants for nothing – perfect and immortal – with which they identify. It is thought to hold the power to seduce, to be desired, while at the same time being free from desire. That Freud made the phallic stage into a stage of development indicates the ubiquitous nature of the phantasy.

As opposed to the binary aspect of the phallic vision along the lines of presence and absence, the structuring and linking function of the penis of the tripartite world of mother, linked with but different from father, and child in relation to the parents, makes for a more complex world. In this position, good and bad, powerful and powerless, masculine and feminine are encompassed rather than being mutually exclusive. It refers to mental bisexuality. This greater complexity is described by Melanie Klein as part of the depressive position when the object is felt to be good and bad at the same time.

Strictly speaking, the phallus refers to a presymbolic mode of thinking in which, for instance, a woman believes her body *is* a phallus in a symbolic equation (Segal, 1957). The penis–as–link on the other hand belongs to the area of true symbolisation and is internalised as a function.

It is the failure to internalise the penis in this structuring function which accounts for the 'claustro–agoraphobic' dilemma (Rey, 1986) central to many different symptomatologies. The person pulls away from his or her objects for fear of being engulfed but then feels abandoned and wants to get back again in a never-ending to and fro. For instance, I described in anorexia nervosa how a young woman was caught between the wish for fusion and the terror of psychic annihilation (Chapter 5). Glasser names this sort of internal situation as the core complex of patients with perverse pathologies (1979); Campbell describes it in pre-suicide states (1993). Limentani noticed, in his reports of "sexual deviants", that the father seemed always to be absent (1991). I suggest that it is the internalisation of the penis in its linking and structuring function that is defective in these situations because it has been attacked, while a phallic omnip-otent phantasy may be clung to with desperation. It is this structur-ing function of the penis that creates the necessary space leading to the possibility of both separateness and link. Without it the possib-ility of psychic engulfment is a mental reality, and only what Steiner calls a 'psychic retreat' can ease the immediate problem (1993).

This structuring aspect of the penis is a reference to more than just the actual father, since the mother's bisexual mental functioning can encompass a structuring function alongside her maternal func-tion of 'being with'. At the same time I do not think it sufficient simply to think of the nipple or the phantasy of the penis inside the mother as the male element, because I believe a fundamental aspect of the penis in mental functioning is that it represents the linking of the two parents. The frightening phantasy of the combined parent figure described by Klein (1932) may be understood as the break-down of the structuring element. When Bion writes that "the prototype for all links ... is the primitive breast or penis" (1957a, p. 308), I understand him to be saying that each exists as basic in its own right, and that there is an a priori knowledge of both. I under-stand this a priori knowledge in the case of the breast to refer to the link between self and other, whereas in the case of the penis it refers to the link between the parents, and therefore the penis brings in from the start the notion of triangulation. Breast and penis represent different functions and are internalised as different functions; the breast has to do with the function of being with and of feeding in a dual relationship, the penis with the function of giving structure (the three-dimensional situation). Containment, in my view, involves a bisexual aspect. I think that it is not a purely maternal function but *already* combines both the maternal function of being

131

with and the paternal function of observing and linking. In order to contain her infant, a mother (and an analyst) has to receive the projections empathically (the maternal receptive function) and also take a perspective on this (paternal/third position function). The phantasy of the phallus is a search for that structuring function but the sort of mental organisation it leads to is a rigid and restricted one which does not recognise the full Oedipal structure made up of the three distinctive positions of mother, father and child. In particular there is no place for a feminine with its specific qualities.

My aim in this chapter is to show how phallus and penis–as–link have a different relationship to mental space.

I will use a moment in the analysis of Agnes to illustrate how I understand the psychic function of the penis–as–link and its relationship to mental space. Agnes is a deeply depressed bulimic bisexual woman whose sexual fantasies include being abused by men in authority. Through her dreams and associations it was possible to see how she also identifies unconsciously with a violent ejaculating phallus when she makes herself vomit. Agnes suffered a very deprived childhood with parents who were themselves deeply traumatised and related to each other in a disturbingly sado–masochistic way.

Agnes started the first of her five weekly sessions not long after an analytic break with this dream:

> She was wanting to walk with this person with long hair but he or she didn't want her. If only she knew who he was, man or woman, she would know what to be in order to be allowed to go with him or her.

This problematic developed over the week and I came to understand that it expressed the way in which she was feeling unwanted and wondered about my own state of mind and who I was more likely to be pushed into being this week, the sadistic male or the masochistic female partner, and therefore which position *she* should adopt in order to get me closely involved with her. She described how, when she feels out of contact with her son whom she finds difficult to tolerate because he is not very expressive, she will provoke him until he cries; then she comforts him and after that she feels better. I think she also wondered how best to provoke me because she felt out of contact with me and which position I was most likely to enact, and, as we will see, she settles for the masochistic position. Agnes' discourse was very muddled and bitty, and none of this was clear to me until the end of the week, as I will describe. The atmosphere during the week was one which is difficult to convey. It was certainly not openly provocative but it was subtly provocative in a way that I encounter frequently with her, and yet I find difficult to spot as it is happening and tend to realise only with hindsight once I have been provoked into saying something which she can feel to be critical.

At the end of the week Agnes brought a dream in which

she felt she needed something and went to the petrol station run by a German man. She wasn't sure what she needed, petrol or cigarettes, she was afraid she would make things explode. The man had little cakes that he was giving away but it's not what she wanted [this said with disdain].

She spoke in this session in a very dead voice with no associations and, as my efforts to get her to expand on the dream were of no avail, I took up in desperation that she was not wanting the cakes on offer here. The explosion mentioned in the dream did then take place. Agnes suddenly came to life and screamed at me that I should have known that German for her means not to be trusted and that I am always ready to attack her and why don't I take up her sexual fantasies. This led me to see more clearly the buildup of the week, the bait she had been throwing, and to see that I was now the German man who was being invited sadistically to penetrate her orally or anally (cigarettes and petrol) which were the sexual fantasies.

I took this up with her. I went over the events of the week, saying something along the lines that she had felt on Monday that I had disengaged from her over the weekend and that this had made her want, as the week progressed, to engage me in a sadomasochistic interchange, because she believed that I would be very interested in attacking her, and that if I did attack her she could then feel wanted by me. Agnes clearly felt understood, she relaxed noticeably, and she and I felt more in contact. The following Monday she reported a dream she had had after the Friday session.

She was in my house; the consulting room was larger than in reality. She was in the next room looking at the books and talking to my husband. On the mantelpiece was Pinocchio.

133

She said of Pinocchio that he becomes a real boy when he can love, which reminded me that six months before, when there had been a marked shift in her analysis and a lifting of her depression, she had said to me that she thought analysis was about learning to love. I understood this dream as my husband representing my masculine function of observing and linking together the week's material on Friday (penis-as-link) and thus interrupting the enactment we had been involved in. This had led to an internal expansion of her mental space (the larger consulting room) and a capacity to dialogue with and introject that function (talking to my husband) and greater separateness from the mother she is fused with in a masochistic way. I thought that the fact that my husband was next door in the dream represented the position of observer, at a distance from the enactment. The situation of talking to my husband next door also expresses the Oedipal wish to take in the penis and be a real *boy* (the ambiguity of *Penisneid*). I want to stress that the penis in question here which is introjected psychically is the penis–as–link (which enables her to observe and relate in a separate way) rather than the phallus (the introjection of which in my view constricts mental space and would have made her more detached).

Following this dream, the remainder of Agnes' weekend was spent preoccupied with a woman whose husband had died of a brain tumour and another whose husband has a brain tumour but is denying its seriousness. She had felt more appreciation for my masculine mental function of observing and linking her material together and she now felt concerned with the virulence with which she tries to stop me thinking clearly. Indeed it has been typical of Agnes to throw confusion at the end of sessions on whatever clarity has been reached, making what I think of as a bulimic mess of vomit out of a productive session, sometimes leaving me in doubt as to the validity of the understanding we had reached. I think that Agnes was concerned about the very real gravity of this malignant process to her analysis and this made her feel very desperate. Material suggested a close connection between vomiting and faecal soiling, and a faecal representation of the father's penis, and I understand the anal attacks as interfering with the introjection of a good penis. Her greater appreciation of the father's function in the fragment I discussed led to Agnes' concern about her hatred of the father's intrusion and her hatred of the link of the parental relationship.

I have found the attack on this link of the primal scene and the hatred of the father's intrusion to be particularly striking in the homosexual women I have as patients who deny the function of the penis in the primal scene (penis-as-link) while identifying with the idealised omnipotent phallus, and it is with their analyses that I first became interested in distinguishing between phallus and penis-as-link. In fact Agnes came into analysis because she did not know whether she wanted to be married or live as a lesbian.

The confusion between the phallus, powerful and self-sufficient, and the symbolic penis in its structuring function also dominated Mr B's mental life. The lack of the latter made him turn to the former. As a child he had spent hours inside a climbing frame. Now, when he felt fragmented and confused, he compulsively sought a perfect, beautiful woman 'with a firm body' he could get inside of, or else fantasised being homosexually penetrated. When, one day, he said, "I'm obsessed with beautiful women and my father", I understood that both served the same function of searching for the phallus to hold him together.

When, after some years of analysis, Mr B developed more of a sense of an internal structure, it was possible to see the difference between times when he felt fragmented and sought this phallus, and times when he had a sense of inner structure and this compulsion waned. He told me one day that for the first time he had a backbone and on another occasion that I was his skeleton. He spoke about structures that are built in the sea, like arms which prevent the sea from flooding and help create a beach. I thought that the backbone and the skeleton, and the arm in the sea, all described the introjection of the penis-as-link, the internal structure which can make him feel that the different parts of himself and his internal objects are ordered, separate but connected to each other and which help him gain some space in which to think rather than be flooded with impulses and sensations. When he can feel that, he need not search for the phallus to hold him up. He then feels less driven by an obsession and less out of touch with reality, the reality of the full Oedipal situation including the parental relationship.

The wish to have or to be the phallus is an attempt to find the structuring function of the penis when it is missing, and a phallic organisation brings temporary respite from fragmentation and chaos. Mr B believed that it would be the solution to his problems, but that solution ultimately fails because it is a manic and concrete solution

135

and because it aims to create a two-person world (those who have and those who do not have) where the function of the penis-as-link is denied and therefore that function cannot be internalised.

I understand the subjective experience of mental space, which Agnes represented in her dream by the larger consulting room, as having to do with the adjunct of the third position that makes for a three-dimensional world and allows for a perspective on oneself and one's actions. It promotes the capacity to dialogue with oneself, to allow for thoughts to come together and the diminution of a compulsion to act. The reverse situation was expressed by Mr B after a summer break: "I couldn't think at all. It's like two skins glued together and thinking feels like ripping them apart. I've been thinking more than ever about how nothing can make up for my father's absence." In fact the actual father had been and continued to be very present in his life.

Mental space and the capacity to think are created by the structure that allows for separateness and link between internal objects, and self and other, instead of fusion or fragmentation. The penis-as-link represents both that separateness and link of the parental relationship and forms the backbone of healthy mental functioning, which is a bisexual functioning.[4] I have noticed with Agnes that being able to dream, in itself, can signal a greater capacity to take a step back and observe herself from a 'third position' after a period in which she has been entrenched in a paranoid relationship to me. She can go through phases in her analysis where she has no capacity at all for self-reflection, when she does not know why she is coming for analysis or what it can possibly do for her. At these times she is extremely suspicious of me and it becomes very difficult for me to make any links in the sessions. Eventually she will have a dream and she will feel better even before we have made sense of her dream. The whole atmosphere shifts and she becomes able to think about herself astutely. I experience this as the passage from a two-dimensional way of being, from being paralysed on one plane as it were, with no perspective, to a three-dimensional way of being where she is able to observe herself and her interaction with me from a third position and where she and I can begin to dialogue about her (a three-person situation). I understand the dream itself in such cases as allowing for the presence of both parents. The dream has the maternal function of holding together Agnes' as yet not understood feelings and the paternal function of taking a perspective

136

on this. Having been able to allow this creative mental intercourse to take place she feels better and can start to observe and think again, for a while at least, until jealousy and envy take the upper hand. The dream is reassuring because it is evidence of the psychic work of representation of that which had been inchoate and disturbing. It is reassuring because it is a sign that the capacity to make sense of and digest experiences is alive again, and because it is evidence of an experience of internal containment. The larger consulting room represents the container/containing object which is also part of the mind, with dreaming in itself expressing containment (see Chapter 9). As in the sequence described, all psychoanalytic processes can be looked at in terms of ongoing micro-experiences and fluctuations between failed and successful containment, with both parties playing a part in it ("bi-personal field": Ferro, 1999), and the overall balance and a repeated move towards containment being necessary for a developmental outcome.

While for some psychoanalysts – in France in particular – the notion of the phallus is central in psychoanalytic theory, others, notably in Great Britain, make little reference to it.

I believe that it is useful to retain the notion but that it is clinically and theoretically important to distinguish the phallus carefully from what I have called the penis-as-link, and that the two are often confused; for instance, when speaking of 'penis envy'. While Freud made a distinction between phallic sexuality and genital sexuality along developmental lines, what I am proposing is not a developmental model but one which considers different mental positions, because I take the view that there are from the start certain innate known structures, the foremost being that of the parental relationship and the role of the penis (Money-Kyrle, 1968); at the same time, the notion of the phallus is so ubiquitous that it may be considered a primal phantasy.

While the phallus belongs to the mental configuration that allows only for the 'all-or-nothing' distinction, hence to the domain of omnipotence, and is an attempt away from triangulation, the penis-as-link, which links mother and father, underpins Oedipal and bisexual mental functioning and hence has a structuring role which underpins the process of thinking.

I suggest that phallus and penis-as-link can coexist or alternate in the unconscious and refer to specific symbolic functions or organisations.

I have illustrated clinically how the lack of internalisation of the penis-as-link and its structuring function leads to a compulsive search for the phallus by men and women in the erroneous belief that it will provide an internal structure, while the introjection of the penis-as-link enhances mental space and thinking. The absence of this structuring function is particularly clear in borderline and perverse pathologies where there is often a compulsive attempt at organisation along phallic lines. More specifically I described how the fluctuations between the two positions within the analytic situation connect with fluctuations in the capacity to think and to dream, to being under pressure or to having more mental space.

Notes

1 Melanie Klein never used the word phallus in her writings. On the very few occasions when Klein used the adjective 'phallic' it was when speaking of girls. In the explanatory notes at the end of Volume 1, the commentator writes that she "speaks of the phallic phase out of a manifest desire not to diverge from Freud" (1932a, p. 426). The fact that Klein used the notion of phallic phase in relation to girls and not to boys has to be considered as having more meaning than simply pleasing Freud, since, after all, for him there was also a phallic phase for boys. I believe it reflects the more complex situation for the girl and the need to describe the particular constellation in women's unconscious to which the concept of 'phallus' refers.
2 As Parat puts it, "le phallique n'est pas mâle, le phallique est narcissique" [the phallic is not male, it is narcissistic], translation mine (1995).
3 R. Steiner, in commenting on my paper 'Penis, Phallus and Mental Space', writes:

   in his book Über dem Traum (1814), the German romantic writer Von Schubert, well known to both Coleridge and Freud, had already noticed that the phallus was also the pyramid of the Ancient Egyptian pharaoh's tombs, the phallus therefore being a symbol of death rather than of life if one also bears in mind the incest practised by the Pharaohs.

   (R. Steiner, 1996, p. 13)

4 The experiential state is connected with what Quinodoz (1991) calls 'portance' (translated into English as 'buoyancy'), which in French makes a reference to how a person holds himself up, carries himself; hence one could say his internal structure.

TIME AND THE *APRÈS-COUP*

Issues concerning time are at the basis of psychoanalytic theory, of the analytic setting and of the clinical phenomena we encounter. They also underlie important technical and theoretical differences in psychoanalytic approaches, implicitly or explicitly. French psycho-analysts have emphasised the non–linear form of the temporality of *après-coup*, contrasting with the more linear developmental model of British psychoanalysts. While the theorising differs in significant ways, clinically in the sessions the two forms of temporality, namely developmental and *après-coup*, go inherently together, one being a requisite for the other, and may be found as such in the British approach, as I will discuss.

Lacan was instrumental and credits himself (1966, p. 839) with extracting the significance of the notion of *Nachträglichkeit* in Freud's work. According to Laplanche and Pontalis (1967), its importance had not been previously recognised due to the fact that the same word was not used throughout in the translation of Freud (this is true of both the English and the French translation). In a later paper, Laplanche (1998b) adds that if the terms '*nachträglich*' and '*Nachträglichkeit*' were not always translated as the same word by Strachey, it was because, in fact, the meaning given by Freud varies between three different usages. The first simply means 'later'. The second implies a movement from past to future: something is deposited in the individual, which is only activated later on – this is based on the model of the seduction theory where the trauma is constituted in two stages. The event leaves a trace, and in a second stage it has a psychic effect. Laplanche compares this to a delayed action bomb. Strachey's translation of *Nachträglichkeit* as 'deferred action', which many people now think is a bad translation and is the reason why it has not been given importance in the English-speaking world, in fact conveys this particular meaning quite well. The idea, in this second meaning, namely that something is deposited but it will only have an effect later on, is a 'deferred action' and the temporality here is from past to present. The third meaning implies that something is perceived but only takes on meaning retrospectively. It is this third meaning, the one least present in Freud, that was picked up by Lacan and developed by French psychoanalysts. According to Laplanche (De Mijolla, 2002), however, while Lacan was the first to draw attention to the notion of *Nachträglichkeit* in 1953, he only pointed out its usage in the Wolfman and it was left to Laplanche and Pontalis (1967) to point out the more general importance of the concept in Freudian theory. The second meaning corresponds to Laplanche's own theoretical developments of Freud. However, other French psychoanalysts tend to use the concept in the third sense, a sense which is not conveyed by the translation 'deferred action'. Le Guen in his dictionary (2008) writes that the idea of 'deferred action', by putting the accent on the first moment which is simply deferred instead of revealed by the second moment, neglects the importance of the double temporal movement (p. 184).

For this reason and because the implications of this type of retrospective attribution of meaning has underpinned a whole corpus of French psychoanalytic writing, I am using in this chapter the French term *après-coup* rather than the German one. Recently in fact it has been recognised that *après-coup* may be thought of as a psychoanalytic concept in its own right and some translations into German are now using either *après-coup* or *Nachträglichkeit* depending on the context. Nevertheless, even *après-coup* can vary in its usage between the different meanings.

Green stresses the differentiation of *après-coup* from a developmental (genetic) aspect when he writes,

One can say that the originality of the French position is due to Lacan's influence; he was a radical critic of any form of geneticism, the ideas of which, in his opinion, are inconsistent with a dialectical approach. For it is thanks to him that the value of the Freudian concept of Nachträglichkeit has been reasserted, becoming a fundamental theoretical axis for French psychoanalysts.

(Green, 2002a, p. 7)

I think that it may be because of the Lacanian rebirth of the concept of *après-coup* and of Lacan's radical rejection of the body and biological development in psychoanalysis that the notion of *après-coup* has been held up as the divide between approaches – French and British. Lacan's modernisation of the concept did not seem to take account of the original description by Freud, which implied5a restructuring following sexual maturation of the child (hence a developmental aspect). In fact, both temporal directions, namely developmental and *après-coup*, are present in Freud in important ways.

In British psychoanalysis there is more use made of the notion of *après-coup* than may appear because it is not referred to in these terms. It seems to me that it is implicit in the 'here and now' mode of interpretation, which may be considered a characteristic of the 'British School' because it cuts across all three groups. Sandler and Sandler, for instance, write, "It is vital that the analyst give first priority to understanding, and if possible interpreting, what is going on in the *here-and-now* of the analysis" (1994, p. 290); and Roth writes, "our sense of conviction about our patient's internal world comes ultimately from our understanding of the *here-and-now* transference relationship between us – this is … the epicentre of the emotional meaning of an analysis" (2001, p. 542). Roth also makes it clear that she does not restrict her interpretations to the 'here and now': "Much of the filling in, the enrichment, the colour of the analysis takes place at a different level, while we become familiar with the quality and variety of our particular patient's particular world" (pp. 542–543).

It should be stressed that not all British psychoanalysts agree with the predominant use of here and now interpretations (King, Couch and Mollon are among those who have spoken against it). It also needs to be mentioned that a number of British psychoanalysts have been particularly interested in the writings of French psychoanalysts (Kohon, Mitchell, Perelberg, Parsons, Bollas, Kennedy and Rose), and they have sometimes specifically discussed the French notion of *après-coup* (e.g. Perelberg and Jozef, 2002). When contrasting British and French psychoanalysis I am therefore not referring to those people who are working at the interface or have been consciously influenced by those ideas. Clearly there are many variations and even cross–overs within each of these ideas.

The liberty I take to generalise is also the one taken by Green who refers to '*L'École Anglaise*' as opposed to '*L'École Française*' and speaks of "the famous 'here and now'" in this context (2002b, p. 78), and I am in a sense responding to him. Strictly speaking there is, of course, more than one *École Française* and one *École Anglaise*, and over recent decades there has been more and more cross-fertilisation, but generalising, while by necessity reductive, also makes comparisons possible.

The 'here and now' approach at first glance may appear to be devoid of temporality altogether, since the interpretation is in the present, but I want to argue that the workings of a complex temporality may be described in the 'here and now'. In fact, the 'here and now' only makes sense insofar as it retains its temporal dimension, and incorporates the ambiguity of the two directions of temporality. It originates in Freud's notion of transference in which the past is reproduced in the present giving the opportunity to work on those issues from the past. Transference is no longer interpreted as resistance but the current interplay, and its modifications are the continual object of study. Joseph (1985), for instance, following Klein, extends it to the 'total situation' and works largely within its parameters. The Winnicottian notions of transitional space and of play also delineate an area of immediacy of experience. The extent to which British psychoanalysts believe that the past can be known from the present, or at least hypothesised, varies, as does the extent to which they believe it is important to make explicit reconstructions or to develop narratives about the past. The interpretation in the 'here and now' rests on the belief that it will carry the most emotional impact and is most likely to lead to psychic change precisely because it is current, and that relating it to the past can serve defensive purposes. Nevertheless, it seems to me that the past has to remain present, so to say, however much it may be implicit or in the periphery. When it is lost altogether it creates the form of impasse which O'Shaughnessy (1992) describes under the term 'enclave'. The greatest danger I believe is when *the analyst* has lost the temporal perspective *in his or her own mind* and is colluding with the patient in a malignantly denuded present. Such an enactment only becomes psychoanalytically useful when the time factor is reintroduced, at least in the analyst's mind.

While the 'here and now' approach has to imply a connection of present to past, most I think would also agree that the 'here and now' is never a pure reproduction of the past, that the past is always a past as reinterpreted in the present, and that the possible

142

and relevant objects of study are the current internal object relations and the way in which they are played out on the analytic scene. The 'here and now' approach rests on the notion that only the present can be known and that, while deriving from the past, it is in a complex relationship to the actual past. But also it rests on the notion that the present will *modify the past*. We can see that, in this sense, in the 'here and now' approach the temporal direction goes from present to past in that it recognises that the analytic setting, and, I would also add, the particular dyad, gives the past its specific shape. It is, one can say, *a new creation of the past*. This direction from present to past is most clearly seen in the notion that one aim of an analysis is the modification of internal objects. Parental objects at the end of analysis are 'known' as different objects from the ones they were at the start of analysis, even though we are still talking about the childhood parents. It is still a reference to the past, but a past which has been retrospectively resignified; that is, a past which is shaped *après-coup*. In that sense, British analysts have often been working with a notion of *après-coup* without naming it. Klein's description of the two positions and the post-Kleinian concern with mental organisations and structures of thinking and their fluctuations does not assume a linear developmental causality, but is concerned with current internal configurations. Each organisation restructures and gives new meaning to previous elements. The reorganisation may be progressive or regressive. This description is very similar to that of the reshaping of experiences *nachträglich* with the castration complex when new meanings are ascribed to that which has been perceived. I do not wish to ignore here that there is a significant difference in theorisation about development when the Oedipal phase is seen as a normative transformational stage from which position the past is apprehended in a new way, and a theorisation in which there is no such normative structural reorganisation around castration.[1] Finally, infantile modes of relating are described as templates but do not assume a simple connection. Most take it for granted that the past cannot be known and that the analytic endeavour is focused on the internal past and not the actual past, a past which is reshaped in the present. In Winnicott's work too, which may seem on the surface to be based on a developmental view, there is, in fact, a much more complex temporal model.[2] Winnicott writes (1974, pp. 104–105):

There are moments, according to my experience, when a patient needs to be told that the breakdown, a fear of which destroys his or her life, *has already been*. It is a fact that is carried round hidden away in the unconscious ... the original experience of primitive agony cannot get into the past tense unless the ego can first gather it into its own present time experience and into omnipotent control now (assuming the auxiliary ego-supporting function of the mother (analyst).

In other words, the trauma needs to be experienced in the here and now in order to become a past trauma.

We frequently find this kind of bidirectional temporality in clinical work. The depressed patient, for instance, fears his anger will destroy his objects while, at the same time, believing that his anger has *already* destroyed his objects. Usually the patient is only conscious of a fear for the future. An interpretation that the destruction has already taken place (internally) is always very meaningful. The analyst usually interprets the future or the past according to rational thought but, in fact, the two are happening at the same time in this non-linear bidirectional form of temporality.[3]

For Freud, the psychic apparatus develops from having to deal with the time element. The absence of the object and the delay of satisfaction forces the ego to find means of dealing with that experience. The capacity to recognise and tolerate the frustration of the absence of the object marks a developmental stage, and goes hand in hand with a sense of time and with the ability to anticipate the return of the object. In the '*fort-da*' game (1920) the child develops symbolic mastery over the unpredictable time span which accompanies the loss of the object. Symbolisation and language are born in that gap. Botella and Botella (2001) stress that by playing the game, the child is attempting to keep alive the 'representation' of the mother and of the self, and that it is the loss of the representation which is the catastrophe and not the loss of the object as such. Boris suggests that in the *fort-da* game the spool might represent not the mother but the child itself, "who felt flung away and needed to be regathered and restored" (1987, p. 357). He continues, "Otherwise why follow the thread to the looming presence of Death when an object-relations view would have been the more obvious and parsimonious one?" I assume that Boris is referring to the fact that this description of the game appears in Freud's paper 'Beyond the

Pleasure Principle' (1920) and therefore has to do with the continual struggle between life and death drives. One could push this further and look at the game as representing the whole interplay between life and death forces with environmental factors played out in the internal world where the internal object and the self are, in turn, destroyed and restored. We can see how the time of separation which brings distress is *also* the time which can promote psychic development. Conversely, underlying many pathological manifestations is the attempt to eradicate the time of experiencing with the consequences we know to symbolic functioning. One would be thinking of this happening when the destructive forces are too great in relation to the life forces or the good experience not sufficiently established. Time is affected by the object being eradicated in what Green refers to as (1997b) "a destructive negative hallucination of the object". He writes: "Non–existence has taken possession of the mind, erasing the representations of the object that preceded its absence" (pp. 1081–1082). There would be some theoretical differences here around whether the object is eradicated leaving a blank or whether what remains is a bad and persecuting object, the Kleinian theorisation.

In any case, time and the 'continuity' or 'survival' of the object in its representation (or of the good object) go hand in hand. A solution to the lack of that representation is to seek timeless states in which the object is no longer searched for. Timelessness is sought in such different states as religious ecstasy, drug-induced states and day-dreaming. In other cases, notably in melancholia, the past cannot be mourned and the future cannot be envisaged, and time seems to be frozen in the moment which lasts forever, like death itself. One of the basic ways of dealing with psychic pain is narcissistic withdrawal, the main aim of which is to create a timeless universe in which there can be no loss. Boschan (1990), comparing the temporality of a neurotic patient with a patient with predominantly narcissistic pathology, describes how the latter stops and freezes time so as to protect himself from contact with the other and with his own emotions, which are experienced as a threat of destruction. I spoke earlier of the psychoanalytic impasse which hinges on the reduction of time to the present.

Klein has described, under the term 'projective identification', the mechanism by which unwanted experience is eradicated. The less pain or frustration that can be tolerated, the more rapid and all-encompassing the mechanism, and the more this affects ego functioning. When pain cannot be tolerated at all, the defensive process has to come in with such immediacy as to prevent all awareness of pain. Bion has gone further in suggesting that the incapacity to tolerate frustration disturbs the development of the apparatus for thinking itself, and instead of an apparatus for thinking there is a "hypertrophic development of the apparatus of projective identification".

> When the pre-conception of a breast is met by no breast, if frustration can be tolerated, a thought develops. If on the other hand frustration cannot be tolerated instead of a thought there is a bad object fit only for evacuation.... The end result is that all thoughts are treated as if they were indistinguishable from bad internal objects; the appropriate machinery is felt to be not an apparatus for thinking the thoughts, but an apparatus for ridding the psyche of accumulations of bad internal objects.
>
> (Bion, 1962b, p. 307)

Instantaneity is a characteristic of the paranoid–schizoid mode of relating when frustration cannot be tolerated; it deals with psychic pain by immediately splitting and evacuating the unwanted feeling even before it can be experienced. It is this instantaneous aspect which I think gives the projection its violent quality. The violence is the rapid reaction of protection by expulsion, which in so doing violently intrudes into the object. The analyst may feel aggressed but I think that the intention is not necessarily aggression, and the violence can sometimes be the result of the strength and rapidity with which the patient protects him- or herself by getting rid of an experience by pushing it into the analyst. What is referred to as 'massive projective identification', a term first used by Segal,[4] describes a psychic phenomenon whose characteristic involves the near-complete eradication of time, specifically the time of sojourn of an experience in the psyche.

Time is first in the mother's psyche in what Bion (1962b) describes as the notion of '*reverie*', the time of sojourn in the mother's mind of the inchoate beta elements and their transformation into elements which the infant is able to assimilate. For the infant, therefore, the time which can be tolerated will be, at first, the time of transformation within the mother's psyche, if the

146

mother is able herself to tolerate the time factor and not have to block or immediately eject the projections. I call 'reverberation time' the time it takes for disturbing elements to be assimilated, digested and transformed. This will be further discussed in Chapter 9. It is the infant's introjection of that process and the creation of a reverberation time which enables the development of the infant's own capacity to develop and tolerate a sense of time. In the analytic interchange, the reverberation time may be of long duration with the analyst having to contain for months or even years the projections before transformation can take place. Carpy (1989) describes how the analyst's ability to tolerate the countertransference, in itself, even without an accompanying verbal interpretation, can over time produce psychic change. Something of the sort takes place with the use of what Steiner (1993) calls "analyst centred interpretations" or Mitrani (2001) "introjective interpretations". The time element is fundamental here. It is the analyst's own capacity to wait, to tolerate remaining in discomfort, which can be introjected by the patient, enabling him or her eventually to remain with his or her own state of mind. As the patient becomes more able to tolerate the feeling, one can see how the time lag before the expulsion of the unwanted feeling becomes longer until, eventually, the patient can stay with the previously intolerable feeling. The word 'work', which is used in connection with the psychoanalytic process as in 'working through' (*Durcharbeitung*) or Klein's "working through the depressive position" and Green's "work of the negative", suggests a different relation to time emphasising the aspect of process, as does the notion of integration to which it leads. This contrasts with the instantaneity of the hallucinatory wish-fulfilment, the immediate gratification or the instant expulsion of the unwanted emotion.

The 'reverberation time' created by the mother's and the analyst's capacity for *reverie*, which includes both a chronological aspect and a back-and-forth aspect between mother and infant, could be represented as spiralling in non-even ways (because the back-and-forth aspect takes varying lengths of time at different moments). The spiralling rather than straight line depicts the inherent necessity for the presence of another, external first, later external or internal. The internalisation of this capacity for *reverie* provides a basis for tolerating the passage of time of which there seems to be some kind of innate knowledge. Money-Kyrle (1968) called the inevitability of time and ultimately death one of the "essential facts of life",

147

although he wonders if it should be regarded as innately predetermined or whether it comes from the repeated experience that no good (or bad) experience can last for ever (1971). Either way, he suggests that the inevitability of death is "a fact perhaps never fully accepted" (1971, p. 104). The anthropologist Edmund Leach notes that the word 'time' brings in two contradictory experiences, one involving the notion of repetition, the other a notion of non-repetition and of something irreversible. He suggests that people put the two together because of a psychological "repugnance to contemplating either the idea of death or the idea of the end of the universe" (1953 [1961], p. 175)[5] as when death is seen as a repetition of birth in religious belief. This makes one think of the '*fort-da*' game, which enables the child to tolerate the passage of time by reassuring him that continual repetition brings the previous order of things back again. I think that the rhythmical aspect of the game also brings the reassurance of one of the earliest experiences of time-as-repetition which is the rhythm of the heartbeat followed later by the rhythm of rocking and sucking. Whether innate, based on a preconception (Bion, 1965a) or learned from early experience, time as non-repetition is particularly hated because it is immutable, inevitable and leading to loss and death. This inevitable journey is part of the biological substrate which Lacan wanted to eliminate from psychoanalysis. And, as we know, he also wanted to eliminate the fixed session length as a given of 'analytic life'. It seems to me on the contrary that it is the interplay between the facts of life of time and the body, on the one hand, and the requirements for psychic survival, on the other, which makes up the psychoanalytic field. The analytic setting itself is anchored in a "contrast of temporalities" (Sabbadini, 1989). The analyst becomes the guardian of time, of the knowledge that analysis has a beginning and an end, as does each session. This fact of analytic life is the third element that stops eternal symbiosis, *the folie à deux*, a fact which can be so persecuting that it has to be attacked. It is linked with the immutability of the Oedipus situation. With the toleration of the Oedipal situation and of the depressive situation, time can 'elongate'. Memories replace 'reminiscences'; thought replaces action. The past can be faced, accepted as past and distinguished from the present. Equally, the present can be lived in the present as distinguished from an idealised or persecutory future. The 'I am my father' becomes 'I am like my father', which marks the process of identification as opposed to the instantaneous projective identification of the presymbolic state. A notion of development and of differentiation emerges. The notion of *après-coup* adds complexity to this with its notion of the influence of the present on the past. Development itself implies resignifications. The depressive position is one which resignifies and gives new meaning to previously disparate states precisely because, in tolerating the passage of time, it brings the possibility of holding in mind different and even contradictory states. Bringing together the good and bad aspects of the mother can only be done because the passage of time is held in mind as a continuous experience rather than fragmented into instants. This is one of the things which patients mention when they emerge from predominantly psychotic states of mind, that they have a new-found belief that a bad experience won't last forever. Paradoxically, while time is elongated in a linear way, in the symbolic mode of thinking opposite asymmetrical relationships are able to coexist. Being in the position of the child in one context and in the position of the adult in another, in the masculine position at times and in the feminine position at times, requires symbolic thinking, the ability to abstract the spirit rather than be tied to the letter.

I am therefore suggesting that both temporalities, developmental and *après-coup* in its meaning of movement from present to past, while appearing so different, in fact go together, and that you cannot have one without the other. If Freud used the same term to refer to progressive and retrospective time I would say it is precisely because there isn't as clear-cut a demarcation between them as seems to be sometimes implied. Laplanche has suggested that, because in the Freudian text *nachträglich* and *Nachträglichkeit* can be open to different possible interpretations, it would be preferable to always use the same term for the translation (unlike Strachey), in order not to impose a single meaning on a multivalent text (Laplanche, 1998).[6] He suggests using the terms 'afterwards' and 'afterwardness', thus leaving open different possibilities.

Looking at it from the point of view of the micro-level of a session, one can say that *après-coup* which describes the movement of time from present to past, a restructuring of the past in function of the present, it can be seen that an interpretation itself operates an *après-coup* by reorganising previous perceptions and understandings. Sodre (1997), speaking of the patient's experience, makes a link between a 'mutative insight', which appears suddenly but is only possible because of a slow maturation, and *après-coup*. Modern conceptions of psychoanalysis on the whole no longer aim at unearthing an objective reality but at enabling a continual reappraisal and modification of the past as internal world. The analytic process is a process of continual reinterpretation in which every new point arrived at encompasses and restructures what has been so far.

I will go on to show the interconnection between the two kinds of time at the micro-level of the session.

Helen is a woman in her early thirties who struggles with a sense that she can never become an adult. For her, you are either a child or an adult and she does not seem to have a notion of development or of integration. (I have noticed something similar to what I am going to describe in a number of patients, and this may be understood in terms of how it is only with the depressive position that it is possible to hold on to the two aspects as being part of the self.) An only child, she had also been a lonely child. The family had had to emigrate in difficult circumstances and she had been left a lot to her own devices. Helen had dealt with her difficulties earlier in her life through the use of amphetamines and still now sometimes relies on marijuana. The drugs induce a state of mind in which she feels relieved of constant persecution from a punitive super-ego; they transport her into a timeless world in which she no longer has to worry about anything, past or future. She has other ways too of being 'out of time', even without the drugs. She will, for instance, stare out of her window, becoming totally absorbed by the play of light and shadows from a tree on a wall, or by the movement of the leaves in the wind, oblivious to how much time has gone by. In the sessions, she resorts to repetitive memories with no modifications, which create that same sort of hypnotic sense of emptiness and of time having stopped. Compulsive day-dreaming is a feature of her life and often centres explicitly around creating immortality. She is keenly interested in newspaper articles relating to such things as the discovery of bodies which have been preserved in bogs or in icy mountains, and she scans the internet for the latest advances in cryogenics and for stories concerned with cryonics: the placing of humans and animals at low temperature after death with the idea of bringing them back to life in future centuries.

In her sessions, there often isn't a process of reinterpretation and restructuring. Her material is very disorganised and confused. I will start by making various partial or trial interpretations in an effort to sort out what is going on. There will be a number of false tracks and eventually I can form an interpretation which feels right and makes sense of and organises the material so far. The interpretation seems also to touch her as being right. A while later, however, Helen will pick up on one of the earlier things I have said. It is done as if what was said earlier has not been superseded by the later interpretation, as if there had been no sequence to the session, as if there had been no restructuring following what had seemed to both of us to be the meaningful interpretation. I think of this as 'unpicking the tapestry', an image another patient had used in relation to not wanting to ever end analysis, and which came from the myth of Ulysses in which Penelope weaved all day and unpicked the tapestry at night, in order that the day would never come when the tapestry was finished and she would be forced to marry someone else. Relevant to my subject is that Penelope is weaving a shroud. My patient Helen will unpick the threads of the image put together in an interpretation so that we will wind up with a collection of threads, all of equal importance, in place of a better picture of her internal world. By dismantling the retroactive resignification – the image built up *après-coup* – she is, in fact, also arresting linear progression and freezing time.

The point I am making is that the same hatred of progressive time produces an attack on retroactive time. One movement cannot be separated from the other because retroactive resignification *is* developmental progression. For there to be progression there also has to be this kind of retrospective resignification. The forward movement necessitates a backward movement at the same time and, equally, the continual incorporation and restructuring of the past in the backward movement necessitates the ability to move forward. The ability to symbolise and for self-reflection necessitate a relationship to time which can allow for the double movement forward and backward in time. When the 'fact of life' of time, with its recognition of the Oedipal configuration of generational differences, cannot be tolerated, we experience the paranoid or melancholic world where time is stuck in a moment which never ends. That moment may be located in the past as a fixed grievance, located in a persecuted and eternal present, or even located in the future as an eternal hope (Mehler and Argentieri, 1989; Potamianou, 1997).

I will now describe another, rather different way in which an attempt is made to stop time, in this case by slicing. A number of

151

patients describe recurrent images of slicing – slicing tops of trees, slicing breasts, slicing brains, slicing testicles. While the action originates in a sadistic phantasy, it is used as a protective device, the strength of the sadism being commensurate with the strength, immediacy and totality of the defence which is felt to be required. In schizoid patients it represents mechanisms by which emotions are separated from ideation, or emotions from other emotions.

With one such patient, Bernard, it seemed to be an attempt to make the outside world manageable by receiving only minute amounts of stimuli at any one moment. He had the recurrent fantasy of slicing a brain as if it were a piece of ham. The slicing of the brain is the slicing of the input, which the patient believes cannot be processed because it is too confusing or too overwhelming or too exciting. This kind of slicing controls the outside world, and the analyst in particular, so that time doesn't move, flow, develop. In the session, there is a slicing from moment to moment. Slicing means that the session becomes a collection of unconnected instants and in that way the patient feels that nothing unexpected will happen. The future is eradicated because, like Zeno's arrow, you never get there. When I took up this slicing of experience with Bernard, this led to his being able to convey for the first time an emotional experience. He spoke of waiting for a woman who never turned up and how this had reminded him of how awful he had felt when he was a teenager being in the company of a girl who did not respond to his interest in her. With this, he had been able to describe to me for the first time an experience that was not sliced up, which conveyed a sense of time and with it the pain of waiting and disappointment. It is relevant that Bernard introduced this after my interpretation, by saying that it would be awful to be frozen in one of the slices, suggesting that the slicing does not entirely resolve the problem which is then dealt with by moving from slice to slice. He described another way of slicing when he told me that he wouldn't mind the coming analytic break because "if you take a scoop out of the pudding and then shake the pudding it all gets mixed up and it's as if there's nothing missing". The whole flow of life was sliced into moments, like frozen unconnected stills, or else shaken into a formless pudding, both of which also made my experience in the sessions very strange and made it very difficult to have a picture of what was going on. We did not seem to move forward, and being able to resignify the material was near impossible.

Freud called this sort of phenomenon, when associative links are severed, isolation. It is relevant that Laplanche and Pontalis (1967) suggest that what is severed is especially the connection to what precedes and succeeds the thought in time.

Riesenberg-Malcolm has written about the slicing of interpretations. She talks about a particular form of splitting when interpretations are sliced longitudinally: "Everything said by the analyst seems to be there, as if each segment had been photocopied and repeats itself, scattered among different situations and people. Each new situation reproduces the interpretation as a faint, thin echo of itself" (1990, p. 129). She suggests that the slicing denudes the interpretation of meaning and is both a result of and a defence against the experience of envy. Riesenberg-Malcolm's description of the use of slicing in relation to the interpretations is relevant to my topic, since she describes this phenomenon specifically in terms of patients who, "instead of using analysis as an emotional learning experience, invest all their energies in keeping it in a static condition" (p. 135). I am suggesting that behind this stasis is the fantasy that time can be stopped. The resignification of the interpretation is the movement forward which is attacked. Slicing separates a whole into thin, minute parts – into moments. A similar though not as all-encompassing dismantling takes place when it is specifically the links that are attacked, as Bion describes (1959b).

Time is intimately connected to the generativity which results from linking. It is the forward movement to the next generation and to the new thought. The attack on linking is an attack on time, the link between the parents which brings the next generation, the link between patient and analyst which generates the next interpretation, the link between one moment and the next, one session and the next, which enables a process of development to take place. A schizoid patient, for whom affect and intellect were almost completely split and who did not want to have children and believed his sexuality to be disgusting, found it extremely difficult for a long time to hear and retain what I had said, to such an extent that he believed I had said nothing in a session, thus stopping any generativity, which would have brought painful affects and opened up a future.

The passing of time is always connected with absence and loss. Fain, in *La nuit, le jour* (Braunschweig and Fain, 1975), refers to the alternation of day and night as that of the rhythm of the presence of

153

the mother and of her absence when she is with the father in the night. '*La censure de l'amante*' describes how the mother 'dis-invests' her baby she has put to sleep and becomes again the sexual woman. "When, having dis-invested her infant, she becomes woman again, it is for the sexual father and she thus remains in the line of symbolic organisation" (Fain, 1971). Looked at in this way one can see that time-as-repetition and unidirectional time may not always be as contradictory as Leach implies, if the repetition of night and day goes with the establishment of the Oedipal structure. Leach does, in fact, also describe how, for the Greeks, the sexual act itself provides the primary image of time. He writes,

> Most commentators on the Cronus myth have noted simply that Cronus separates sky from earth, but in the ideology I have been discussing the creation of time involves more than that. Not only must male be distinguished from female but one must postulate a third element, mobile and vital, which oscillates between the two. It seems that the Greeks thought of this third element in explicit concrete form as male semen.
>
> (Leach, 1953 [1961], p. 179)

The notion of penis-as-link discussed in Chapter 6, and which is reminiscent of this, is inseparable from time; it is the time of the parental intercourse. It implies separateness and bringing together. As a function it is represented in the analyst's interpretative mode which makes links – links between affect and ideation; between image and meaning; between past and present, and present and future; between one event and another, engendering a new configuration. It contrasts with the phallus which refers to an atemporal state: no change, no beginning and especially no ending. There is no deflation and no mourning and actually no satisfaction, since that, too, requires a time which comes to an end. With that narcissistic shield, the self is immune to all states of mind which bring in the past and the future: need, desire, regret, sadness, sorrow, guilt, shame. Patients who function primarily in this way think they desperately want to move on but, in fact, aim to abolish the continuity of time, their own past and their own future; they attempt to create stagnation and make their analysis atemporal. There is a reduction of time to a moment (Perelberg, 1997), or the wish to eliminate the frightening past or the frightening future. A 'psychic retreat'

(Steiner, 1993) is such a temporo–spatial psychic immobilisation, as is a developmental 'fixation' (Rose, 1997). Bion states that, in the paranoid–schizoid phase, the question 'why?' cannot be solved because 'why?' has, through guilt, been split off:

> Problems, the solution of which depends upon an awareness of causation, cannot therefore be stated, let alone solved. This produces a situation in which the patient appears to have no problems except those posed by the existence of analyst and patient.
>
> (Bion, 1959b, p. 312)

Even within the analytic situation there is a reduction to a 'now', or a jump from one 'now' to another 'now'.

One important curative factor of psychoanalysis is precisely that it is a process, that the time element is central to it. For some patients the analysis is more of a collection of sessions, and process is something of which the analyst is a guarantor. An aspect of this is the psychic work which takes place in the analyst when the session is over. The analyst's *après-coup* understanding between sessions is an essential part of the analysis, even though the interpretation can no longer be made, and enables the process to develop over time. The patient also resignifies the session between sessions, either in the direction of greater self-reflection or, on the contrary, with increased projection and paranoia. While the patient may be struggling with hatred of the analyst who has been in 'the other room' (Britton, 1998) between sessions, the patient returns to an analyst who has had time to process and sometimes resignify the meaning of the session. A concrete version of this is, of course, supervision and we know that the good use of supervision does not reside in repeating what the supervisor said, in the next session with the patient, but in the supervisee's own developing understanding which furnishes a different perspective on the material. The analyst's ability to continue the psychic work of the sessions between sessions will be important to the analysis and to the patient becoming able to live in the spatio–temporal world.

With Freud's basic discovery of unconscious processes came his understanding of a different type of thinking, which does not abide by the usual time and spatial requirements that we normally take for granted. This type of thinking, which he called 'primary process thinking', was evidenced in dreams and led to his writing about the

155

'timelessness of the unconscious'. More recently, there has been a preference for speaking of a different kind of temporality, rather than of no temporality in the unconscious (Hartocollis, 1980). Green coined the term 'shattered time' (*'le temps éclaté'*) to describe this other kind of time as seen prototypically in dreams. He writes,

> The dream 'clearly indicates' the existence of 'shattered time', that is a notion of time which has very little to do with the idea of an orderly succession according to the tripartite past/present/future. Everything in my dream is pure present.
>
> (Green, 2002a, p. 1)

French psychoanalysts emphasise the analytic aim of freeing the associative process with its lack of concern for ordered succession in time. This becomes not a means to an end but the end in itself. It is this freeing of the associative process which is seen as the cornerstone of the analytic endeavour (Donnet, 2001). A number of French psychoanalysts, in particular those following Lacan, are largely working with Freud's topographical model and see the lifting of repression as the aim of psychoanalysis, hence the emphasis on the primary processes of free association with its atemporal aspects.[7] I want to suggest that their emphasis on *après-coup*, which rests on gathering disparate elements of past and present, reintroduced the importance of temporality, both retrospective and progressive.

While British psychoanalysts have been talking *après-coup* without always knowing it, French psychoanalysts have been, sometimes in spite of themselves, bringing in developmental time through attaching importance to the *après-coup*, since for the continual restructuring of experience to take place, developmental time needs to be tolerated psychically. Drawing attention to retrospective time is important for freeing psychoanalysis from the deterministic model it has sometimes had, but the subtlety of psychoanalysis rests on the paradoxical interconnection of the two movements, forward and retrospective, which it is aiming to free. The fact that both developmental and retrospective time have simultaneous importance has to be accepted as a paradox which cannot be completely described in words.

Winnicott's notion of the fear of the breakdown which has already taken place can be enlarged to describe the way in which the analytic experience 'becomes'/'is' the trauma. Notions of representation, narrative, constructions are relevant in the context of such things as 'nameless dread', which are given a representation (*après-coup*) in the analysis, one which was not there before but which also does not exclude the role of the past. In my clinical descriptions, I brought out the way in which some patients fight off the trauma by dismantling the development of meaning in the *après-coup* of the session, but in so doing they are impeding the development of the symbolic capacity itself which is necessary to make time more tolerable.

Notes

1 Perelberg (2006) proposed the term 'dynamic *après-coup*' as a reference to a theorisation implying something more than the directionality of temporality and indicating a metapsychological link between castration, trauma, sexuality and temporality.

2 Faimberg pointed out this form of temporality in Winnicott at the conference on Psychoanalytical Intracultural and Intercultural dialogue, IPA, Paris, July 1998.

3 Matte–Blanco discusses the lack of contradiction in his notion of the 'principle of symmetry'.

4 The first reference I found to 'massive projective identification' was in Segal's paper 'Notes on Symbol Formation' (1957). Before that, both Segal and Bion spoke of the "massive use of projective identification" or "massive resort to projective identification" (e.g. Bion, 1956, p. 345).

5 I am grateful to Elizabeth Spillius for bringing to my attention two papers by Leach on the subject of time.

6 In French: 'imposer une signification sur un texte essentiellement ouvert' (Laplanche, 1998).

7 More recently the point has been made that both models can coexist and need not exclude each other.

8

THE WORK OF INTERPRETATION

In psychoanalysis the notion of 'work' is used to describe a process which takes place over time, mixing both conscious and unconscious factors, to produce a transformation. In this way we speak of 'the work of mourning' or 'working through'. The 'dream-work' is a particular instance of this, one in which a pressing emotional situation is put into a graphic representation using, to do so, recent available situations and images (day residues). The work of the dream sometimes in itself brings mental shifts in the patient, because something has been psychically worked at and transformed into dream representation, even before it is consciously understood. In that sense the work of the dream is not only the process of transformation into graphic representation but also a process of working through psychic distress, making it more manageable by using the dream space as a container, as will be discussed further in the next chapter.

I am suggesting in this chapter that the work of interpretation belongs in this category of 'work'. In the literature I found that 'the work of interpretation' usually refers to the conscious work the analyst does when making an interpretation, and sometimes to the effect of the interpretation on the patient. Freud refers to the work of interpretation in relation to the interpretation of dreams to describe the unravelling of the dream thoughts which proceed as the reverse of the *dream-work* (Freud, 1942, 1943), suggesting a conscious, ego-orientated process.

I use the notion of 'work of interpretation' or 'interpretation work' (as opposed to 'giving an interpretation' or 'interpreting') to emphasise the unconscious work of transformation, related to what Bion calls "dream-work-α" (1992).

In recent years we have become very adept at describing the analyst's unconscious collusions and enactments and have found these to give invaluable clues to the patient's internal world and defensive modes when the analyst looks at what happened after the event. I think that sometimes this focus on the analyst's enactments has overshadowed the importance of the analyst's role as receptor of direct unconscious communications from the patient and has also overshadowed the importance of the particular mode of attention necessary to maximise receptivity to this communication.

What was revolutionary about Freud's method was not just the requirement for the patient to free associate but, equally important, the necessity for the analyst to use his own unconscious mental processes in the service of the patient's treatment. Freud wrote in 1912: "The doctor's unconscious is able, from the derivatives of the unconscious which are communicated to him, to reconstruct that unconscious, which has determined the patient's free associations" (p. 116), and, in that same paper, he advised the use of "evenly suspended attention" (p. 111). In 1923 he put it even more strongly when he wrote that the most advantageous attitude for the analytic physician is

> to surrender himself to his own unconscious mental activity, in a state of *evenly suspended attention,* to avoid as far as possible reflection and the construction of conscious expectations, not to try to fix anything that he heard particularly in his memory and by these means to catch the drift of the patient's unconscious with his own unconscious.
>
> (Freud, 1923, p. 239)

We note that this time Freud puts "evenly suspended attention" in italics, suggesting that he now sees it as even more important than he did previously.

While psychoanalysts pay lip-service to the notion of evenly suspended attention, I think it is often not given the place and importance it deserves as an essential ingredient to the forward movement of the analysis. It is also in danger of disappearing if interpretative activity is too great.

This mode of attention is part of the setting which includes as its foundation the patient's demand for help and the analyst's commitment to receiving the communications without acting. The scene is thus set for unconscious communication to take place from the moment the patient arrives at the door, and in fact sometimes important communication takes place as the patient enters the room. It is precisely because patient and analyst are both involved in this same setting, although in an asymmetrical way, that the analyst is able to make use of her unconscious alongside her conscious psychic processes. This does not mean that every analyst will function in the same way and with the same associations to a particular patient. Each analyst comes with "an implicit scheme of reference", as Baranger points out, which is part of the "analytic field" (1993).

I also consider that the interpretations thought but not made by the analyst, as well as the analyst's psychic work outside of the session, are part of the setting. By this I mean that the setting is not just analyst and patient meeting at set times and in a set environment; the setting is also the analyst's commitment to making use of his or her thought processes both during and outside the sessions. During the sessions the analyst is subject to powerful defences of her or his own which sometimes means that the appropriate interpretation is only available the moment the patient has left the room.

I would like to note here that this view of the analytic mode which Freud comes to advocate, of "*surrender* to unconscious mental activity", is a feminine receptive mode, in contrast to the hypnotic inducement he originally practised, in which the analyst acts on his passive patient. Gubrich-Simitis writes about Freud (1997, p. 30): "Listening so intensively and patiently to the person being treated, whatever she had to say, was tantamount to admitting her inside oneself." This feminine receptive attitude is one which is not usually credited to Freud who has many times been described as having repressed his feminine side, and it is interesting that there is a 'return of the repressed' in his consulting room.

Since Freud, more 'active' techniques have gained ground within various very different models. Brenner (2000) even suggests that: "Those analysts who still believe that evenly hovering attention is the proper analytic attitude are ... mistaken in citing Freud in support of that belief" (p. 548); he gives as a reason that by 1925 Freud had recognised the importance of listening to the interplay between wish and defence. Indeed, as has been suggested, a different kind of attention is necessary when the focus changes from the analysis of the id to the analysis of the defences of the ego (Gray,

1982). This change also comes about with an attention and analysis of the more psychotic phenomena in which the splitting of the ego and of the object and their complex interaction become the focus of analysis.

It could be said with Carlson, in his review of a debate in the USA between those who maintain the importance of evenly suspended attention and those who see it as a technique which is obsolete, that "most of us, most of the time, are swinging back and forth between evenly suspended attention and focus" (Carlson, 2002, p. 740).

However, this obscures some important differences. I think that different theories and different ways of working can be characterised by the kind of attention usually privileged by the analyst, whether focused or unfocused, by how much the analyst gives space for her own unconscious processes to develop and by the extent to which the analyst thinks that the interpretation needs to be filtered through the analyst's secondary processes and communicated for use by the patient's secondary processes.

De Urtubey, for instance, writes:

the interpretation springs up following a regressive 'descent' of both unconsciousness towards the repressed, from which the analyst returns with thing presentations to be transformed into word presentations, the repressed having been transformed by his own psyche; the patient, at least momentarily, understands the interpretation.

(De Urtubey, 1999, p. 87)[1]

Klauber (1981) explicitly attacks the notion that an interpretation should always be filtered through the analyst's secondary process.

At the other extreme end of the spectrum, Gray suggests that instead of "evenly hovering attention" the analyst should use a "close process attention" as a way to examine the psychical surface for evidence of underlying ego activity (Gray, 1982).

When the analyst is focused on minute-to-minute defensive manoeuvres, a more conscious processing of the interaction with the patient is also required. A certain amount of evenly suspended attention will still be taking place concurrently, as the psychoanalytic setting always involves a level of listening which suspends the immediate response and gathers cues at a less conscious level.

Nevertheless, the analyst does not use the same kind of regressive mode of unfocused attention when attention is focused specifically on defensive shifts. There are quite considerable differences among analysts in this respect.

Bion with his notion of '*reverie*' comes back more directly to the original attitude of mind prescribed by Freud. With his recommendation that the analyst should avoid "memory and desire" (1959a, p. 56), he extends Freud's recommendation that the doctor "should withhold all conscious influences from his capacity to attend, and give himself over completely to his 'unconscious memory'" (1912). This state of mind is also captured by Botella and Botella when they speak of the work of representation, "le travail de figurabilité". They are speaking about the sorts of patients for whom there are areas of non–represented traumatic experiences and for whom the analyst has to lend himself as a 'double'. As I understand this, they are suggesting that the analyst receives the unconscious communication and does the work of figuration which the patient has not been able to do.

Grinberg puts it clearly:

> The receptive attitude of the analyst reveals itself by consenting to be invaded by the analysand's psychotic anxieties and fantasies and containing them so as to be able to feel, think, and share the emotions contained in such projections with him, as if they were a part of his own self, whatever their nature may be (murderous hate, fear of death, catastrophic terror, etc.).
>
> (Grinberg, 1995, p. 103)

A focus on defensive manoeuvres, which requires a more ego-directed attention, can make us forget the importance of the particular mode of attentiveness which allows for maximal receptiveness to unconscious communication not only from the patient but also from the analyst's own unconscious, and which comes before interpretation can be made. Or, as I prefer to say, maximal receptiveness enables unconscious and partly conscious 'interpretation', in the sense of 'giving meaning', which may or not lead to the verbal intervention of the analyst. This may be what Bion has in mind when he writes: "the state of free-floating attention, usually regarded as desirable in the analyst, is the more effective the more it approximates to being represented by a wide spectrum of grid categories" (1965a, p. 50).

I want to show how, in my view, this mode of attentiveness with maximal receptiveness, of *reverie,* is what promotes the forward movement of the analysis. I use *'reverie'* in the restricted sense which Bion gave it when he writes of *reverie* "as the psychological source of supply of the infant's needs for love and understanding" and as "a factor of the mother's alpha-function" (1962a, p. 36). One could even speculate that at moments when it is lost, for instance, during acute enactments, hate comes into the picture.

A clinical moment

Pedro had started analysis in a very broken-down state with little capacity to speak about his emotions, but, feeling heard, he immediately 'latched on' to analysis. Pedro was troubled by intense jealousy accompanied by cruel and disturbing fantasies.

At the time of this session, some years into his five-times-a-week psychoanalysis, Pedro had recovered and was functioning reasonably well in all areas of his life but the analysis could get stuck around repetitive issues of his wish to control his analyst in ways which impeded his own development. Greater psychic freedom was immediately followed by panic and regression, in particular into a masochistic position.

Pedro is often late or misses sessions. He starts this particular session by telling me that he found it hard to come today. He talks about how unequal it feels between him and me, and he doesn't like to be hanging around waiting to see me; it feels like 'unrequited love'. He mumbles, his speech becomes vague. I hear something about how my window could be open. I wonder if I have misheard or missed something. I feel puzzled and confused about who is at whose window. I have a vague image of Romeo and Juliet, or was it Cyrano de Bergerac, and scenes at the window – Pedro talks more about the humiliating situation he feels it puts him in, that I am like an 'emotional prostitute' and eventually he says that he wanted to stay in bed with his girlfriend and I should be the one left waiting for him.

I was struck that he had been on time when usually he is late and without much thought I said:

You had to fight the feeling of wanting to have me waiting for you, and to use me as an emotional prostitute in whom you

163

could get rid of feelings that seem hard to bear, but *in fact you didn't do that and you came on time.*

This had a great impact on the session and it took an interesting turn. Pedro told me that he thought he had made progress recently, that he was able to bear not turning to alcohol or food. It's "like being able to take the sensitivity of not having alcohol at night, or like not being scared of going to bed for fear of not being able to sleep". He then surprisingly told me about a gesture he had made towards his father in the face of a recent bereavement in the family, making good some photographs of the relative who had suddenly died. He then said that maybe it was to make up for all the jealousy he had felt towards him: "maybe it's an anti-jealousy thing, to go against how I've been jealous of his contact with others".

At some point in the session however Pedro started on the subject of times when his father hadn't helped him when he was in acute physical pain and appeared not to know how to help. It started to escalate and he seemed to be getting carried away with a series of complaints.

I wondered at this point if there was a complaint about me and what it was, what it was that I had not known how to help him with, or if he felt I was forgetting about all the bad things and his grievance because I was taking up his warmer and reparative feelings. As I wasn't sure what the complaint was or why, but I tended to think he was covering something up, I said:

> Earlier you were talking about '*sensitivities*', emotional hurts, the difficulty when you feel not helped with those. You feel it's safer to rely on yourself.

Pedro paused and then said: "I remember a television programme when I was young, maybe seven, there was this group of independent rebels."

I said: "So it's an attitude that has been with you from way back."

He gave a little laugh.

What was on my mind was that the unbearable pain, the 'sensitivity' at this point, was a more depressive feeling, feeling sorry for what he's done, wishing to repair the father (and his analyst) and that the rebellion is a wish to get away from that pain into an 'I don't care' attitude.

164

He said:

I was looking at your plant and then I started thinking of a science fiction film I saw, I wish, again, it would go out of my mind [pause].

Me: "You don't like your mind" [encouraging tone].

He said: "In this film there were two people who looked the same, the good twin who was able to be good and have proper relationships and the renegade independent twin who exploits his resemblance with him."

This seemed to fit with what was going on in my mind at this point. I had felt anxious that I had been completely mistaken, that I had been thinking that he prefers me to see him as bad because it's safer and he doesn't have to face the pain (and persecution) of having hurt his object, when in fact the image of repairing the object was in some way false. I now felt very unsure which it was and I had an uneasy feeling.

I said: "So I might get confused as to which twin I am talking to."

He responded immediately: "Or when I'm late, which one twin is responsible for that?"

Me: "Which one finds it hardest to be here?" (meaning his loving self, or the hateful one, and whether he is protecting me or attacking me by being late).

That was the end of the session. Just after Pedro left the session I suddenly remembered that he was taking Friday off to go on a long weekend away with his girlfriend, something very unusual. I could see that he may have been concerned by what I would feel about this and wanting to make up for it by being on time, or perhaps keeping my anger and retribution at bay. I was left wondering which is the 'real' twin. Or was the point that he can slide between the two so that he is always hiding the real one? At any point, either twin can be the mask for the other one. Or is it that he himself lives in a state of confusion about who he is, good or bad, and whether it is his love and appetite or his hate which can hurt and make his object unable to help. Even speaking of twins would offer some clarity and respite from that anxiety. A state of unease and confusion had been transmitted to me during the session.

165

In the next session Pedro was again on time and he told me he had felt for the first time in the evening that he had space to do what he liked rather than "curl up in a ball and be frightened". He spoke of his anxiety about having a full session today (as he was on time again) and the possible disappointment. Perhaps he wants something extra; he said:

> to stay here all the time, to live here with you and see the others coming and going from my different position. That would mean competing directly with your husband and maybe then I think of your husband growling at me.

Pedro then spoke of seeing part of my family tree on the internet and being reassured that it didn't say that my husband was deceased. Now that it was back on my mind that he was taking the Friday off, I took up at some point in the session that he was relieved that when he was away on his weekend I would have someone too; in that way *I* wouldn't want to growl at him. He said: "it didn't say that your husband was alive, it just didn't say he was deceased. It makes me think of the pictures which we made pretty, like an undertaker beautifying the dead."

I was struck by how his making the old pictures whole for his father had now become "beautifying the dead", a perversion of the reparative gesture, and I had an uncomfortable, rather sick and shivery feeling (Pedro used to shudder in the early years of analysis). He went on to talk about the time I had cancelled two sessions which I think was an attempt to make me into the guilty one but also to get away from something very disturbing about dead people. This continued the theme of hiding.

It was only when I wrote up these sessions that I remembered I had had a fleeting image/thought about the window, Cyrano under the window, and also of Romeo and Juliet. Cyrano is about this theme of one person hiding behind the other. Cyrano hidden by the shadow of the night agrees to woo Roxanne with his poetry on behalf of his inarticulate friend, and in this way Cyrano, who thinks he is too ugly to woo Roxanne directly, can speak of his own love. Pedro has both great difficulty articulating his feelings and a dys-morphic body image. The images that came to mind combined romantic forbidden love in Romeo and Juliet, the sexual imagery of the window and the disguise in Cyrano.

166

What I want to get at is that my fleeting thoughts/images *anticipated* in the session what Pedro said about the twins and that I only remembered them with effort. The complexity of the transference and countertransference makes it impossible to know how much I was picking up of what he was bringing unconsciously and how much the session took the turn it did through something coming from me which made me pick up the discrepancy of his arrival in the way I did. Certainly the particular form my thoughts and images took in the session had to do with the personal significance of the theatre play for me, and of my own resonance to the analytic situation, but the twinning aspect of the imagery would have been something I unconsciously picked up at the beginning of the session, anticipating what came up.

After the event it is possible to do much reinterpretation or further interpretation, looking further into the countertransference, thinking about the sexual imagery of the open window, as well as looking at the session in terms of the whole week, his taking a day off, notions of hiding, fake and real, and the uncertainty and wrong-footedness I experienced.

I could also fruitfully study how in these sessions Pedro moved astutely so that what is real one moment becomes a mask the next so that I am continually left unsure when it's a good him hiding behind a bad him, or a bad him hiding behind a good him, in this continual and rapid footwork which takes place. I could also consider how the 'good work' gets continually undone and how he can feel safer in the 'bad self' position.

All this is the more conscious work which goes on in and outside the session. But this is alongside or subsequent to the unconscious process which takes place in the session. I had forgotten my fleeting associations to the open window, even during the session, and only recalled them because I wrote up the session and they slowly came back. I could then see how much they had been part of the session, *pre-empting* the later material about the twins.

They were my unconscious response and would have impacted unconsciously upon how I understood and interpreted the material, even if I cannot say exactly how. In fact I later wondered if the open window might itself have been a free associative image as I could not be sure he had actually said that, and it seemed to come from nowhere.

There is of course no activity free of unconscious process whether in the analyst or in the patient, and, as psychoanalysts, we are unique in using our minds as an instrument, even though it is an instrument which is far from recording an objective reality. Most of the time we do not know what lies behind that which we notice, our associations, what we choose to take up. The interpretation itself later becomes part of the situation to be interpreted. This is why psychoanalysis is a process rather than a collection of interpretations. We lend ourselves, our psychic apparatus, through our receptive position, to do unconscious work which we can only capture in its outcome and, with the help of conscious work, becomes the spoken interpretation.

The unconscious processes lead to enactments when the analyst acts out a scenario but when they remain contained in the mind of the analyst in the form of *reveries* they form part of the data which will be transformed into an interpretation. The images which float into the mind of the analyst are derivatives of unconscious processes. These images and *reveries* which only sometimes reach consciousness will impact upon the analyst's understanding of the patient without the analyst being aware of it. When they are fully conscious, I think that they are not necessarily useful in providing conscious understanding during the session, and that they are often more useful in their unconscious effect in directing the mind of the analyst to that which is of relevance and importance. The fleeting images only become meaningful after they have found expression in the session. Usually they won't be remembered but they help us arrive at interpretations without our knowing how we got there. Freud writes of "ideas which come into our head we do not know from where, and with intellectual conclusions arrived at we do not know how" (Freud, 1915b, pp. 166–167).

Bion (1962b, pp. 86–87) describes an optimal state in the analyst when he writes:

> a state of reverie conducive to alpha-function, obtrusion of the selected fact, and model-making together with an armoury limited to a few essential theories ensure that a harsh break in observation ... becomes less likely; interpretations can occur to the analyst with the minimum disturbance of observation.

Baranger (1993, p. 18) describes the danger of obstructing the receptive frame of mind:

The psychoanalyst ... must beware of mentally obstructing access to the unforeseen, to 'surprise', which is precisely what he hopes for as the emergence of the unconscious. Yet it is not a passive or ingenuous form of listening. It is guided by the analyst's entire listening resources. Analytic theory, which need not be formulated, provides him with an implicit framework to accommodate his discoveries.

He goes on with the warning:

The analyst must steer a course between two contrasting dangers: the forced application of a pre-existing theory, which will ultimately lead to spurious interpretations, and the whole complex of chaotic theories. The analyst's scheme of reference is what guides both the search for the point of urgency and the formulation of the interpretation.

(Baranger, 1993, p. 19)

There can be a danger in trying to utilise the *reveries* directly. Ogden (1997a, p. 569), who values the role of the conscious *reveries* of the analyst, also believes that

The experience of reverie is rarely, if ever, 'translatable' in a one-to-one fashion into an understanding of what is going on in the analytic relationship. The attempt to make immediate interpretive use of the affective or ideational content of our reveries usually leads to superficial interpretations in which manifest content is treated as interchangeable with latent content.

'Reverie' is not the same as 'countertransference'. The latter usually refers specifically to affects (Grinberg, 1962; Heimann, 1950). Reverie is largely unconscious but guides the analyst's thoughts in directions and ways which can subsequently be more directly utilisable by the secondary processes of the analyst. Ferro's (2002) Bionian notion of the "waking dream thought" which he describes in the patient is close to what I have in mind, but I am talking about a *reverie* taking place in the analyst, in particular when the analyst is in a state of evenly suspended attention. In the material I described, the open window and Cyrano de Bergerac were derivatives of this kind of thought, and although I was not

169

conscious of it, they both anticipated and contributed to the development of the session, as I could see later on, opening on to the material about the twin selves which are a mask to each other, and this gave the analysis a sense of movement. Most of the time we do not capture those thoughts but they lead to those moments when greater 'intunness' with the patient is achieved beyond a response to the patient's verbal communication. They are a 'window' on to something new, something which comes with a sense of surprise.

I am mindful of Britton and Steiner's warning that "It would be arrogant of an analyst to suppose that he was immune to the unconscious processes that might lead to the emergence of an overvalued idea masquerading as an intuitive insight" (1994, p. 1071). They go on to write:

> We will therefore discuss the emergence of a selected fact, which we see as a creative integration of disparate facts into a meaningful pattern, and contrast it with an alternative phenomenon, namely, the emergence of an overvalued idea, which can likewise be used by the analyst to give a sense of integration to otherwise disparate and confusing experiences. In the case of an overvalued idea, the integration is spurious and results from the facts being forced to fit an hypothesis or theory which the analyst needs for defensive purposes.
>
> (Britton and Steiner, 1994, p. 1070)

I want to stress that what I am describing as the *reveries* and images fostered by the unconscious communication which accompanies the analysis in an ongoing way is only the raw material from which will be constructed an interpretation which will be creative or defensive, or lead to an enactment. I think, however, that the receptivity to *reverie*, fostered by the setting, is what brings the potential for something creative, by which I mean something new developing in the analysis (which may not be quite the same as what Britton and Steiner were meaning by the word 'creative' in the above quote). It is interesting that Freud recommended 'evenly suspended attention' which not only fosters a more regressive mode of thinking but also the suspension of action and hence the reduction of enactment. It is this which promotes the life force of the analysis.

I am also not ignoring the fact that the analyst too will be subject to countertransferences. As Racker (1957, pp. 307–308) writes:

> The first distortion of truth in 'the myth of the analytic situation' is that analysis is an interaction between a sick person and a healthy one. The truth is that it is an interaction between two personalities, in both of which the ego is under pressure from the id, the superego, and the external world; each personality has its internal and external dependences, anxieties, and pathological defenses; each is also a child with its internal parents; and each of these whole personalities – that of the analysand and that of the analyst – responds to every event of the analytic situation.

This will always be the case, and it is this which requires a 'third position' and a conscious attempt to 'know' as far as is possible. But I am suggesting that it is the openness to 'dream thoughts' coupled with a suspension of 'activity' that is an essential part of the 'work' which moves the analysis forward. It is also what makes for 'an experience'. Further work of understanding and 'analysis' of countertransference will also be required, bearing in mind that the complexity of the 'field' means that understanding is always very partial and in constant evolution.

Of course, the receptive attitude can also be excessive. Racker (1958, p. 561) points this out when he writes:

> our masochism may ... lead us into being exaggeratedly passive and not fighting for the patient.... Excessive passivity implies scant interpretative activity and, this, in turn, scant working through on the patient's part with a consequent reduction of therapeutic success.

Indeed, the receptiveness to unconscious communication is only part of the work of interpretation, the more unconscious aspect, while there is also a more conscious activity which involves looking for patterns and conceptualising. There needs to be a balance and a coupling of evenly suspended attention with a more focused interpretative activity. It is the latter which can enable an understanding of the 'stuckness' and in particular of the masochistic pull upon which it is based. In Chapters 10 and 11 I discuss further the notion of *reverie*, and also the use of fleeting images in the session.

Too often the unconscious is described as if it is an enemy in the analysis, that which leads only to enactments and impasses. I am suggesting that the unconscious work which one sometimes catches a glimpse of through the analyst's *reveries* and images is the motor of the movement forward of the analysis. It is not something which takes place sometimes, but is a continual processing by the analyst. I have suggested that the notion of 'the work of interpretation' may be used to describe the unconscious processing in the analyst in individual sessions but also over the whole analysis; it is 'the work' of receptivity and transformation which takes place in the analyst's mind. 'Interpretations' will be in a loose connection with this work. Like the dream work, the interpretation work (or work of interpretation) is a 'particular form of thinking', a form of processing in the analyst made possible by the setting and the mode of attentiveness to the patient, and is the life force of the analysis. The work of interpretation in the analyst has a counterpart in the patient's working through insofar as in both of these 'works' there is a process in which a repetition is not an identical and every moment has an influence on the next moment, and where forward and backward are part and parcel of the movement in a complex way.

Note

1 Translation mine; in the original:

l'interpretation surgit à la suite d'une 'descente' régressive communed des inconscients vers le refoulé, don't l'analyste revient chargé de representations de chose à transformer en représentations de mots, le refoulé ayant été traduit par son psychisme; le patient, momentané-ment du moins, comprend l'interpretation donnée.

9

REVERBERATION TIME, DREAMING
AND THE CAPACITY TO DREAM

A patient dreams:

I am walking in this dark, cold place and I come across a DeLorean car that is covered in ice. The ice was melting. I feel excited to be able to use the car. He explains: "The DeLorean car is a futurist car, a 'Back to the Future' car, with doors opening up rather than out, a time-machine. As well as the two dimensions of the ground it can move in time, backwards and forwards. It's a vehicle of freedom."

At the start of that week the patient had said: "I feel stuck in a well"; I took up the double meaning of 'well'. This seemed to 'unstick' the session and melt the ice. I knew this patient became worried whenever he felt more normal and I thought he feared no longer relying on his grievances as the better, safer food. He then brought in the idea that 'being well' led to expectations that he will 'do well', 'be good', repay his analyst's investment of time, make reparation for his meanness, live up to expectations; he started to think of harpies circling around ready to attack and tear bits of his flesh, and of his mother with a scolding look. He then thought of the danger of being 'too well', a flight into mania. He now had the idea, which he had not voiced before, that being too well had preceded his depressive breakdown.

And so he dreams of walking in a dark, cold place and finding a DeLorean car. The dream, like all dreams, is a vehicle of freedom. Freedom to do, without actually doing. Being where you want,

173

when you want. Inventing solutions which do not conform to the reality of time and space. In the film *Back to the Future* Marty is flung 30 years back in time and stuck there unless Doc Brown can help him. Marty's own mother, now a teenager, falls for him instead of for his father. Manic solution to the Oedipal scenario.

The dream always has a dreamer. The dream is inserted into the temporality of the analysis with its own strange ways of moving, like the DeLorean car, back and forth in time, one does not always know why or how. My patient's dream is about time in more than one way. It represents a wish to deny chronological time, to collapse the generations, but also to fly off omnipotently and then be brought back safely – the dream was dreamed not long before an analytic break which he was pre-dating by a week, albeit for necessary work reasons, and he would indeed be flying off abroad where he was going to some very important meeting with important people and he feared becoming manic. The analyst too has her own temporality, and the Oedipal meaning of the dream was only understood *après-coup* when she found out the story of *Back to the Future*.

If the patient is able to have this dream, it is a sign that it has been possible, on this occasion, through the 'work of the dream', for him to transform thoughts, anxieties, desires into dream images, to have an internal 'conversation' which resulted in a wish-fulfilment (the DeLorean car). And in bringing the dream to the session, the dream in its recounted manifestation after secondary revision becomes a 'clinical fact' of the transference situation and inseparable from it. The patient is asking for the 'doctor's' help with his anxieties about being destabilised by losing touch with reality when he gets 'too well'; that is, his fear of breaking down during his 'high-flying' activity and absence from analysis, and a wish to be 'brought back' to reality. Within the analysis the 'work of the dream' is inseparable from the 'work of psychoanalysis'. Communicating these anxieties offers the possibility to go back in time and find a better solution in order to move forward, to unfreeze his life, and not to stay stuck in either mania or masochistic gratification. The DeLorean car is psychoanalysis, vehicle of freedom if the compulsion to repeat can be put in the service of development rather than malignant arrest.

I started with the presentation of the dream because it makes direct reference both to time (the time-machine) and to an interpersonal and directly transferential situation (Doc Brown, a

174

resonant name to that of the analyst), and also to a specific temporal moment in the analysis (an interruption of the sessions). It speaks of stasis (freezing) and movement (unfreezing), past and future, and even of *Nachträglichkeit* (back to the future). It speaks of time as a marker of the difference between the generations and the wish to erase the reality and 'down-to-earthness' of chronological time and its Oedipal implications. It shows the patient in his dream life 'discussing' all these issues in the graphic and pithy way characteristic of dreams. We recognise in these the fundamental issues related to the passage of time which each individual has to negotiate, and we can see why temporality is at the heart of psychoanalysis.

My aim in this chapter is to suggest that the most primitive subjective sense of time which I proposed to call 'reverberation time' (Birksted-Breen, 2003, p. 1504) develops out of the first relationship to the maternal object and shares its roots with the development of an 'apparatus for dreaming dreams' (Grinberg, 1987). I also suggest that psychically it is the building block for the depressive position and the acceptance of the Oedipal situation. Hence, at the core of all deep disturbances we find an inability to negotiate the passage of time, leading to a psychic 'freezing' of time such as we find, for instance, in melancholia, in the 'psychic retreats' of borderline states (Steiner, 1993) or in the 'telescoping of generations' (Faimberg, 2005). In psychic reality a frozen mental state is a 'real' stoppage of time, as discussed in Chapter 7.

It is no surprise that psychoanalytic controversies themselves so often centre on issues of temporality: history versus psychic reality, 'here and now' versus 'there and then', as if there could be a 'here and now' without a 'there and then', and vice versa. To put it another way, it is the reconnection of the temporal link between the two which is the psychoanalytic endeavour. Psychoanalysis, one could say, operates in that 'transitional space' which is the ambiguous play between temporalities.

There has been a tendency to concentrate on the opposition between chronological time which is what distinguishes the generations, marks the uni-directionality of the earliest relationship to the breast and signifies the inevitability of death and, in the analysis, termination, on the one hand, and the timelessness of the unconscious on the other. This distinction also marks the opposition between the pleasure principle and the reality principle, primary process and secondary process, conscious and unconscious, life force and death

175

force. Sometimes an opposition is also made between 'real' time and subjective time. Here, however, I am interested in the subjective experience that 'time passes' and how it first develops, and not whether or how closely it corresponds to a reality. It is sometimes assumed that time is something simply imposed from the outside – objective, chronological time. However, psychoanalysts recognise some more internal origins:

> Freud told Marie Bonaparte (1940) that 'when consciousness awakens within us we perceive this internal flow and then project it into the outside world'. The succession of time, therefore, according to this finds its psychological birth in the very nature of consciousness rather than being the consequence of something imposed from outside.
>
> (Abraham, 1976, p. 464)

Freud also wrote that the origin of the sense of time had to do with the sampling of the external world periodically, the discontinuous method of functioning ensuring a 'periodic non-excitability' which offers the infant a 'shield against stimuli'. He writes: "[the] discontinuous method of functioning of the system Pcpt.–Cs. lies at the bottom of the origin of the concept of time" (Freud, 1925, p. 231). Primitive temporality has also been linked to other biological rhythms, in particular the rhythms of frustration–satisfaction but also to rhythms such as breathing and pulse, and to the intervals between defecation (see Hartocollis, 1974).

It is important to remember that rhythms are not pure repetition of the identical, as Barale and Minazzi point out:

> [There is] a grain of the variation or transformation inherent in any rhythm, if only because every presence, even if the same as its predecessor, is also new because it has behind it the entire sequence that precedes it; it has a 'before' and 'after' and belongs in a time – it 'goes towards' something, alluding to an anticipated future, in expectation of the coming of something identical which might, however, not occur.
>
> (Barale and Minazzi, 2008, p. 948)

In that sense this primitive temporality is one which already has in it an experience of directionality.

176

All these rhythms, however, do not exist independently of the mother, and from the start of the infant's life that infant's experience is mediated by the mother's care and her psyche (Denis, 1995; Künstlicher, 2001; Laplanche, 1997); she has in particular a direct influence on the variations of the rhythms. Not only are the rhythms of hunger and satisfaction directly related to the mother's feeding of her infant, but also to the quality of her presence.

The mother has been described as taking on the function Freud gives to the outer layer of the mental apparatus which protects from excessive excitation (Khan, 1964). When the infant is given "too much or too little psychic space in which to be mentally creative on his own" (McDougall, 1974, p. 447), this leads to deficiencies in the area of representation and mentalisation. This is of relevance to the topic at hand because such deficiencies lead to the tendency to act out, that is, to act rather than wait and think; in other words, to an intolerance of the passage of time. Fain (1971) describes the consequences of infants whose mothers overdo the role of protective shield because "they unconsciously wish to bring their children back to foetal bliss inside their own bodies" (quoted in McDougall, 1974, p. 446), and cannot disinvest the baby sufficiently for that baby to develop its own autoerotic activity and the capacity for psychic development. The womb-like existence, or, more precisely, the fantasy of it, has a timeless quality which in turn prevents the child from being able to develop means of dealing with time.[1] These mothers, Fain also says, are not able to disinvest the baby at night and turn to the father of their baby to become the father's lover rather than the baby's mother ('la censure de l'amante'). Here we have another rhythm clearly mediated by the objects, that of day and night. This rhythm of day and night and its psychic representation is a basis for a notion of time, and the foundation, via absence, of the Oedipal structure and psychic development.

The toleration of absence and of frustration is the basis of cognitive development. In the 'fort-da' game (Freud, 1920) the child develops symbolic mastery over the time of waiting for the return of the mother, but also anticipates her return with the rhythm (Barale and Minazzi, 2008). Absence creates the thought (Bion, 1965b) and the word and representation (Botella and Botella, 2001), and the capacity for psychic survival (Boris, 1987). Thinking is what detaches one from the immediate reality into symbolisation and brings the possibility of moving backward and forward in time.

All pathologies deal with problems to do with time and the inability to accept change, that is, a movement in time: fixation, regression, psychic retreat, repetition compulsion. An imaginary future can also act as a retreat and stop movement. Psychoanalysis itself may be used as such a timeless retreat. Mourning and melancholia typify the two opposite relationships to time. Vertical splits enable different parts of the personality to have different relationships to time, by which I mean that neurotic parts of the personality may function according to a notion of time passing, while psychotic parts of the personality function on the omnipotent stoppage of time passing. The task of psychoanalysis is, via repetition, to enable an unblocking of a present frozen in the past on to a possible future of open possibilities. A different sense of the present, less enslaved to the past or to a fantasy future. A new sense of time is almost always mentioned, in my experience, by patients in the latter phases of their analyses, a new sense of time which has been mediated by the analyst's psyche in the interchange between patient and analyst. In Chapter 12 I describe the changed experience of time at the end of analysis and how it connects with the analytic process.

I am putting forward the idea here that central to the development of the sense of time are not only the biological rhythms or the rhythm of presence and absence of the mother, but that a primitive sense of time and the toleration of time develop with the transformation effected by the mother's *reverie* and the transformation that takes place via this *reverie*, and that this is also something of central importance in an ongoing analysis.

Bion, as far as I know, does not relate reverie specifically to temporality but his description of the transformation of beta elements projected into the mother, into alpha elements, brings in a time element. I suggested giving the name 'reverberation time' to this whole process in order to emphasise the time element inherent in this transformation: it includes the infant's projections, the mother's *reverie*, the sojourn and transformation in the mother's psyche, the return of the transformed projection to the infant and its reception by the infant. I wrote in Chapter 7: "It is the infant's introjection of that process and the creation of a reverberation time which enables the development of the infant's own capacity to develop and tolerate a sense of time." It could also be called 'reflection time', but this would suggest a more fully conscious and intellectual process than what is actually involved. Maternal *reverie* is not a conscious process;

178

it is not day-dreaming, though it may have conscious elements attached to it. Reverberation, importantly, also points to an auditory aspect. Architecturally, reverberation describes the way sound travels back in modified form after coming up against a surface. It accounts for the echo. 'Reverberate' is akin to the word 'resonate' which is used metaphorically to describe the attunement of one person to another person's meaning. Reverberation, the echo, describes an ill-defined area between narcissism and object relation, and is thus appropriate for the earliest mother and infant experiences. It is, in Winnicott's terms, a transitional space. The infant sees himself in his mother's face as Winnicott (1967a) describes in his notion of the mother as mirror, or, one could add, hears himself in her sound response to the sounds he produces. But the mother is not like a physical mirror which would just reproduce mechanically. The mother brings herself, her feelings, her unconscious into the interaction, so that transformation is always taking place. It is in that sense, in my view, that there is no clear delineation between primary narcissism and primitive object relation, which is why I call it 'ill-defined'.[2] It is an 'echo' which comes back slightly transformed, or, in Winnicott's terms, it is 'me and not me'. What is mother and what is infant are not clearly differentiated. From the point of view of the infant what comes back is something of herself, with a difference which involves the object. The time of reverberation is part of the experience of having feelings contained and made manageable. It is only when the response is not adequate or takes too long that 'objective time' will 'impinge', and either compliance in the sense described by Winnicott (1955) or defences against 'objective time' will set in. Using Winnicott's notion of the breast which is created by the baby, one could say that the time it takes for the breast to be 'created' is 'me' and 'not me', and it is in that space that a sense of expectation and a sense of time develops. Finding the breast includes the transformation of anxieties.

Sound is central in prenatal and early postnatal life. Anzieu (1979) has written about the importance of the auditory environment in the earliest development of the self. The "sound bath," he writes, "pre-figures the skin-self, with one half of its double face turned to the inside and the other half to the outside" (Anzieu, 1979, p. 30). This describes the non-differentiation and intimate connection between the relationship to the self and the relationship to the other. He suggests that before the visual mirror described by

179

Winnicott and Lacan there is "a sound mirror or ... an audio-phonic skin". In the same paper he points out that in Greek mythology Echo and Narcissus are brought together, and he writes:

> This legend appropriately illustrates the precedence of the sound-mirror over the visual-mirror, as well as the primary feminine character of the voice, and the link that exists between the emission of sound and the request for love. But it also provides us with elements for an understanding of pathology. If the mirror, whether of sound or vision, only reflects back the subject to himself — that is, his request, distress (Echo) or quest for ideal (Narcissus) — the result will be a defusion of instincts. The death instinct is freed and becomes economically predominant over the life instinct.
>
> (Anzieu, 1979, p. 32)

This captures, though via a different framework, what I want to say about reverberation; reverberation is not just reflecting back something identical but is reflecting something *transformed* by another psyche. I refer to it as an ill-defined area between narcissism and object relation because, from the infant's point of view, it is not clearly delineated as self or not self, but it is the basis, in my view, of differentiation of self and other, and of a sense of time.

While this paper is dealing with the "clinical infant" rather than with the "observed infant" (Stern, 1985, pp. 13–14)[3] and with maternal *reverie* and the development of the primitive experience of time as adduced from the psychoanalytic setting in which there is no one-to-one direct relationship to the historical infant, it is interesting to note that what is discussed here is congruent with the findings of infant researchers. In particular, Beebe *et al.* describe the centrality of the back and forth between caretaker and infant and write that very young infants are able to abstract a sequence of interaction. They write that very young infants have "a remarkable capacity to perceive temporal sequences" which is evidence of a "presymbolic representational capacity" (p. 141), and suggests that "the temporal coordination of the interaction is an important dimension in the organization of development, representations, and the child's experience of relatedness" (Beebe *et al.*, 1997, p. 170).

Confirmation of the importance of sound is also given by infant researchers who have discussed the importance of the 'chatter' of the caregiver based on pretending that a dialogue is going on (see Lichtenberg, 2003), emphasising again the interplay of differentiation and non-differentiation of mother and infant. Lewkowicz (1989) writes that the discrimination of duration is one of the most basic functions of the auditory system.

Interestingly, the auditory channel is also privileged in psychoanalysis, through language obviously, but psychoanalysts have also been interested in the communication which takes place between patient and analyst through non-verbal sounds (Scott, 1958) and through the qualities of the voice. Mancia writes of the 'musical dimension' of the transference, as evidenced in the tone, timbre, volume, rhythm and timing which are rooted in the unrepressed unconscious and give clues about the earliest childhood relationships (Mancia, 2003, 2004), and for Ogden (1999) the 'music of what happens' in the session is to be found in the analyst's *reverie*.

Bion describes how, when there is no transformation via the mother's *reverie*, the infant is left with 'nameless dread' and is prey to the death instinct. Nameless dread is subjectively an a-temporal state – patients describe how in that state of mind the experience is of terror which has no end because there is no object, external or internal, imagined or expected to hear and respond. It may also be thought of as 'timeless dread'. The experience is terrifying because it is experienced as eternal. Death is imagined by some to be such a terrifying state with no end. In that sense it may be said that the mother is not primarily protecting against the painful awareness of time by creating an illusion of timelessness, but on the contrary is helping to protect against the pain of timelessness, the state of terror without end. The work of Bion on containment, it seems to me, helps understand how her function of transformation of unbearable stimuli is also the basis of a primitive temporality. The notion of containment describes borders and limits in space and time. Baranger *et al.* in this line of thinking write:

> [Psycho] Analysis could be defined as historicization [*Nachträglichkeit*] versus death instinct. Nachträglichkeit is the attempt to constitute the trauma as such within a new historicization, that is, to make it comprehensible.... We are thus led to differentiate the extreme form of the inassimilable 'pure' Trauma, nearly pure death drive, from the retroactively historicized forms

181

which are reintegrated into the continuity of a vital flow of
time that we 'invent' in analytic work.

(Baranger *et al.*, 1988, pp. 126–128)

I understand this to mean that the analyst gives the 'pure trauma'
representability which means placing it in space and time. The time
of reverberation may be understood as the time of giving meaning
retrospectively within a shorter or longer time framework insofar as
the mother and the analyst are bringing 'history' into their response.
In this way the repetition of the 'identical' can become a repetition
of 'the same', to use a distinction made by De M'Uzan to speak
about patients for whom nothing is remembered, only identically
reproduced (De M'Uzan, 2007) in contrast to those for whom repetition includes subtle differences when an elaboration of the past is
possible.

Within a different framework, Winnicott also talks about the
role of the mother in protecting the infant from 'unthinkable
anxieties'. Although he does not relate this directly to time, Winnicott does use the expressions 'continuity in being' and 'going-
on-being' which imply a time factor. He writes that failures of
adaptation and impingements, which disrupt 'going-on-being'
recurrently, lead to a pattern of 'fragmentation of being' (Winnicott, 1965), which means there is no integrated unit able to
continue to have a self with a past, present and future. Of psycho-
analysis he says: "It is a long-term giving the patient back what
the patient brings. It is a complex derivative of the face that
reflects what is there to be seen" (Winnicott, 1971, p. 117).
Implicit, it seems to me, is the idea that there is psychic processing in the mother's mind before recognition and reflection in her
face so that she is always more than just an impersonal mirror.

It is in this sense that I think of reverberation as being between
narcissism and object relating, a relationship to the self via the
mother. Anzieu puts it another way:

The sound and visual mirrors contribute to the structuring of the
self and then of the ego, on condition that the mother expresses
to the child something of herself and something of him, as well as
something about pleasure and pain which are the primary psychic
qualities of the beginning of self.

(Anzieu, 1979, p. 32)

182

For the mother, in the earliest stages, it is also a state between narcissism and object relating in that state which Winnicott calls "primary maternal preoccupation" (Winnicott, 1958). The echo reverberates back and forth, with mother and infant recognising themselves in the other.

Continuity over time is also the basis of Klein's depressive position insofar as the infant needs to be able to keep together different moments so that bad object/bad experience can be connected with good object/good experience, and this gives an indication of the fundamental importance of this earliest ability to perceive a temporal sequence. I am suggesting that it is the early 'reverberation' which creates the sense of continuity while its absence supports fragmentation and the stasis of the paranoid–schizoid mental state.[4]

Within the analytic situation, transformation occurs in the area of temporality on the basis of the time of reverberation between patient and analyst which promotes the expectation of response and the toleration of frustration and of loss, and therefore the possibility of symbolisation and acceptance of the Oedipal situation. The characteristics of the setting with its strict boundaries in time and space demarcate a particular temporality inside the boundaries, not so much a-temporality or timelessness it seems to me as a bi-temporality. A specific temporality is given by the analytic pair who will speak of past or present. But whether the analyst chooses to interpret now or then, the time within the analytic setting is always now *and* then. The essence of psychoanalysis lies in that double register. Within the boundaries of the session times, the discourse takes place in two different times simultaneously. This is what typifies the psychoanalytic session. It is neither completely 'past' nor completely 'present', and it is a matter of preference how the interpretation is made, hence a mode of working often favoured by French psychoanalysts of working 'in the transference', a mode of interpretation which assumes that interpreting the past or the external object is implicitly an interpretation of the transference. Whatever the locus of discourse, the boundaries demarcate a metaphorical language which is about speaking at once of different times. What Freud invented with his method was the possibility of a space where this bi-temporality could be played out. The mode of attentiveness on the part of the analyst which suppresses reaction and favours *reverie* creates the temporal particularities of the space within the boundaries. It is the reverberation between patient and analyst, within a space where it is both now and then, in a rhythm which favours a temporality facilitating modification of the internal world and integration. A patient in the last phase of analysis said: "Time seems so different, it's like an extra dimension; now I see that it's not like there is a baby who was traumatised long ago, but I am that baby now, it's inside me now." It is interesting that the patient found it a liberating thought that 'now' and 'then' had come together.

So far I have discussed the link between the reverberation between mother and infant, patient and analyst, and the development of a subjective sense of time. Dreaming has been largely discussed in relation to temporality from the point of view of the content of the dream and its timelessness. It is, however, important to distinguish between the timelessness of the dream content and the capacity to dream (Pontalis, 1974), and it is the latter which I suggest has more to do with reverberation time. My contention is that this reverberation is also the basis of the capacity to dream. When I talk about the capacity to dream I am meaning it in the same sense that Bion (1962a) talks about alpha function making the dream possible.[5] It is the introjection of a particular kind of relationship which becomes involved in the capacity to dream, to put inchoate elements and anxieties into representation.

Freud's (1900) description of the 'dream work' gives some understanding of what is required for the capacity to dream. He describes how the 'dream work' makes a current situation which would provoke anxiety because it revives repressed childhood states of excitation into a dream, thus enabling the expression of it in a disguised form which escapes censorship. More recent advances have considered situations where transformation is not possible and instead the aim is to rid the psychical apparatus of an excess of painful stimuli (Green, 1977) or to use the dream to evacuate states of mind which cannot be metabolised (Segal, 1981). Bion (1962a) linked the capacity to dream to the capacity to transform beta elements into alpha elements, to turn inchoate elements into something more coherent, and in that sense the dream performs the same function as the containing mother, of transforming unbearable anxiety into something bearable. The dream, he writes, "preserves the personality from what is virtually a psychotic state" since the capacity to dream "is related to differentiating conscious from unconscious and maintaining the difference so established" (Bion,

184

1962a, p. 16). When containment fails, in Bion's terms, there is not a dream but acts of evacuation; hence psychosis is the opposite of a dream. Segal (1981) describes the 'evacuative dream' of borderline and psychotic patients, when the dream, indistinguishable from reality, is enacted in the session.

The capacity to dream is built on the internalisation of the *reverie* or mental digestion by the mother, in Bion's terms requiring an alpha function, or, more specifically I suggest, on the reverberation between the infant and mother, or the patient and analyst. From this derives the dream in its transformative function. The dream space, one may say, is the maternal container in which operates the transformative work of the dream related to the reverberation back and forth between the mother's receptive *reverie* and the infant's experience. Within that space the dreamer can process conflicts, or else reorganise the world in a less conflictual way so as to fulfil a wish (Freud, 1900). The evacuative dream is a failure of containment within the dream and a lack of satisfactory transformative work, hence the traumatic dream or nightmare. Bertram Lewin's notion of the dream-screen (Lewin, 1946, 1955) connects the screen necessary for the projection of the dream directly to the maternal breast. He understands this quite literally as a preconscious memory of the surface of the breast. If we think of it more as a place for transformation, a three-dimensional idea of the dream seems more appropriate and is reflected in the use of the notion of 'dream space' (Pontalis, 1974). It has been described as a female space (Roheim, cited in Lander, 1953), much as the notion of the 'container' has been represented by the female symbol by Bion. One could say that the dream of the borderline or psychotic patient has a 'screen' but not an internal container which can work through the anxieties. Without the internal container for elaborating anxieties the patient seeks an external place to rid the self of those anxieties. In this case one could also say that the evacuative dream is a dream in search of a container when the internal one is deficient, even if it is more of a 'toilet-breast' (Meltzer, 1967) than one which is expected to be able to transform. Grinberg (1987) also speaks of evacuative dreams as "primitive dreams, dreamed essentially in order to discharge their contents into object containers" (p. 159), for example, into the analyst. In my terminology, it is a dream in search of reverberation, external if internal is deficient.

185

The fact that psychotic mechanisms can interfere with the capacity to dream was also noted by Winnicott (1971), who distinguishes the withdrawal into fantasy or day-dreaming from the capacity to dream. Fantasising, he says, interferes with real life, "but much more so it interferes with dream and with the personal or inner psychic reality, the living core of the individual personality" (p. 31), and he writes about a patient for whom "fantasying remains an isolated phenomenon, absorbing energy but not contributing-in either to dreaming or to living" (p. 26). For what I am wanting to say about time, this is of central importance because fantasising is a withdrawal into an a-temporal state, connected to the wish for Nirvana, an expression of the death drive according to Freud and to be distinguished from the capacity to dream which involves a transformation and enables life to go on. The capacity to dream has its root in that primitive reverberation which I suggest creates a subjective sense of time and the forward movement of life. The patient who has internalised this reverberation has a dream space in which anxieties can be represented and transformed unconsciously in the dream. In the same vein, Grinberg and Grinberg (1981) have linked the development of a continuity of representation of self over time, which they call the 'link of temporal integration', to maternal *reverie*.

Psychosomatic cases afford a view on states in which this kind of temporality – maternal *reverie*, reverberation time, dreaming and symbolisation – are deficient. Marty and de M'Usan (1963) stress that many of their severe psychosomatic patients either do not dream or appear incapable of telling their dreams, or, if capable, have great difficulty in associating to them. McDougall (1993, p. 217) notes:

> Clinical experience has frequently led me to observe that adults who suffer from severe sleeping problems appear to have no representation, in their inner psychic world, of a caretaking maternal instance with whom they could then identify toward their own child self.

I would put it that the capacity to dream as internal dialogue and processing of anxieties has its basis in the reverberation between mother and infant.

Clinically I have observed the constellation of a deficiency of maternal containment and cathexis, refusal of feminine receptivity, inability to bear frustration, concrete thinking, dream as symbolic equation, inability to mourn and to bear the passage of time, including the generational distinctions. I understand this as centrally related to a failure in the area of reverberation and its consequences in the organisation of temporality.

I have also been struck by how, conversely, we often see how patients who have been in a state of great disturbance for a period of time may feel a sense of relief when they experience having dreamed, even if the meaning of the dream is not consciously understood. They feel less disintegrated and agitated, and able to wait for their own associations and their analyst's interpretations (that is, to tolerate the passage of time). And not being able to sleep is equated with madness. This is reminiscent of when Winnicott writes that, when the mother stays away for too long the baby's distress cannot be mended, and this leads to a break in life's continuity. This is the experience of madness which means a breakup "of a personal continuity of existence" (Winnicott, 1967a, p. 369). The psychotic, Bion tells us, "cannot dream and therefore cannot sleep" (1962a, p. 7), and I would add that, because his internal world is so persecuted there is no trust that in sleep he can find the internal dialogue which can reflect and 'reverberate' his anxieties. And we know how not being able to sleep makes people feel in turn very persecuted and disintegrated, and that they are going mad; they lose their reflective capacities and feel that there is no help available which in turn makes it difficult for them to receive help. Bion writes of the "felt need to convert the conscious rational experience into dream" (1992, p. 184).

I will describe this in connection with Amy, whose mother was depressed in the early months after her birth and for whom issues related to time were central. Femininity, which she associated with the passage of time and change, was very problematic for Amy and she had severe anxieties about the inside of her body and of her inner world. She wanted to stop the passage of time, to create interminability in her analysis and she often retreated to superficiality, concrete thinking and somatisation. The fear of death had been a central theme in Amy's analysis. She dreaded death as the ultimate and never-ending punishment. I had taken it up in this way and also in terms of final separation, but it was only late in her analysis, when I connected her fear of death to a fear of falling into a black hole for ever, that something shifted. In the session which followed this, the idea of ending analysis came up; she spoke about feeling more grounded and how she was now interested in the solidity of her house, in the bricks rather than in her own appearance. I heard little more about her fear of death during the rest of her time in analysis.

The black hole is the experience of the infant whose anxieties are not responded to. To put it another way, there is no reverberation, the cries fall into infinite and timeless nothingness rather than resonate against another psyche. Amy's severe sleeping difficulties could be understood in terms of the fear of falling into that black hole of timeless nothingness. My putting back to Amy that this was what lay behind her lifelong fear of death reverberated her experience and put some containing and solid walls to that black hole.

After a long interruption in the analysis due to a work assignment which took her partner abroad for two years and from which she had to return early because she felt so disturbed, Amy said: "I know I'm not right. I feel I'm living superficially, I can't get in touch with myself. I can't dream which is also why I can't sleep properly. A whole part of me is gone." She then told me that, the night before coming to see me again after this very long interruption, she had dreamed again for the first time and felt very relieved and believed she had made contact with a lost part of herself. When Amy came back in a state of distress saying she cannot dream and that is why she cannot sleep well, she could have been paraphrasing Bion:

> Failure of alpha-function means the patient cannot dream and therefore cannot sleep. As alpha-function makes the sense impressions of the emotional experience available for conscious and dream-thought the patient who cannot dream cannot go to sleep and cannot wake up. Hence the peculiar condition seen clinically when the psychotic patient behaves as if he were in precisely this state.
>
> (Bion, 1962a, p. 7)

It was the loss of the capacity to dream which disturbed Amy. She did not particularly want to know the meaning of the dream she was able to have when she came to see me. It was the dream as dream and not its meaning that felt important to Amy. Indeed, Amy had often withheld dreams or repressed them, but there were times, like during this long interruption, when a more psychotic process was at work and she could not process her experience in a way which could bring relief in a dream. During the interruption she had not been able to keep analysis and her analyst alive in her mind, and hence neither the capacity to use dreaming to process experience. Through 'symbolic equation' the dream itself was the analyst and the analysis, and she was in a panic about not dreaming, believing that the dream/analyst was dead. I assume that there would have been some non-remembered dreams during that time, but her early return from abroad was linked to a partial destruction of the capacity to use her own mental apparatus, both during the day (as 'waking dream thoughts') and in sleep, which threw her in a state of panic. She referred to this loss of the dream space as living 'superficially' and linked it to when she had been severely anorexic. Had she been able to retain a more symbolic mode of functioning, the dream space could have been used to work through her loss during the interruption of analysis.

This contrasts with a time some years later when Amy could process conflicts or else reorganise the world in a less conflictual way so as to fulfil a wish (Freud, 1900), as evidenced in the following dream: "I was going to be bridesmaid to Fiona but then I was wearing the bride's dress and a sort of top hat, which was strange." Amy associates the top hat with the Mad Hatter in *Alice in Wonderland*.

In the dream space she can imagine being both bride and bridegroom, and with the breast permanently available — at the Mad Hatter's tea party it is always four o'clock, time for tea. The mad world is restricted to the dream world and in her waking life at this time, by contrast, she was no longer making her analysis timeless, she could accept the passage of time and the ending of her analysis. She could dream and therefore she could end her analysis — to transpose Bion's words. The dream with its wish-fulfilment meaning could be dreamed and night could be distinguished from day. She had a sense of the passage of time as something with borders rather than feeling on the precipice of a timeless black hole, and this made it possible to represent the wish for interminability and limitlessness in her dream and work through ending.

There has been a tendency to focus on the spatial characteristics of the psyche, in particular in the notions of internal world, internal objects and of 'container/contained' (Bion, 1970).[6] Space and time go together, and temporal relations can be represented by spatial ones (Freud, 1933), but I think that focusing on the time dimension brings out directly the thread which connects the mother's capacity for *reverie* understood as implying a time of reverberation, the back and forth between mother and baby, the infant's development of the capacity to wait, the capacity to mourn which is essentially a temporal phenomenon, and the capacity for symbolisation which derives from it. Conversely, at the basis of all the more severe disturbances is the inability to mourn and hence to symbolise, which has its basis in the inability to deal with the time factor and a freezing of time, and the lack of an internal object capable of *reverie*.

A primitive subjective sense of time is created by the reverberation between mother and infant, something which is internalised and becomes the basis of the capacity to dream. The dream then becomes the container of the 'back and forth', of an unconscious dialogue. In the analytic situation, for there to be a psychoanalytic process, the 'here and now' has to be mediated by *reverie* and the analyst's capacity to give meaning, a meaning that is at the same time 'now' and 'then' which is what brings in the third dimension of time. It is that mediation by the analyst's psychic processing in the 'now' and 'then' and the reverberation of the patient's experience which enable a change in temporality in the patient's psychic functioning. On this is built the capacity to wait, to detach from the immediate and hence to symbolise, to tolerate loss, and also to dream. Interminability can then be dreamed rather than enacted in the analysis. 'Black holes' can become internal spaces with 'walls' within which internal reverberation is anticipated.

Notes

1 It is relevant that Klein suggests that: "The change from intra-uterine to extra-uterine existence, as the prototype of all periodicity, is one of the roots of the concepts of time and of orientation in time" (1926, p. 99).

2 In her study of Poussin's Narcissus, Tutter (2014, p. 1235) also writes:

Poussin's reflective vision supports a radical reappraisal of the enigmatic myth at the heart of psychoanalytic theory and practice, in which Narcissus is construed as a far more object-related figure that seeks the formative, affirmative mirroring of the other.

3 See Perelberg (2008, ch. 11) for a discussion of the difference between the infant and the infantile and what constitutes the object of analytic research.

4 Projective mechanisms, changing states, non–lasting failures of *reverie* and containment, minimal traumas and innate factors all, of course, contribute to what happens to the 'reverberation' in individual cases.

5 Yu (2001) writes in *Neuro-Psychoanalysis*: "in agreement with the current neuroscientific findings ... dreams are representations of emotionally charged 'object–relationships'" (p. 55). From the clinical perspective, however, it is the emotionally charged object relationship which is relevant to dreaming.

6 The point has been made by cultural theorists that modernity has represented time by space (Lefebvre, 2000), which coincides with the development of Freudian theory.

10

TAKING TIME, THE TEMPO OF PSYCHOANALYSIS

The transformation we seek in psychoanalysis is twofold: a transformation into language and a transformation into using language in a way which supports symbolic thinking. Symbolic thinking underpins psychoanalysis and yet we are confronted repeatedly with how fragile such thinking can be and how easily concrete thinking takes over in ways which are not always immediately evident when it is the analyst who becomes prey to it. Impasse may always have a form of concrete thinking on the part of the analyst, as well as of the patient, as its foundation.

In this chapter I suggest that the increasingly popular 'here and now' technique lends itself to this pitfall if it is not grounded firmly in a theoretical and technical approach resting on the form of temporality described by Freud as 'evenly suspended attention' (in the Strachey translation of 'gleichschwebende Aufmerksamkeit'; Freud, 1912, 1923), sometimes also referred to in the literature as 'evenly hovering attention' or 'free-floating attention'.

Its main characteristic is an unfocused state of mind. Such a state of mind implies a withholding of immediate response and thus a duration. While the issue of time in psychoanalysis is usually mentioned simply in relation to the fixed duration of sessions, I am here ascribing a central place to time as a function of the specific modality of the psychoanalytic interchange itself, which stems from the analyst's evenly suspended mode of attention. Paradoxically, while in the analyst it privileges a more a-temporal primary process mode of thinking, for the patient, while a-temporal modes are being fostered, it also brings to the fore issues around time that are at the heart of psychoanalysis: to do with the toleration of frustration, the apprehension of and positioning within the Oedipal situation and the generations, the depressive position (which involves connecting different moments in time), mourning, and the capacity to conceive of a past and of a future. These issues are being worked through via the particular temporal mode which I refer to as 'reverberation time', the time of suspended/unfocused attention and mental digestion, on which is based the back and forth between patient and analyst. While spatial metaphors are used frequently in psychoanalysis, and imply an element of time, such as 'triangular space' (Britton, 1989) or 'potential space' (Winnicott, 1967), they do not focus directly on it (Noel-Smith, 2002).

So-called 'here and now' interpretations cover a whole range of types of interpretation (see Blass, 2011; Busch, 2011); I speak of 'here and now' technique in a wide sense to cover a way of working which is characterised by frequent interventions aimed at describing the patient's experience and feelings towards the analyst throughout the session. It is a particular way of conceiving of the 'transference interpretation'.

I argue here that the rise of interest in using a 'here and now' approach – I now use this notion in the widest sense of staying purely with what is happening in the moment – makes it particularly essential that analytic attention be rooted in the kind of temporality engendered by the analyst's evenly suspended attention, albeit the focus on defence analysis has often led to a decline in its perceived value (Carlson, 2002), and it is even considered by some to be out of date (Brenner, 2000; Hoffman, 2006). Contrary to this, I suggest we can link an increasing interest in Bion's (1962) notion of *reverie* (Ogden, 2004; Ferro, 2002b), which grows out of and extends the notion of evenly suspended attention, with an increasing use of the 'here and now' approach and as part of the necessary development of a more complex understanding of this type of attention (De Bianchedi, 2005). In fact I would go so far as to say that to be psychoanalysis a 'here and now' technical approach *necessitates* the notion of *reverie* or its equivalent. My argument is that *reverie* places the time element at the centre of the enterprise, of which it becomes the necessary third element.

This type of attention is fundamental. I call this attitude 'theory in practice' because it is more than just a technique, and rests on the whole theoretical corpus and basic structure of psychoanalysis. I also call it 'theory in practice' because in the clinical situation, the theory to which it refers need not be conscious, at least not in its many ramifications which go beyond being a basic position. In that sense, theory is not prioritised over experience but is a necessary implicit accompaniment. I previously argued (Birksted-Breen, 2008) that the analyst's theory is the essential 'third' of the two-person analytic situation. I am here suggesting that the theory of temporality is this crucial aspect of the theory, its embodiment being in the attitude of 'evenly suspended attention', a term I use here in a very wide sense to include, for instance, what De Bianchedi calls 'evenly suspended mind' (De Bianchedi, 2005), and also its Bionian further development *reverie*, the temporality or tempo which in my view characterises psychoanalysis. Without some version of this, we have 'two people in a room' but not psychoanalysis which requires this third temporal element. The absence of this 'theory in practice' may be observed in situations of impasse. In fact I consider that impasse always has at its root the absence of that third temporal element, giving rise to concrete thinking on the part of both analyst and patient.

To be clear, evenly suspended attention and *reverie* are psychoanalytic concepts to be distinguished from 'day-dreaming', an everyday term which describes a conscious experience and often implies a state of withdrawal. *Reverie*, on the other hand, is a concept developed by Bion to describe the mental processing and digestion of the patient's material via the psyche of the particular psychoanalyst, most of which takes place outside of consciousness and by definition implies a basic receptive attitude on the part of the analyst. It was in fact Marion Milner who first mentioned the importance of *reverie* in 1956 in the Appendix of the second edition of *On Not Being Able to Paint* (2011, p. 191), where she writes: "For the word 'reverie' does emphasise the aspect of absent-mindedness." And indeed her work on this is relevant and important.

We owe it to Bion to have developed *reverie* into a psychoanalytic concept within a theoretical framework. Speaking of the mother's *reverie*, Bion writes, "Leaving aside the physical channels of communication my impression is that her love is expressed by reverie" (1962a, pp. 35–36). Day-dreaming, on the other hand, is often more akin to what Winnicott calls 'fantasying' (Winnicott, 1971), a turning away from the other. In the analytic situation, studying the countertransference helps distinguish *reverie* from instances of day-dreaming.

It is recognised that both symbolic and non-symbolic modes of functioning are present in everyone (Bion, 1957), although one or other mode predominates in some patients and at certain times. This is important in that we often meet in psychoanalysis patients who are highly capable of symbolic thinking in their professional lives, but appear to be very concrete in their psychoanalysis. They belong to a category Brown (1985) calls 'interactional concreteness', a concreteness which takes place as a protection from the emergence of painful affects and as a category of resistance to treatment; it is not always clear-cut, as these patients can also show other forms of concreteness such as what Brown calls 'topographical concreteness' in which there is a move from abstract thinking to an action or sensory or perceptual mode; for example, 'acting out' or psychosomatic symptoms. The patients I am specifically thinking of are those who fear intrusion within the intimacy of the psychoanalytic setting, in part due to their tendency to project their own needs and intrusiveness or wish for fusion, but also sometimes due to having been excessively projected into. For this reason it is the interpretation in the 'here and now' of the session, pointing to the interaction and relationship of patient and analyst which arouses maximal anxiety and thus engenders non-symbolic modes of functioning. Chiesa *et al.* describe "non-reflective internal working models [as] triggered within the context of emotionally charged attachment relationships" (Chiesa *et al.*, 2003, p. 647). Fonagy and Target link the capacity to hold multiple perspectives with a development that comes from the Oedipal period: "what only comes with development [from the Oedipal period] is the capacity to hold multiple perspectives, to mentalize" (Fonagy and Target, 2004, p. 511). These are also the patients who are particularly intolerant of the analyst reflecting about them, as Britton describes in his paper "Subjectivity, Objectivity, and Triangular Space" (2004, p. 48) and for whom he writes, "what is missing in these cases is the third position".

Concrete thinking attracts concrete thinking. When the analyst forgoes the basic temporal attitude of 'suspension' the analytic structure collapses; the analyst is in danger of also resorting to concrete thinking and an absence of the third position, thus leading to impasse, as will be shown in the following clinical situation.

Impasse: Jennifer and her analyst

Jennifer is a middle-aged successful professional in an allied profession, who suffered an early separation from her teenage mother, and, when she was three years old, the death of her grandmother who had been caring for her. She was presented in a workshop by an experienced and sensitive analyst.[1] Jennifer's analyst had the idea that she found it hard to accept interpretations, considering her to prefer her own interpretations to that of the analyst's, just as in childhood Jennifer had preferred a neighbour's food to her mother's food. At this point in the analysis Jennifer had had a plan for more than two years to have breast enlargement surgery, a plan which kept recurring with greater intensity, and she was now announcing that she would go ahead with it during the forthcoming analytic holiday. The analyst reported that she was very concerned about what she saw as an acting out, since there appeared to be nothing in reality wrong with the patient's body. The analyst understood this surgery as a wish to find an alternative treatment to the analysis, just as Jennifer had preferred another woman's food as a child, and to find a treatment that was meant to give instant gratification. The plan had been put off a few times and Jennifer was now very insistent on getting her analyst's approval. She was insistent that the operation would make her feel more normal, although she also said at another point that the difference would be barely noticeable.

Although the analyst took up that Jennifer wished her to take sides, it could be seen in her way of interpreting that she believed that the surgery was a mistake and a failure of the analysis. She believed that her patient was acting rather than thinking and trying to find an alternative treatment during her analyst's absence. She took up with Jennifer how this plan recurred just before holiday breaks, in particular a year ago and two years ago at the same time of year. These interpretations appeared to bounce off the patient ("yes, but...", she kept replying) and had no effect on her patient's decision. Nor, it seems, could the patient see her analyst's point of view that there could be unconscious meanings to her plan, and she simply felt disapproved of.

The location of the plastic surgery magnified the discordant points of view, since the breast has a particular psychoanalytic significance for the analyst and fits in with her view of Jennifer as a patient who refuses the mother/analyst's food and indeed, in the sessions presented, there is material around anxiety about an anorexic girl and a problem of two psychotherapists who disagree with each other over her treatment.

At this point, patient and analyst are indeed like the two psychotherapists in conflict, each stuck in their single-minded way of thinking and belief, and unable to entertain the other's viewpoint. We thus have a dialogue between two people which operates on different planes: the patient is thinking about her body and wishing to make it more attractive, thinking along a concrete mode, and the analyst is thinking symbolically that the patient feels herself to have an unsatisfactory and frustrating 'analytic breast' and wishes to provide a better one for herself, one that never lets her down. The patient believes that a surgical operation will make her feel better and the analyst believes that thinking differently is what will bring relief. The patient proclaims that the analyst is not unsatisfactory; quite the contrary, she says, she thinks her plan is part of the good outcome of her analysis and all she asks is that her analyst should agree about this and be pleased. The analyst, on the other hand, believes that she is for her patient a 'mother who has nothing in her fridge', a transference from the past, and that Jennifer has developed a defensive attitude of wanting to provide 'a breast' for herself. In this way she believes that Jennifer is trying to short-circuit the experience of feeling deprived by her analyst. Indeed, it is possible to see the urgency and her need for action when Jennifer says that she is aware that she speaks like an addict who pleads "just once more and then I'll stop" and then adds: "let me have it or I will die or become mad". Jennifer insists that she does indeed know that analysis is the true nourishment and that her analyst is helpful, but it is precisely because of this help that she is now able to seek the plastic surgery. She insists that this is not an alternative to the analysis. She simply wants her analyst to be pleased that she is doing something to enhance her physique and her feelings about herself. In fact she wants the analyst to feel that this plan is a good therapeutic result of her analysis. Instead, the analyst feels a sense of despair and is overcome by a belief that this is the end of any hope for the analysis.

In my way of looking at this, each of the parties here is operating with a different model and has a different project. The patient feels she has taken something good from the analyst and wants it confirmed that she is loved by her, while the analyst feels that her job is

not about content but about the possibility of symbolization being undermined because the patient is not taking the analytic food in the way it is intended, in order to develop symbolic thinking. This disturbs the patient. The analyst in the sessions gets increasingly despairing, interpreting the 'false breast', the plastic solution. So we see in this interaction that analyst and patient are speaking two different languages. The impasse presented at this moment of the analysis rests on the fact that the analyst and the patient have two different models: the analyst, with her psychoanalytic model, is thinking symbolically of the maternal feeding breast which the patient hates and attacks and melancholically identifies with; the patient, on the other hand, does not hear any symbolic meaning and wants her analyst to concur that it is progress that she wants to make herself more attractive. She wants above all to value her analyst and be valued by her, and instead she just feels criticised, which has now become her main problem. Even while the analyst struggles not to appear to take sides, the patient knows that her analyst is against this plastic surgery, and she speaks of her partner who thinks that the plastic surgery is an offence against his love and against her own body. This is a fairly accurate assessment of what her analyst now feels in her countertransference. In spite of some apparently productive sessions, the patient announces that the surgery has been arranged to take place during the break, causing the analyst to feel deceived and despairing.

We can see how, at this point, the problem rests on the fact that, while apparently upholding a symbolic mode of thinking, the analyst herself has slipped into concrete thinking. She believes that the plastic surgery means the literal and irreparable damage to the analysis and to any potential for thinking, as if the 'analytic breast' – that is, the analyst's capacity for thinking – will be literally destroyed by the surgeon's knife. In fact at this point it has indeed been destroyed insofar as the analyst believes it is the end of the analysis.

I spent some time describing this impasse because I believe that this sort of situation is not at all infrequent; a situation in which the analyst is upholding a supposedly 'psychoanalytic view' in which there is implied dissatisfaction with the patient's lack of progress (towards symbolic thinking) but which itself has become a form of concrete thinking, while the patient, on the other hand, is satisfied with the benefits of the analysis but cannot convince the analyst of this. At this point the analyst has lost her ability to hold multiple perspectives, including an imaginative development of the patient's perspective.

After much discussion in the workshop where this material was presented, the analyst was able to regain her capacity to think and came to understand that she had felt guilty, believing herself to be responsible for this whole situation because, due to a bereavement of her own, she had had to impose a break on the analysis and had also been preoccupied. Under the tyranny of a psychoanalytic super-ego which demanded 'symbolic thinking', and her guilt about having let her patient down, the analyst had resorted to concrete thinking in the form of 'symbolic equations'. Analyst and patient, each in their one-dimensional mode of thinking, had hit an impasse. Time for reflection became possible again with the help of the group's *reverie*. This enabled the analyst to have a dream between the two days of the workshop and enabled her to recover a more complex and psychoanalytic mode of thinking and to feel she could continue with the analysis, about which she had been in doubt.

In the sessions she reported on, the analyst had maintained a 'here and now' mode of interpretation, taking up, for instance, the patient's refusal of the analytic breast or the patient's attack on the analyst but, at that point of impasse, what was lost was the 'suspension' of her attention which would have allowed for a new development to emerge in her mind. The pair were frozen in time, they had become two single-minded people trying to convince each other, and no movement could occur.

Such impasses occur more easily with patients who have difficulty with symbolic thinking within the analytic situation due to unbearable anxieties, and in these cases the analyst can get drawn into a stance in which symbolic thinking takes on the role of an 'overvalued idea' (Britton and Steiner, 1994) when, due to the awakening of her own unprocessed anxieties, the analyst is unable to wait in a state of evenly suspended attention. In the above case the overvalued idea was used as a defence by the analyst against the depressive anxieties of fearing that analytic intervention could not provide enough for her patient, against her feelings of guilt at having abandoned her patient during her own bereavement, and against her own helplessness. She was struggling against her feeling that she was in reality now 'the mother who has nothing in her fridge', and by imposing 'psychoanalytic' ideas she was hoping that these ideas were 'putting something in the fridge'. Only with the help of an outside position and a state of *reverie* could the analyst become aware of her own one-dimensional position which was preventing development, causing a spiralling sense of despair and threatening the future of the analysis.

199

About impasse

The dictionary definition of impasse is "A road or way having no outlet; a blind alley; a 'cul de sac'" (Shorter (2 vols) *Oxford English Dictionary*). It is a good metaphor for an analytic situation which cannot evolve due to the 'blindness' of both parties who are stuck in this one way of thinking, thereby threatening the life of the analysis (see Roth, 2009).

Rosenfeld (1987) describes three causes of impasse: envy, destructive narcissism and what he puts under the title of "confusion, collusion, and the role of history" (p. 268). The latter refers to complex transference and countertransference interactions which lead to "chronic misunderstanding". What I have described would belong most immediately to the latter but the three are not mutually exclusive because envy and destructive narcissism in the patient often create interactions in which two points of view collide which can lead to the sort of misunderstanding and concrete thinking of the analyst I have described.

However, as Rosenfeld also writes (1987, p. 32),

> even the most disturbed and tricky patients, whose pathology may cause them time and time again to defend themselves against anxiety by distorting and undermining the analytic process, not only seek to communicate their predicament but also have a considerable capacity for co-operating with the therapeutic endeavour, if the analyst can recognize it.

For these reasons I would argue, as does Ferro (1993), that impasse is always a 'couple-related problem', a bi-personal situation (what Baranger and Baranger call a 'bastion' (1983)), one in which the analyst is caught up in his own one-dimensional thinking, which may masquerade as psychoanalytic theory, when anxiety which cannot be faced is aroused.

When Freud discusses impasse in his female patients as being a wish for the male organ as the only solution, and calls this a biological bedrock (Freud, 1937, p. 250), it seems that both parties have become entrenched in a one-dimensional way of thinking. Both resort at this point to a single and concrete idea and away from further thinking about what this "refusal of femininity" could be defending against and which would turn the bedrock into being

200

psychological rather than biological (Gibeault, 1992). Concrete thinking in the sense of loss of multiple perspectives, I would say, is the psychological rock which psychoanalysis hits against. Freud's paper is written in the context of a discussion of the repetition compulsion and the death drive, and as Bégoin (1994) points out, further analysis is only possible if "a fundamental despair about being unable to develop" can be borne over time by the analyst without expectation. This in fact requires of the analyst a 'feminine' position of waiting (suspended attention, *reverie*). Deadlock can only be avoided if activity is sufficiently balanced by this more passive receptive mental attitude of 'taking time' in order to give space to a potential for new ways of thinking to grow in the analyst's mind. I use the word 'passive' purely in contrast with 'active' (that which is necessary for the making of an interpretation), since the receptive attitude is not just 'doing nothing' and requires refraining from usual modes of listening and reacting and an active openness to a more intuitive modality. Bion refers to this refraining as necessitating "negative capability"[2] (1970, p. 125). This receptive attitude is in the service of Eros, if despair and anxiety can be tolerated, as too is the mother's capacity for and use of *reverie* for understanding her infant.

When I speak of impasse I do not necessarily have in mind the sort of impasse which can lead to the demise of the analysis, nor am I referring to the moments of misunderstanding and misrecognition which inevitably happen in all analyses. I am using the word impasse in the sense of a prolonged period in which analyst and patient seem to each get stuck in their own unmoving and restricted view. This could be for a number of reasons, including a *mise-en-scène* of an internal situation of the patient which comes to be enacted, something which forms part and parcel of all transference situations. However, when the situation is prolonged to the frustration of both parties, it can be because something significant has also been unconsciously mobilised in the analyst. Conversely, the overcoming of the impasse is important and fruitful, and psychoanalytic work proceeds by phases of restructuring following such a working through of impasse. If we include both minor or major impasses, 'acute' or 'chronic' impasses (Cassorla, 2001) and extend this also to enactments, it is of course the case that this is not only inevitable but necessary. Here I am highlighting the aspect of temporality in these phenomena.

201

In the case of Jennifer's analyst, the impasse was lifted when temporality could be reintroduced into her thinking. On the second day of the workshop she told us that she had had a dream during the previous night that had led her to the following thought which she wanted to share with the group in the morning:

> A Winnicottian colleague would say that the grandmother of this girl died when she was 3, now she has been in analysis for three years. I have often thought that I couldn't find a place for this grandmother in the analysis, a place for the loss of this grandmother who was this patient's support, that there is no representation for her in the analysis although she had been a support for this patient. A Winnicottian colleague would have linked my own unplanned absence which took place at Christmas two years ago with it, because there seems to have been no trace of this loss.

We assume from this that the analyst is not a Winnicottian. The third object, Winnicott (brought to life by the 'presence' of the group as other), was called upon internally to offer a different perspective, and this could happen once a space had been created in which time could be taken to 'dream up' an alternative way of thinking. What I call 'dreaming up' refers to a creative process made possible when there is a relibidinising of the analytic situation which had become deadened, enabling the analyst to call upon and create new avenues of thought and to be 'surprised' (Laub and Lee, 2003; Faimberg and Corel, 1990; Smith, 1995; Baranger, 1993), something which is only possible when a 'non-expectant' attitude is basic. Enabling such a relibidinisation is a fundamental aspect of a supervision or consultation in cases of analyses which have become stuck or are accompanied by hopelessness in the analyst. The consultant functions as an auxiliary for that lost capacity.

I am suggesting that the basic and necessary 'theory in practice' in the mind of the analyst which acts as the 'third' of the analytic situation involves temporality, the time of suspension and *reverie*. Paradoxically, being 'without memory and desire' which suspends chronological time (past and future) enables a different temporality to predominate, the non-chronological time of *reverie* and one which creates a necessary temporal space within the analytic situation. It is opposite to an orientation to goals, which includes the goal of promoting symbolisation. The mental contents which this attitude leads to has been described differently by different authors. Ogden tends to describe lengthy conscious reveries occurring in the analyst's mind during the session and which, if the analyst does not dismiss them, can elucidate an unconscious experience of the patient. He writes (1997b, p. 727):

> Reverie is a principal form of re-presentation of the unconscious (largely intersubjective) experience of analyst and analysand. The analytic use of reverie is the process by which unconscious experience is made into verbally symbolic metaphors that re-present unconscious aspects of ourselves to ourselves.

Ferro describes what are more like associations of his own to the material of the patient and which he will use as metaphor with the patient, or else 'dream–like flash' which help him come closer to an understanding of himself and his patient. Botella and Botella (2005) describe a more regressive state of mind that enables dream–like states in the analyst which will produce helpful representations where the borderline patient has an absence of representation. De M'Uzan (1994) describes a state of necessary 'depersonalisation' in which the analyst 'becomes' the patient. Both Ogden and De M'Uzan in fact speak of the creation of a third: for Ogden it is the 'analytic third', for De M'Uzan, the 'chimera'. Ithier (2016), discussing Ogden and De M'Uzan, suggests that the 'chimera' touches on traumatic areas of both analyst and patient.

While there are important variations and each of these belong to different and specific conceptual models, one may say that, at the most general level, they come under the umbrella of Bion's notion of *reverie* (which I will discuss further in Chapter 11), and bring to the dual relationship a third element grounded in a 'suspension' of focused attention and of immediate response.

In this chapter I will focus specifically on the single images which this state of mind gives spontaneous rise to from a less conscious part of the mind of the analyst. This is only one of the manifestations of the work of *reverie*. I will not discuss here but would like to note how this state of mind also enables interpretations which 'spring to mind' without being 'worked out'. These images are not only helpful for understanding the patient and the current analytic situation but these images, a product of *reverie*, can act as metaphors and become a 'third' element which is more easily tolerated by those more borderline patients who become concrete within the close affective relationship of the analytic situation and are also intolerant of any indication of a 'third' object. These images springing from the analyst's *reverie* are a 'third' in the sense that Winnicott speaks of the transitional space, the 'not me' and 'not you' space and are a development towards symbolisation. They can anticipate the development of the session as described in relation to Pedro in Chapter 8. They introduce an 'other' or an 'otherness' which does not produce intolerable jealousy while also allowing a space between patient and analyst, thus avoiding claustrophobic reactions. The images offer the possibility of a meeting place between patient and analyst in these situations of potential impasse. Also importantly, they promote relibidinisation of the analysis in both parties when repetitive patterns have taken hold. *Reverie* is in that sense in the service of the libido, against the repetition compulsion. This type of attention thus creates "optimal conditions for symbolization" (Green, 1975, p. 295) and development, as I will describe in the following clinical situation.

A way out of impasse

Eugene is a patient in analysis with whom I continually hovered on the brink of impasse.

I found it very difficult to make helpful contact with him. He wanted advice and solutions, and would not find my attempts to make sense of what he brought meaningful. At the same time Eugene would convey an experience of something utterly catastrophic, even though the situations described were quite ordinary, and in such a way that I would feel acute pain at not being able to help. I felt drawn to the same desperation as I think Jennifer's analyst experienced and, like Jennifer's analyst, I felt that my patient was unable to engage at the symbolic level I was wanting to engage in, and which I thought would relieve Eugene's terrible pain. I came to realise however how much I was being drawn away, with this wish, from a state of evenly suspended attention and was trying to make my patient think and talk as I thought he should. This helped me regain the potential for *reverie* which produced an image in my mind that enabled me to make meaningful contact with Eugene.

Following some sessions I had had to cancel at short notice, Eugene spoke for a while about situations in which he felt intensely and delusionally jealous of his partner's involvement with other people. I knew from previous experience that there would be no point in making a direct connection between his jealousy and my absence but, after he started worrying about various aspects of the future, I took up how it made him anxious when he becomes aware that he is not in control of what happens. He brushed this aside and was irritated. Aware of my part to play in a potential impasse in which we would take up 'usual' positions, it seemed more possible for me to stay silent and regain an unfocused state of mind. Eventually Eugene could say something about my absence; he said that he had felt disorientated when he didn't have his sessions; he supposes, he said, it is "when you expect to do something and be somewhere and it isn't there". At this point I had a powerful visual image of someone underwater, adrift in the open sea after the rope holding a boat to a rock has broken. As is the nature of dreams, it does not make complete logical sense. In the image, which was strong but happened quickly, there was no boat and I was only aware of the rock, the piece of rope and the person drifting, but the idea was there that the rope had broken loose and this was why the person was drifting dangerously.

After a pause, I simply responded: "like a rock". Eugene hesitated and to my surprise, since I was used to his rejecting what I said, he said "yes". He relaxed and his tone changed. He now himself said it was difficult when he could not predict the future. I responded that that is like not having a solid rock. He then went on to discuss a warm interaction with his family (something rare) and spoke positively of his partner and how he could even imagine having a child with her (this had not been mentioned before). He then went on to muse about some new acquaintances and how surprising it is that he can like someone who has different political views to himself and dislike someone who has similar political views. This used to be impossible to think, he added.

In this fragment one can see how Eugene is able to speak about an experience of disorientation when 'something' isn't there. Picking up on this cue of his being able to speak of this experience in a non-personal way, I responded with the image which had come to my mind unsolicited, namely of an inanimate hard object, the rock, but one which can enable a solid connection. It is a metaphor which uses a concrete image for an emotional experience. The rope connects two objects, rock and boat, not people. I did not think this through when I said it, and it came to me as an image while I could also feel the bodily experience, and anxiety of drifting out to sea, unable to do anything about it. The image condenses many aspects of which I was only dimly aware; for instance, thinking about it later I thought there was something foetal about the person in the water and the image could hint at a broken umbilical cord, but I thought it relevant to the patient that a non-human object, the rock, came to mind.

The point is that around the simple image of the rock we were able to make a connection, via the bodily experience of feeling grounded by a solid hard base versus drifting dangerously away when the connexion is gone; this made Eugene feel that his experience of the absence which he experienced bodily and in terms of a 'something' and a 'somewhere' was received, which indeed it had been. By keeping to the image and its resonance to a *sensorial* experience (which was also my experience), he felt understood. We had been able to meet over a concrete image without having to refer more directly to the experience of need or dependency which involves a more complex thinking about the analytic relationship. At the same time, the image opened up a space which led to more complex thinking, the idea that it is possible to like someone even if you don't agree with their views. He showed a movement from rejecting the 'not me' thought as threatening and bad (spitting out the bad) to the sense that it is possible to hold on to my view and think about it, even if I am different from him. Eugene had made a move away from one-dimensional thinking which is the essence of concrete thinking, while I too had allowed my thoughts to 'drift' when I suspended focus and interpretation. We also moved away from impasse in that a meaningful exchange was taking place, thus indicating a development.

Due to the powerful projections which can lead to an impasse when the focus on the 'here and now' becomes the breeding ground for two incompatible perspectives (and two "wilfully misunderstanding objects" (Bion, 1962a)), the metaphoric visual image springing from the time of 'suspension' fosters, on the other hand, the possibility for the two parties to communicate, each coming from their own perspective. The metaphoric visual image is produced out of an unfocused state of mind, a maximally receptive state of mind which is paradoxical in that its characteristic is effortlessness and purposelessness, while the maintenance of such a state of mind requires purposefulness and "a positive act of refraining from memory and desire" (Bion, 1970, p. 31). The word 'hovering' is apt in conveying a position which is sufficiently detached to encompass the whole situation from a certain distance. Again paradoxically such an attitude, while 'neutral' (Tuckett, 2011), is also on the side of the life forces.

Closer to dreaming it enables the mental work of 'figuration' (Botella and Botella, 2005), of transformation of elements inhabiting the field between patient and analyst into a condensed evocative image which thus is meaningful to both patient and analyst and hence an important potential meeting ground between them. The more 'regressed' expression of drive and affect in the visual image offers the possibility of meeting in the concrete realm, and bringing together the two perspectives, concrete and metaphoric. The unfocused state of mind in this way creates the optimal conditions for symbolisation.

It is important that when I spoke of rock, I myself thought of it in its concrete form, that I had the idea in its pictorial form in my mind and could feel the sensorial qualities of drifting dangerously and worryingly in the sea, which I wanted to convey to my patient, rather than thinking of it as, and what I could see in retrospect it is, a common linguistic metaphor. At the moment of speaking of it, what predominated was the visual image grounded in a frightening bodily experience and it is this which provided a meeting ground. The concrete image then moved to a more symbolic register in my own mind, though I continued to make use of the image and it became possible to stay with the ambiguity for the rest of the session.

Rather than a conflict of registers, both registers can be held together via the image, first both patient and analyst immersed in the concrete realm, later the patient thinking in terms of the safety of a physical hard indestructible object and the analyst thinking of an emotional state of dependency. The coming together of the different points of view into one image, in contrast to what happened with Jennifer, functions as a building block towards more complex and abstract thinking. We see this development taking place in the fragment above.

The visual image

While some approaches have moved away from free-floating attention, others have built on the importance of a particular form of attentiveness that this points to. French psychoanalysts in particular, building on Freud's notion of 'formal regression' in dreams, in which "primitive methods of expression and representation take the place of the usual ones" (Freud, 1900, added 1914), have been interested not only in the need for the patient to have a capacity for 'formal regression' but have also developed this in relation to the state of mind of the analyst. With their notion of 'figurability', Botella and Botella (2005) express the idea that the image in the mind of the analyst is the product of a complex work akin to that of the night dream, thanks to "the existence of a capacity of the psyche to create a sensorial quality from a singular and complex unconscious process" (p. 10). In the realm 'beyond' representation they suggest that floating attention is in fact not enough (p. 112) and that the analyst is required to tolerate a more important regression of his thinking (p. 122) in order to access that which lies beyond the mnemonic trace.

For the purposes of this chapter however, as I said earlier, I am not distinguishing between the various forms of 'non-purposeful' attention but suggesting that the development of the popularity of the 'here and now' technical approach, with its frequent interventions often addressing the shifts in defences in the sessions, has been in danger of reducing or even eliminating these various forms and degrees of regressive modes of listening which give space to more primitive modes of expression and representation and the complex but non-purposeful mental work of the analyst – which also of course take place in the 'now' of the session. I am therefore not only talking about those patients described by Botella and Botella or Green in the notion of 'blank psychosis', although it is also the case that there are 'blank' areas in all patients. The patients I have specifically in mind in this context are those who are intolerant of the affective closeness of the analytic relationship. Interpretations which address the patient's emotional experience as related to the relationship to the analyst which stands as a metaphor in relation to their internal and external object relationships require complex symbolic functioning within a highly charged affective situation. For the sorts of patients I have been discussing, the use of a concrete image with its "sensory strength" (Freud, 1933, p. 21) is simple and direct and more facilitating. Furthermore, an image is more easily tolerated by these patients because the image can be felt to be 'outside' the relationship, and reduces reactions of shame or humiliation. The image offered by the analyst from her *reverie* also reduces reactions of jealousy and envy because analyst and patient are together looking at the image as the outside object. The image acts here as a third element which is felt to belong to some extent to both parties, or to neither, as Winnicott describes with his notion of transitional space, and in that way is easier to tolerate than that which directly represents an Oedipal situation. In operating as a third element, the pictorial image coming from the analyst's *reverie* fosters a greater psychic space and the necessary triangulation for the development of symbolisation. The image brings in a third element without bringing in the third object and is thus easier to tolerate by the sorts of patients I am describing. The metaphoric visual image, by combining metaphoric and concrete into one, brings together two perspectives and thus supports this development. It also makes a direct sensory connection to the body, bridging a gap between body and mind. Kristeva (2007) describes the "sensory substratum of language as a relay between signs and drives"[3] (p. 429). When patient and analyst meet in the visual image, each from their own point of view, two levels of meaning are brought together, thus furthering the potential for symbolic thinking. These images work as building blocks (Avzaradel, 2011). Hence the importance of the state of mind of 'suspension' (of action and of focus), and of *reverie* which provide the space and time necessary for this to take place.

The image coming out of *reverie* is the analyst's own move towards concreteness and towards meeting the patient in that area of thinking grounded in the body and taps into a more primitive experience of connectiveness. It is that which requires 'taking time', or should I say 'time out' with the "particular form of thinking" (Freud, 1900, p. 506; footnote added 1925) akin to dreaming. From there can develop a form of communication in the 'here and now' in which there can be a play and movement between concrete and metaphoric with analyst and patient each able to hold on to their perspective which may move between being different or similar, without creating an impasse.

Green (1975, p. 13) suggests that:

> For the most part symbolic structures are probably innate. However, we now know, as much through the study of animal communication as through psychological or psychoanalytic research, that they require the intervention of the object in order to move from potential to realization at a given point in time.

With the patients for whom symbolisation is deficient I have wanted to think about how the 'intervention of the object' can be enhanced with a bi-personal potential path out of impasse via the metaphorical image grounded in the analyst's affective and bodily experience as I described with Eugene. This requires the analyst to remain in a maximally receptive state which enables the transformation in her own mind, the transformation which the patient is not able to do, from concrete to symbolic, from factual to dream representation. This requires also 'abstinence' from 'explanatory' interpretations.

In recent years there has been an increasing interest in the mental work which needs to be performed by the analyst and in what is evoked in the analyst's mind. Ferro (2002) and Ogden (2004), following Bion, who writes that "the analyst must be able to dream the session" (Bion, 1992, p. 120), use an evocative image 'dreaming the patient' to convey this necessary state of mind.

Evenly suspended attention is opposite to enactment.[4] Although enactments inevitably happen, they always imply the loss of that state of 'suspended attention' and can lead to impasse as we saw with Jennifer. Bion writes that "anxiety in the analyst is a sign that the analyst is refusing to 'dream' the patient's material" (1992, p. 43). On the contrary, the formation of the pictorial representation necessitates a 'formal regression' requiring a certain passivity on the part of the analyst (Botella, 2010, p. 47) which is not always easy for the analyst to tolerate, and requires "an act of faith in unconscious process" (Parsons, 2000, p. 201). I discussed in Chapter 8 the importance of an openness to the unconscious processing in the analyst's mind while suspending action. I am suggesting here that there is a particular danger when the psychoanalyst uses a technique of actively interpreting in the here and now without a grounding in the temporality of *reverie*, in particular with the sorts of patients who have difficulty with 'thinking about' experiences and with 'dreaming' their experiences. This type of 'suspended' or 'unfocused' attitude and of *reverie*, coupled with suspended action or interpretative (over) activity, is the necessary space for transformation, allowing for the passage of time, as something necessary, not just desirable, for transformation. The images this produces enable patient and analyst to meet in an elaboration of the here and now affective relationship that is simultaneously concrete and metaphoric and linguistic, thus avoiding impasse and promoting movement towards more complex thinking in the case of those patients whose symbolic capacity within the analytic situation is problematic. The loss of this type of attention is a good indicator for the analyst that an enactment or a temporary impasse is taking place. In that sense they can be in the service of furthering analytic work (Ferro, 1993) as long as there is a return to a baseline attitude of suspended attention and *reverie*.

I have argued in this chapter that in order to be psychoanalysis, the 'here and now' technical approach requires the preservation of the time element via the notion of 'evenly suspended attention' and of its more developed and contemporary derivative, '*reverie*'. This temporal element, which is also happening 'here and now', is the 'theory in practice' which forms the essential and necessary third element of psychoanalysis. Without this type of attention we have two people in a room but not psychoanalysis. In situations of impasse this third element is often, if not always, missing. *Reverie*, on the other hand, opens a way out of impasse, in particular via the visual image, especially with patients whose symbolic capacity, either within the affective transference relationship or more generally, is limited, and when destructive repetitive processes take the upper hand. This visual image, emerging out of a libidinal investment of the analyst when a more regressive mode of attention is adhered to or regained, opens up a space and a meeting ground between patient and analyst.

'Taking time' refers to this 'theory in practice' which requires a time of digestion and transformation, a 'reverberation time' which is in danger of getting lost with some contemporary active techniques.

Notes

1 The workshop which I moderated was part of the Clinical Comparison Method project (see Birksted-Breen *et al.*, in Tuckett, 2008).
2 A term borrowed from John Keats: "Negative Capability, that is, when a man is capable of being in uncertainties, mysteries, doubts, without any irritable reaching after fact and reason."

3 Italics in the original.

4 While I can agree with the view that enactments are ubiquitous, I nevertheless think it is important to distinguish the understanding of the whole of the analysis as an enactment of internal object scenarios from specific enactments when the attitude of the analyst is in contrast to his or her more general analytic stance. I use the term 'enactment' here in this latter sense.

11

BI-OCULARITY, THE FUNCTIONING MIND OF THE PSYCHOANALYST[1]

The psychoanalytic situation with its constructed, clearly defined setting, coupled with a particular kind of attentiveness on the part of the psychoanalyst, sets in motion the most primitive, undigested and traumatic aspects of the analysand's psyche, engaging the psychoanalyst in processing their own experience in the knowledge that what takes place in themselves or in the patient will never be completely within their grasp.

In this chapter I will argue that the essential function of the psychoanalyst is to maintain what I call bi-ocularity as an essential function of the setting, the aim of which is to foster symbolic thinking.

To define my terms. For me, 'setting' includes the mind of the psychoanalyst in relation to a Now and a Here. Because the maximal affect and meaning is Now and Here, the setting is one which conjures "a piece of real life", as Freud put it (Freud, 1914, p. 152); Freud contrasts this with hypnosis which "could not but give the impression of an experiment carried out in the laboratory". Therefore, Freud goes on, "analytic treatment ... cannot always be harmless and unobjectionable" (Freud, 1914, p. 152). While it is a piece of real life – it is happening Now – the setting is indelibly connected to a There. But a There understood as – and this is the essence of the psychoanalytic approach – a reference to the 'other' place, that of the phantasy world, psychic reality, the unconscious and traces of the past continually reshaped *Nachträglichkeit*.

In order to produce this 'piece of real' life, the setting needs to be preserved if it is to bring forth the 'illness' via the "highly explosive forces" which Freud describes in his paper on transference love

213

(1915a, pp. 170–171). Within this setting 'madness' irrupts. And also 'psychosis'. I'm using the important distinction made by Green (1986) who links madness to 'passion' and Eros, which is not the prerogative of pathology, while psychosis (with its mechanisms of splitting and disavowal) is linked to the destructive instincts. It is the latter which relates to an absence of representation and a decathexis of the object.

In this setting 'madness' is to be welcomed in the fight against the absence of cathexis and representation in those patients who consult us because their life feels meaningless.

I introduce the term 'bi-ocularity' to indicate the necessity of maintaining a position which gives maximal potential to filling that 'hole' by having one 'eye' on the understanding and interpretation of defensive mechanisms, while the other 'eye', unfocused, preserves a gap for a 'something else' to develop, first in the mind of the psychoanalyst. There has been an increasing interest in regressive states in the analyst's state of mind which enable representation where there is none. I have in particular been interested in the sudden and often fleeting visual image to which this can give rise (Chapters 8 and 10).

This dual way of listening in itself, with one eye/I in the moment and the other eye/I receptive to something not yet formed or thought, in itself fosters a triangularity. Hence I would say that the setting (in a wide sense) itself contains the mind of the psychoanalyst in relation to different temporalities and modes of experience and topos, forming a triangle as a necessary if not sufficient condition for the development of symbolisation.

Interestingly, Freud uses the idea of the cry of 'fire' during the theatrical performance to discuss the moments when reality and fantasy are in danger of collapsing in the mind of the psychoanalyst (1915). He writes that it would be as disastrous for the analysis if the patient's craving for love were gratified as if it were suppressed. For this, Freud writes, "there is no model in real life" (1915). I understand this to mean that the specific characteristics of the setting of psychoanalysis, which is a 'piece of real life', including the attitude of the psychoanalyst, does not exist in any other situation outside of psychoanalysis. The necessary paradox is that while it is 'a piece of real life' it is not 'real life', and requires a transformation away from action and an implicit reference to something else.

214

Bion echoes the difference: "Everything that happens in a consulting room has happened commonly to both participants before, but *never in quite the same way*" (Bion, 1992, p. 92, italics added). He later adds:

> the interpretations appear to a layman to be far-fetched and bizarre, a quality they owe to the extension that ordinary interpretative capacity receives through development of the analyst's intuition and the aid he obtains from the body of psycho-analytic theory with which he is familiar.
>
> (Bion, 1992, p. 92)

Psychoanalysis operates in a space 'between' – between fantasy and reality, between primary and secondary process thinking, between theory and experience, between conceptualisation and intuition, between 'Now' and 'Elsewhere'. The function of the psychoanalyst is to maintain and make use of that tension. It thus involves a temporal 'gap', the gap necessary for transformation. In that sense it is the opposite of an enactment (or mutual enactment).

To give a brief example. A patient, before an unusually long interruption of his five-times-a-week psychoanalysis, comes in a panic telling me that there is a fire in the wood next to my house. He is very insistent that I should phone the police and the fire brigade and that the situation is dangerous. I am overwhelmed with his anxiety but manage with difficulty not to get up from my chair, to digest what is being bombarded at me, and finally I am able to take up the panic which he wants to communicate to me. The setting had enabled a presentation of his psychic reality, as in a dream. For him and for me for a while it was not a dream or a psychic reality, it was external reality. The concrete thinking which erupted in the face of acute anxiety around loss, and the feelings set alight by it, needed to be contained and transformed in my mind, introducing a temporal dimension. I needed to know at the same time that there was a fire in the consulting room and that there wasn't a fire in the consulting room for the session to be able to continue. The patient left the session in a calmer state of mind. I did not feel the need to rush out and I continued with my work with other patients, but the next time I left the house I did find myself having a brief look towards the wood.

In the consulting room everything has meaning in the here and now but none of it is pure here and now, nor pure you and me. One of the pitfalls of the so-called 'here and now' way of working is that it can collapse into a 'you and me'; that is, a 'you and me' as whole and real objects whose actual relationship is the focus of interpretation and is the 'real life' without any otherness. Blass describes an instance of this in what she refers to as "the interpersonal approach", in which "the analytic focus shifts to the actual relationship between the patient and the analyst – what is being experienced and what may be understood – but the unconscious depths are downplayed" (Blass, 2011, p. 1141). While Blass links it to certain schools, in my view it is always a danger if otherness and the non-represented are ignored.

While there may be two people in the room, the analytic object is about more than two people in the room. Or, put another way, Here and Now always refers to that which is not apparently 'here' *or* 'now' – the unconscious, the lost connection, the non-represented. These may take time to get hold of, or the meaning may be obscured by the explosiveness of the affective surge. In my view, the non-represented can also get lost in the trees of too much interpretative activity, or too narrow a focus. Above all, they necessitate 'taking time' (see Chapter 10) because the phenomena taking place within the psychoanalytic pair can only be seen and understood over a period of time and necessitate "countertransference metabolisation" (Ferro, personal communication), and also because the movement towards the new and away from repetition involves the time of *reverie*, a non-purposeful state.

Bion uses the word *binocular* to refer to two different perspectives: the conscious and unconscious coming together, correlating two views of the same object. He writes, "The use in psycho-analysis of conscious and unconscious in viewing a psycho-analytic object is analogous to the use of the two eyes in ocular observation of an object sensible to sight" (1962b, p. 86). Binoculars integrate two perspectives;[2] in order to distinguish what I wish to describe from this, I use the words *bi-ocular* and *bi-ocularity* to indicate that the two images are overlapping but distinct, and need to retain or regain coexistence in the mind of the psychoanalyst. I am putting the emphasis on holding on to the disjunction. I see the function of the psychoanalyst as safeguarding the tension in a space which is 'now' *and* 'then', 'here' *and* 'other', so that it does not collapse into the immediacy of just a 'now' of a relationship, while at the same time remaining maximally present.

I am not here referring to the question of the place of the material past of the patient or of whether to speak about the past to the patient, but about transforming the moment of experience into the mental sphere which requires a gap where something 'other' resides. Symbolisation necessitates that gap – the loss of the concrete spatial and temporal moment, while that which cannot be symbolised remains in an ever a-temporal present (as discussed in Chapters 9 and 10; Weiss, 2013, Scarfone,[3] 2014, pp. 197–199). *Reverie* inhabits that gap, the gap in which 'a something else' happens or can happen. 'Bi-ocularity' puts a stress on the gap and disjunction. One could say that it is a variant of binocularity, as when the binoculars are out of focus. It is closest to the meaning given by Bion in his Brazilian Lectures (1973/1974) when he writes, "We need a kind of mental binocular vision – one eye blind, the other eye with good enough sight" (Bion, 1973/1974, p. 101).

For transformation to take place, the Now of the analytic situation requires more than an automatic translation or a parallel discourse, which are monocular and unitemporal. Speaking of linguistic translation, Diderot writes, "Woe to the makers of literal translations, who by rendering every word weaken the meaning! This is where we can say the letter kills and the spirit gives life."[4]

Transformation in the psychoanalytic situation necessitates the *more than* literal translation. It involves the psychoanalyst being receptive to multilayered messages and at various levels of consciousness, giving space to the communication from unconscious to unconscious, experiencing and digesting consciously and unconsciously that which is received – a process which takes place continuously but may also require a lengthy period of time before it becomes sufficiently available for an interpretation. The transformation via the psyche of the analyst is thus not pure translation but involves '*work*'; it has a temporal element. I have referred to this as 'the work of interpretation', as a reference not to what results in an interpretation but as a reference to conscious and unconscious processes, just as we speak of the work of mourning or dream work (Chapter 8). The 'work of interpretation' may or may not result in a verbal interpretation. It includes what Bion calls "dream-work-α" (1992) or "unconscious waking thinking" (1962a, p. 9), as well as the analyst's continual ongoing processing, conscious and unconscious, of the analytic situation. I am giving 'work of interpretation' the meaning of 'making sense of' rather than simply describing the utterances of the analyst. It happens in the present but is also the result of a buildup over time. I described how this work of interpretation rests in large part on unconscious processes coming from the encounter between analyst and patient, and I described (Chapter 8) how a fleeting image at the beginning of a session, forgotten and later barely remembered, anticipated the unfolding of the session.

The time of transformation via *reverie* in the mind of the psycho-analyst, which I call '*reverberation time*', preserves that temporal gap between that which is and is not – the moment of loss which leads to its transformation into something else, a something other. It is in the gap that meaning is formed.

The notion of *reverie* needs some discussion, since it is used to mean, in my view, somewhat different things. My use of '*reverie*' I believe stays closer to Bion than some other approaches and includes three things which I think are implied by Bion: a mode of attentiveness which is passive and receptive; an 'orientation' to the patient, as Ceglie describes (2013), since it is an expression of the mother's love; and the time of sojourn in the mother's or analyst's mind, resulting in a transformative mental process. The mother's and the analyst's *reverie* obviously differ insofar as the mother's *reverie* and love are accompanied by bodily ministrations, but both involve a receptive attitude in the service of the infant or patient. Bion puts it that "Leaving aside the physical channels of communication my impression is that her love is expressed by reverie" (Bion, 1962a, pp. 35–36). Bion goes on to say, "The term reverie may be applied to almost any content. I wish to reserve it only for such content as is suffused with love or hate" (p. 36). I understand the latter to mean that *reverie* is concerned with the emotional tie of infant and mother, patient and analyst.

In that sense, thoughts in the analyst's mind which would be the result of a detachment from the patient, for instance as a defensive reaction, would not be '*reverie*' in Bion's sense (even if this could also provide useful information). Ogden, on the other hand, extends the notion of *reverie* to describe it as elaborate con-scious narratives and "a motley collection of psychological states that seem to reflect the analyst's narcissistic self-absorption … daydreaming" (Ogden, 2004, p. 177). As I understand it, maternal *reverie* is not a conscious process and is to be distinguished from

218

day-dreaming which is more akin to what Winnicott calls 'fantasying' (Winnicott, 1971).

While I agree that useful information may be gleaned from the
mental activities that Ogden describes, in particular the apparent self-
absorption brings to the fore affect which may be out of the patient's
reach, these forms of mental activity are not the same as *reverie* in the
sense used by Bion, which is mainly the unconscious process of
'dream-work-alpha'. For that reason the visual images which suddenly
appear and are the product of that unconscious work seem to me to
be of particular interest. Ferro refers to this kind of sudden image as a
"dreamlike flash" (Ferro and Basile, 2004, p. 678).

It is also not the same as an image that may come to mind to
represent, as a metaphor, what is taking place. The single images I
am referring to are closer to dream images than 'thoughts', and may
seem quite unconnected with anything conscious occurring in the
material, as I will describe. A narrative, when one can be added, has
the characteristics of the secondary revision of a dream. The images
derive from "sense impressions being transformed into alpha elements" (Bion, 1962a, p. 26). They result from the buildup of
impressions and in turn unconsciously guide the analyst's attention.

Reverie is not *any* experience of the analyst; it is not the equivalent of countertransference (which concentrates on the affect and
includes defences, etc.). *Reverie* necessitates the state which Bion
characterised as "without memory and desire". It is a maximally
receptive state which involves not looking for anything in particular, such as the patient's response to an interpretation. By definition, *reverie* refers to the product of alpha functioning. In that way,
it may be said that *reverie* brings in something new, and in that sense
it opposes the repetition compulsion. *Reverie* is thus a reference to
the gap or space made for something different to develop. For this
reason it relates to the 'madness' of Eros.

The state of *reverie* is in tension with another necessarily more
focused attitude of the mind of the psychoanalyst, whose function is
to identify – 'analyse' in its etymological meaning of dismantling
and investigating – the psychic mechanisms displayed by the patient
in the session, leading to putting into words. Looking for the
patient's response to the interpretation would be one of them. This
is at times important and forms part of the overall data, but in my
view it brings in the 'desire' of the psychoanalyst in a way which
can interfere with *reverie*.

219

With the notion of 'bi-ocularity' I hope to convey the importance of maintaining both perspectives simultaneously: with one
'eye' on movements in defensive positions, repetitive patterns, anxieties, etc., and one 'eye' on the product of *reverie,* or rather on preserving the 'negative capability' which may give rise to it. In my
view, the latter is often drowned by the former via too much interpretative activity or explanatory type interpretations, while it is the
reverie which is the life force, Eros, which can help overcome repetition and deadness, and enable transformation.

Bi-ocularity describes the need for both states of mind to coexist:
on the one hand, the conscious processing of the material, understanding the defences, looking for the deeper anxieties; and on
the other, the maximal receptiveness to unconscious communication and its transformation into visual images. I am using
'unconscious communication' here as a shorthand because what is
received is something more in the form of what Bion calls beta elements, in conjunction with a mixture of beta and alpha elements
coming from the analyst based on present and past experience with
the patient. I don't think it would be possible to completely disen-
tangle this.

One can think of the two modes as representing two necessary
aspects of containment: the maternal taking in and 'holding inside'
and the paternal separating and taking a 'third position'. Together
they enable being affected while retaining a 'balanced' attitude: "An
understanding mother is able to experience the feeling of dread, that
this baby was striving to deal with by projective identification, and
yet retain a balanced outlook" (Bion, 1959b, p. 313).[5]

How the two modes interplay is in itself of particular clinical
interest and this can be a fruitful subject of enquiry. The interplay
of the two 'I/eyes', the predominance of one over the other, the
loss of one or the other, will reveal information about the state of
mind of each party and echo other phenomena in the consulting
room. Bion, for instance, discusses how free-floating attention can
be attacked by the patient when he writes:

> Free floating attention, regarded as necessary in analytic work,
> might then be described as that state of mind in which the analyst
> allows himself the conditions in which dream-work-alpha can
> operate for the production of alpha-elements. The psychotic
> patient knows this and sets himself out specifically during the

sessions to attack anything and everything that makes the production of alpha elements possible either in himself or the analyst.

(Bion, 1992a, p. 150)

Thinking about the two components of bi-ocularity in terms of maternal and paternal describes the triangulation with differentiation of the sexes, necessary for engendering new thoughts. The interplay of the two components gives maximal information and guidance, as long as they can fertilise each other rather than wipe each other out. Too much emphasis on one squeezes out the other. How they interplay in the session will also be a product of unconscious forces, so what I am describing is about what is to be strived for rather than achieved.

My focus in this chapter is more specifically on one side of bi-ocularity , on the function of *reverie* and on the more general maintenance of the gap in which otherness resides, and which I think gets lost in some contemporary, more active approaches.

The clinical encounter

I turn now to describe aspects of my work with a man whose capacity to represent is deficient and whose thinking could be characterised by what has been called "operational thinking" (Marty and De M'Uzan, 1963), in which the individual protects him- or herself from trauma by rejecting all libidinal cathexis – narcissistic and object related.

Lucas is a mathematician who came from the United States to join a department at one of the prestigious universities. He specialises in the area of logic. Indeed, he deals with my interpretations and his own thoughts as if they were part of a logical whole to be figured out. Reducing things to logic in this way makes him reflect on his own 'normality' and to conclude that he is 'normal' and has no big problems. At times though it is palpable that he is terrified that he could fall apart.

Lucas consults for a sexual problem and is not aware that anything else is wrong with him, and he would like to be reassured that this is the case. He seemed interested however when I said in our first meeting that he did not seem to know who he was or what he wanted, and I think that my seeing this kept him coming, that and the fact that he knows that he is in the grip of crippling anxieties

221

which he feels his sessions are able to calm. I find that Lucas is also tormented by obsessional thinking which at times seems to stave off a fear of disintegration or fill a frightening void. Lucas has almost no access to his feelings, except for rage when he feels diminished, but which he has learned to control because he fears he could kill or be killed. In the sessions he listens eagerly, finds what I say 'interesting', but the emotional impact is largely absent. On some rare occasions he tells me of a bodily reaction to something I say, the only clue to an emotion, although he does not know why.

At the time I describe, his talk is very factual and repetitive, though willing, and I would wonder if anything would ever develop.

One day Lucas throws his coat on the armchair before going to lie down. I am listening to him and his repetitive obsessional and intellectual speech, not finding anything emotionally salient. I suddenly see on the armchair in the folds of his coat a lion or panther lying on its haunches and looking straight at me. The image looks real and sharp, even as I keep looking back at it, thinking that it will disappear. I am wondering what sort of wildcat it is; it looks more panther than lion-like because it is black and relatively small, maybe more like a female. It has pointed ears and is looking straight at me. It is not threatening or aggressive but looks at me extremely intently, as if waiting to see what is going to happen. I am intrigued by this unbidden image. I am thinking of the animal side of my patient – he has been physically violent in the past. The waiting and looking is the most apparent aspect. My own frustration and waiting for something to happen could be part of this, with myself as the one paralysed, waiting, curious. Certainly this could describe the state of play, but in the session itself it seemed disconnected from everything else, as Lucas kept talking in his usual detached but willing way. The beast was there on the chair for a few sessions and then disappeared as mysteriously as it appeared. I add that although many of my patients put their coats on the chair, this experience has not happened before or since.

A few months later Lucas relates a dream he had during an analytic break. He is lying in bed with his wife, and on top of him is a lion asleep with his head on the patient's shoulder. The lion is heavy and stifling. On the floor there is a cheetah looking up at him. His associations link the lion directly to his father and the cheetah to his mother. Both parents are in reality frightening figures who were apparently prone to unpredictable and violent behaviour. It seemed that the consulting room was filled with potentially dangerous beasts and I was struck by the voyeuristic curiosity and control, as well as the opposite asleepness of the lion. The stifling 'keeping watch' so that no incest is committed certainly related to his sexual problem with his wife. Looked at in another way, the lion/father in whom the child's feelings are projected is preventing the primal scene from taking place. Lucas' very first dream depicted being swept off his feet in a tornado and the image of a woman in white going up into the sky, a virgin mother/analyst. Certainly something was impeding a penetrative and emotionally fruitful interchange, in spite of Lucas' efforts at being a 'good', hardworking patient.

In response to the lion dream I may have said something simple like, "your father is stopping you having intercourse and even living". I was deliberately playing with temporality and polysemy, with the different meanings of 'father'. By using the present tense (your father *is* stopping you) I was making clear that I was discussing the current psychic reality with a reference to the different 'fathers': the father in my consulting room whom Lucas fears will attack him if he is not kept paralysed, the actual violent father of his childhood, the father on whom were projected his own sadistic impulses and curiosity and envy of the primal scene, the castrating father ensuring that little Oedipus does not commit incest, the Father with a big F of the Oedipal basic structure, and the father in the homosexual position. By using the present tense I was purposely making room for and bringing together the 'then' and the 'now', and talking at the same time of the different fathers: childhood father, internal father, analytic father and prohibiting father.

It would have been equally true to take up with Lucas directly and simply that which was preventing a deeper interchange between him and me (for instance, the fear or even wish of waking up the dangerous lion/father, or the lion in him, or in me), but at this point this would have had no meaning for him, as he would have found it difficult to see what about his interchange with me was superficial and he would have felt criticised. A more explicit type of interpretation, I felt, would also be fuel to intellectualisation. My aim at this point was simply to open something up in his associations that could be more specifically interpreted, and to develop a space for multiple perspectives. I was keeping the bi-ocularity by fostering a space for different possibilities rather than explaining the meaning of the dream in terms of him and me, which he would have been happy to discuss. By using the present tense I wanted to foster his awareness of a psychic reality and enable the non-factual to develop.

As I went back to consider the image on the chair still vivid in my mind, I found a resemblance to certain depictions of the sphinx. I was also aware of a resonance with the Wolf Man's dream, now embodied in Lucas's dream of the cheetah on the floor looking up at him, and I thought that a primal scene situation was central. Waiting, watching, paralysis seemed to be the main features of what was going on, and in my mind too it seemed that Freud, the father of psychoanalysis, was present.

Some while later Lucas reports another dream. He says he had a sexual dream about his wife but, he says, "it didn't happen". His wife is lying on top of him and, on the bed next to them, there is a grey shape. He explains that he means it is grey because it is in the shade. Perhaps, he adds, it was only a cat, and he further adds that he does not think that the shape was spying on them. This brings to my mind the lion of the other dream, my 'vision' on the chair and the primal scene again. The session continues rather superficially; he goes on to describe in his usual obsessional way his torturing ambivalence towards his wife. Something is 'not happening' in the session.

I ask him more about the grey shape in the dream. He says that it makes him think of sarcophagi. At first I thought he might be talking about a dead/depressed part of himself but he starts speaking about how when he was a child he became very interested in the Egyptians, reading up on this, the sarcophagi, how they protected the tombs so as to not have any precious things stolen. Something seemed to come to life in the session. I had never heard him describing a real interest or anything meaningful in his childhood. He was telling me with the dream that in the shadow lay a story of intense desire and curiosity for the precious things inside the mummy and her body, but that this came with huge dangers which required strong defences. I could see for the first time how the concrete walls of the quasi–autistic state he presented entombed his powerful instinctual desirous urges, which had previously appeared to be non–existent. It also linked with my sense that behind his lack of desire for his wife lay an intense fear of her body.

224

There are of course a multitude of ways in which one can understand these condensed images in the Now, the There and the Then. And of course in the session the patient, as in the dream, is lying on his back and there is an issue about how much he can allow to 'happen' in the session. To me what was important, however, was that after a long time of repetitive material, a dream space was opening up in which he could begin to have some access to a non-factual inner life. I thought he could begin to represent a phantasy around the danger of arousal of desire in the face of the precious things inside the mother/his wife and myself in the transference, with all the attendant dangers and the persecutory fears connected with this desire. Above all, I thought he made contact with a sense that there were precious things inside the mother's body, in stark contrast to his apparent emotional indifference to his analyst and his actual rejection of his mother, which could also open the door to symbolising desire, dependence and loss.

Because my patient takes everything intellectually I did not go into the details of the imagery at this point, and felt it was sufficient that with his dream and his associations something was developing in his capacity to represent a central unconscious dynamic, evidence that psychic processing and psychic work was now more possible for him. It helped me to have a glimpse, behind the walls erected in terror, of his instinctual self and the dangers of the mother's body and his curiosity. It also gave me hope that something more alive could be reached. Some time after this session Lucas reported that his wife thought that he was more able to take some pleasure in things. This also moved events in the direction of Lucas eventually being able to come for a full five times a week of psychoanalysis, in spite of his terror that it would result in a loss of control. When he started with the five sessions, the problem could be expressed more symbolically and directly in the transference when Lucas said in a session, "I want to know what you think. It excites my curiosity, I'd like to be *inside* your head. I feel frustrated, I feel crushed."

It became more possible to take up such things as Lucas' cruel revenge on his object through his indifference; but in my view in order for this to be meaningful Lucas needed to know about his passion for the object, the mummy he had entombed along with his love, desire and curiosity, and the experience of having been left utterly destitute, without even a containing intact skin – something he projects into the future in his terror of winding up penniless and homeless. We began to see that behind his self-righteous attitude lay an extremely low self-esteem and the thought of having been an unwanted child (he was born as 'an accident', 10 years after his two siblings).

Concluding remarks

Many things take place in the Now of a psychoanalysis and there are many ways of being in the Now of the session. In describing this material, I want to illustrate how I see the function of the psychoanalyst with this patient to be that of providing a space in which something more than a fearful and rigid adherence to 'the factual' and the intellectual devoid of emotion can take place, and to reach that which has been paralysed by severe persecutory and catastrophic anxieties, while also not avoiding reaching those anxieties. In order for this to happen, and to give a shape, affect and eventually thoughts and words to the "nameless dread" (Bion, 1962a, p. 96), or "unthinkable ... agony" (Winnicott, 1974, p. 104) which paralyses him, a capacity to symbolise needs to develop – a development which goes hand in hand with a temporality which is less frozen and more 'ambiguous'.

A screen memory points to a possible breakdown in early childhood when the world went dark, leading Lucas to a restricted emotional range and to fear for his future sanity in the way that Winnicott describes in his paper "Fear of Breakdown" (1974). The Barangers write about patients who cling "to a temporality that is already oriented and determined out of fear of ambiguous temporality, in other words, of the joint experience of a present situation with the analyst and a past relation with archaic objects". They add: "We could say that the temporal dialectic of analysis progresses from a fixed and determined temporality to a different type (more mobile, with more of a future and a different content), passing through an especially ambiguous temporality" (Baranger and Baranger, 2008, p. 800).

Put another way, we could say that the patient is clinging to a present due to a terror of going back to a past which is remembered but not recollected, as Botella puts it (2014), and a fear of the future which signals the breakdown. In that restricted space of the Now an ambiguity needs to be restored, one which is 'polytemporal', as I tried to show. I use 'polytemporal' as a particular aspect or category of 'polysemy'[6] in order to stress the opening to multiple temporalities.

The analytic function, as I see it, is to maintain bi-ocularity, a conjunction but also disjunction between the immediate and something other. The two need to be held together in their slight disjunction and not collapsed with explanations or literal translations. It is that disjunction which creates a gap, a *time*, a structure in which a process of *reverie* provides the soil for symbolisation to develop. Baranger and Baranger write, "It is essential for the analytical procedure that everything or every event in the field be at the same time something else. If this essential ambiguity is lost, analysis also disappears" (1961, p. 8). Here my focus is specifically on the disjunction in the functioning mind of the psychoanalyst with the need to maintain bi-ocularity, in which one 'I/eye' is separate from the other, but each provides important material for the other; the connection may happen only much later or outside of the sessions, and each needs to be foregrounded at different times, creating the necessary space. In the case of Lucas, bi-ocularity could enable the beginning of a move out of the restricted space of a two-dimensional world. It also enabled a relibidinisation of a 'dead' analytic situation and enabled a contact which I believe did touch Lucas emotionally.

Da Rocha Barros discusses the pictorial representation in dreams as "a first step towards thinkability" (2011, p. 270) and points to the necessity of symbols for the storing of emotional experience and for conveying our affects to others and to ourselves (Da Rocha Barros and Da Rocha Barros, 2011). With the kind of patient I describe, the pictorial representation may need to take place in the analyst when it cannot take place in the patient, via a regressive state. The visual image opens up a space on to the something new, and a first step towards a potential for greater symbolisation. This is different from a more conscious work which also takes place. At particularly arid times, for instance, I felt I needed to do even more than 'dream the session', as Bion puts it (Bion, 1992, p. 120), and needed to 'dream up' a something more, hoping it wasn't too way out.

A number of authors have been specifically interested in regressive states of mind of the analyst in order to work with those patients for whom areas of blankness prevail (foremost are De M'Uzan (2005) and Botella and Botella (2001)). For Perelberg the analyst's work of figurability is not equivalent to *reverie*, as it contains the capacity to create a *"substitutive scene"* triggered by the negative of the patient's experience that is "inaccessible and without memory" and "equivalent to an earlier scene that cannot be reached". "It has the capacity of replacing the *memory without recollection by a substitutive memory that is destined to become a screen memory*" (Botella and Botella, 2013, p. 119, italics in original) (Perelberg, 2015).

While there are different conceptual models and variations in what is described, for instance, in terms of whether one is talking about a rare and centrally significant 'scene' or the piercing into consciousness of ongoing unconscious processing, and in particular in terms of the conceptualised connection with the past, in my view the notion of *reverie* may be used generically to describe the 'work', whether we think of it as 'figurability' (Botella) or 'waking dream thought' (Ferro).[7] Bion (1970, pp. 35–36) writes:

> Receptiveness achieved by denudation of memory and desire (which is essential to the operation of 'acts of faith') is essential to the operation of psycho–analysis and other scientific proceedings. It is essential for experiencing hallucination or the state of hallucinosis. This state I do not regard as an exaggeration of a pathological or even natural condition: I consider it rather to be a state always present, but overlaid by other phenomena, which screen it. If these other elements can be moderated or suspended hallucinosis becomes demonstrable; its full depth and richness are accessible only to 'acts of faith'.

In the case of my hallucinosis one may be thinking in terms of the representation of impulses which have not been representable by the patient, who describes a blank where a primal scene would be. On only one occasion did a vague hint of a primal scene come in the form of a dream of being haunted by frightening supernatural forces in the context of a bedroom scene.

By using the word 'bi-ocularity', I am pointing not to something different from binocularity so much as placing an emphasis on the need to retain both attitudes of mind at the same time – the one which 'analyses' and the one which remains maximally receptive – in a disjunctive manner. De Masi gives the title of 'delusion and bi-ocular vision' to a recent paper. The term 'bi-ocular vision', he writes, was given to him by his psychotic patient. De Masi (2015) writes:

Lorenzo says he realizes that he has a *bi-ocular* vision of reality. I note the great precision of his statement: he does not say that he has a binocular vision because his vision lacks integration, as would necessarily be the case if the two visions could meet and be compared with each other. In this case, the two visions, one delusional and the other real, remain distinct and differentiated from each other because they both possess the same perceptual character, that of reality.

I had not read this paper when I first wrote mine and was struck by the similar use of bi–ocular to describe the unintegration of the two visions. This unintegration, I am suggesting, is the necessary gap which needs to be fostered as part of the analytic attitude. In the situation I described it led to the wildcat on the chair, a hallucinosis which anticipated something yet to take place and which could only reach a representation by the patient later on. By 'gap' I am referring to the gap which I argue needs to be maintained in order to allow for the necessary 'something other' to emerge, a 'something' which is often not to be immediately understood and remains unintegrated until a later date. It tends to happen in the form of images appearing in a flash and which can easily disappear and not be remembered. I assume it is happening much more often than one is able to be aware of, but will nevertheless play an important role in the development of the analytic process. I have also high-lighted the aspect of anticipation, an important factor promoting the forward movement via the psyche of the analyst. In the case of the visual image I described, or of a flash which disappears quickly, it is part of its characteristic that if remembered the image may appear to be out of context and with no apparent links to the material. In the case I describe here, the visual image anticipated material which appeared not in the same session but a month or two later. It is a necessary madness if representation is to fill psychotic holes.

Notes

1 An earlier version of the paper was presented at the English Speaking Conference in London in 2014, "Here and Now, There and Then".
2 Bion also uses 'binocular' in related meanings such as: "those two people [analyst and analysand] are required to produce a binocular vision, a binocular observation" in *The Complete Works of W.R. Bion*,

Vol. XV, p. 54 (unpublished works 1977); or when he discusses the psychoanalytic approach through the individual and through the group, and writes: "the two methods provide the practitioner with a rudimentary binocular vision" (1961, p. 8). Bion also discusses the need to blind ourselves to what we know so that our intuition can "have a chance of seeing something.... We need a kind of mental binocular vision – one eye blind, the other eye with good enough sight" (Bion, 1973/1974, p. 101).

3 Scarfone refers to this a-temporal present as *impassé* (2014, pp. 197–199), a neologism combining the idea that it is not 'the past' as it is active in an a-temporal way, and that it hasn't moved into being 'past'.

4 "Malheur aux faiseurs de traductions littérales, qui en traduisant chaque parole énervent le sens! C'est bien là qu'on peut dire que la lettre tue, et que l'esprit vivifie" (Lettres philosophiques (1734), XVIII; Citations de François Marie Arouet, dit Voltaire Références de François Marie Arouet, dit Voltaire).

5 Vermote (in preparation) picks this out as one of Bion's earliest definitions of containment.

6 In music, 'polytemporal' refers to different tempi occurring simultaneously which is a slightly different idea, although the notion of different 'tempos' intermingling in a session and in an analysis, is also fruitful, and may be related to what I call 'reverberation time' as one of the tempos.

7 Hock (2014) also points out that even in Freud's early work there is no real division between construction and reconstruction.

12

TERMINATION IN PROCESS

In this chapter, I focus on a specific manifestation of readiness to end which has come to my attention. It is the patient's spontaneous representation of the *process* of psychoanalysis, something which indicates a different relationship to time and a greater connectedness to the 'human world'.

Albert Camus, in his essay "The Myth of Sisyphus", suggests that Sisyphus is condemned because of his passion for life and his hatred of death (Sisyphus had chained death), and for revealing the God's secrets. What is tragic, Camus explains, is that Sisyphus is conscious. In other words he is aware of the hopelessness and futility of his predicament, condemned to the repetitive and hopeless task of pushing a rock up the hill, only to see it roll down again when he gets to the top. However, Camus writes, he can find happiness when he can look at his life and see that his destiny belongs to himself. Camus makes a comparison with Oedipus who starts by following his destiny blindly. His tragedy starts when he knows. But at the end, linked to the world by the hand of a young girl, he says, "Despite so many ordeals, my advanced age and the nobility of my soul make me conclude that all is well." For Oedipus and Sisyphus destiny has become a human affair through their own self-awareness.

This could be an essay on the process of psychoanalysis and its termination: the confrontation with the destructive forces in the guise of the cruel Gods who hate life and punish those who want to live and tell the truth, and the possibility of acceptance consequent on self-awareness and on having an overview, a better contact with reality, and a greater connection to helpful internal and external objects. The power of the Gods is to impede development, so that

231

progress is forever undone, and hence instil interminability. While the recognition of this state of affairs leads at first to despair, it is also this recognition which allows for freedom and happiness. "There is no sun without shadow and it is essential to know the night", Camus writes. He then ends the essay by saying that once he has become master of his destiny – through his knowledge – "this universe henceforth without a master seems to him neither sterile nor futile". The last sentence reads: "The struggle itself towards the heights is enough to fill a man's heart. One must imagine Sisyphus happy." Representation has replaced 'repetition' so that the struggle is not quite the same and the repetition is not quite identical when there is self-awareness.

The decision to end does not itself come without a painful struggle. It also maximally implicates the psychoanalyst, touching on the psychoanalyst's own theories, values, expectations, illusions, omnipotence and limitations, conflicts and defences. Ferro describes an impasse with a patient until he realised that "It was I who had to mourn for my therapeutic ambitions and resign myself to the thought of finishing the analysis" (1993, p. 920) as well as thinking that "in my pain at this termination, I may perhaps have taken on the projective identifications of the patient, who was having more difficulty with the separation" (p. 921).

Alongside the processes which unconsciously influence the situation such as the patient's masochism or the psychoanalyst's depressive anxieties, and which can lead to delaying or, on the contrary, precipitating an ending, consciously psychoanalysts base themselves on an array of indicators which, as a constellation, build up to a sense that change has been sufficient to give confidence that the patient will manage the future.

In my view indicators coalesce around two major dimensions; one is to do with a better psychic functioning (less rigid defences, increased symbolic capacity and ability to reflect rather than act, ability to hold a more complex view), and the other is to do with the growth of a greater capacity and experience of a loving connection to others. The latter will affect the relationship to external objects but also to internal objects (including the modification of internal objects and in particular the diminution of a punitive superego). The two clusters are of course interconnected and lead to an overall picture in which there is a greater ability to face psychic reality, a greater sense of responsibility without masochism, a better

232

self-esteem and toleration of separateness and loss, a better toleration of the more disturbed parts of the self and capacity to contain these, a better protective 'shield'/'skin' or a greater sense of an internal structure when these have been deficient.

Contemporary literature stresses in particular the better psychic functioning and the creation of the tools which will enable the patient to face future situations, the capacity for self-reflection and for representation (Ferro, 2006; Ithier, 2005). An analysand put this graphically to me at the end of her analysis: "It's like someone describing mountain climbing when iron bars are left in the rock for future use." I wrote in my notes "crampons" rather than "pitons" and I cannot say if that came from me or from my patient, and it illustrates the coexistence of opposites which make up the field.

Insofar as psychoanalysis is interminable, and that to the end there will be a back and forth of progression and regression, it is only a question of balance, and of patient and analyst together feeling it is possible to contemplate bringing the analysis to an end, albeit with an inevitable background of a resurgence of primitive terrors.

In my experience, in the final phase of a satisfactory psycho-analysis, patients very often also describe in one way or another how they have 'learned to love', or to connect with other people in a new way. As one of my analysands put it, "I don't understand how this analysis worked but when I look back at how suicidal I was, I don't see how I could feel that again." He spoke about this in the context of having learned a new way of connecting with people and of having a greater sense of "human connection".

These two aspects, namely the tools for thinking and the greater ability to connect, are accompanied by a sense of greater confidence in the future, and a reduction in the feeling of being hampered by the past, a different temporal experience.

The development of a symbolic capacity is a central trans-formative aspect of the psychoanalytic process; that is, of the development of what Bion calls "the apparatus for thinking". Throughout this book I have pointed to the relationship between symbolisation and temporality. Representing *the process* of psycho-analysis involves both of these. After speaking of the mountain climbing, the patient mentioned above said that time now seemed very different to her – "it's like having an extra dimension" – and in the next session she spoke of feeling that she can accept ageing

233

and the end of analysis, and the limits of what can be repaired. The mountain which she had referred to could be understood as a reference to having lived under the dominance of a powerful super-ego, the 'punishing Gods' which had a grip on her and kept throwing her down. Another analysand who was trying to make up his mind about ending wondered whether he had the confidence to end and said, "I suppose I don't have to become a saint, being less fragmented and knotted is still a good result". I responded, "not having to become a saint is a good result".

Patients are of course continually describing their experience of the psychoanalyst and of the psychoanalysis in dreams and associations, and this is a focus of interpretation. There comes a time however when a patient may bring, as a dream or an association, an image or an idea which conveys the *process* itself of psychoanalysis, and not simply how they experience the analysis or the analyst at a particular moment (such as a punishing teacher, a devouring mother, a place of retreat or, on the contrary, of impingement). This conscious or unconscious representation of the process, by dint of being a process, necessitates the representation of a temporal element. The representation captures aspects central to the process of psychoanalysis such as the idea of repetition, of a struggle between the life and death drive, of working through, and an idea of time as movement. The spontaneous representation is evidence that the process *itself* has been internalised. It is particularly significant in the case of patients for whom processes of symbolisation had been deficient. I am using the word 'representation' in a wide sense to include both 'idea' and 'image'[1] and to cover both conscious and unconscious aspects. What I am describing requires a deep understanding *from experience* and at various levels of consciousness of the process itself and implies a great degree of abstraction but also of integration over a long period of time.

Insofar as it is the representation of a process, it is evidence of an internal experience of time as duration. The patient who is fragmented cannot grasp a process. Most severe pathologies show a psychic 'freezing' of time in which only a moment exists, a moment which may be placed in the past (in a grievance or a trauma), or in the future (fantasising an ideal) or in a present devoid of past or future. Steiner captures this lack of movement in his concept of "psychic retreat" (1993), a term which immediately evokes a spatial image but is also temporal insofar as it implies that there is no movement except in the sense of 'retreating' from the dangers of both 'paranoid schizoid position' and 'depressive position', so going back to a 'no change' position. Weiss distinguishes between the borderline patient who deforms the experience of time while for the psychotic patient concepts of time and space dissolve (2013).

In Chapter 7 I use the image of 'unpicking the tapestry' to describe the attempt to omipotently prevent endings and stop the passage of time. Laplanche, also referring to Penelope, mentions Homer's use of the Greek word for 'undoing' which is the same word as 'analysing', and points out that unweaving is necessary in order to create a new fabric. In that way the story may be looked at in an opposite way; rather than not letting go of Ulysses, Penelope is doing the work of mourning. He writes: "Perhaps (Penelope) only unweaves *in order* to weave, to be able to weave a new tapestry. It would thus be a case of *mourning*, mourning for Ulysses" (Laplanche, 1998a, p. 254, italics in original). Whether the unpicking is a freezing of movement or a necessary work of mourning will depend on the phantasy behind the unpicking, whether it is aimed at keeping something static, at preventing the experience of loss or if it is the first step in a working through, installing in memory the lost object, a work which reconfigures and "requires time", as Laplanche points out. (op.cit.). It is the difference between 'identical' which the unpicking aims to keep in an unchanged state, and the 'similar' which the unweaving can allow by releasing threads to be woven in a new way. Similarly, while it is said that the analyst must be 'killed' in order for [the patient] to achieve freedom to grow (Orgel, 2000, p. 734), and that every psychic act is an act of murder (Chervet, 2009), there is also preservation in the mentalisation itself. Or, to put it another way, the absence of the ability to symbolise makes the end of psychoanalysis impossible if it is experienced as actual murder. In a similar vein, Potamianou suggests that for some borderline analysands even minor changes in the psychic economy are felt as a loss of 'pieces of their self' (1997), making development towards an end problematic.

The aim of psychoanalysis is to enable the development of the capacity to reconfigure the threads in a symbolic form, enabling separation via the creation of memory of the process.

Towards the end of a long analysis in which she tried to freeze time into an ever-present 'now' because endings seemed so catastrophic, and following a discussion about the setting of an ending date, Beatrice (Chapter 4) brought the following dream.

> There was an aquarium and two fish were dying. There was going to be a ritual, the other fish, very colourful fish, were going to do a dance. Someone asked him if he wanted to watch and he said yes enthusiastically.

Beatrice spoke of the people who used to go and watch the guillotine during public executions. She had written a thesis on the French Revolution, which she was particularly interested in. The dream is rich and overdetermined and could be understood in different ways. I took it to depict in the first instance Beatrice's favourite hysterical defensive posture, making something very painful and frightening into a spectacle, a drama to be enjoyed. Importantly however it also depicted an understanding of how analysis had been turned into a glass bowl existence where analyst and patient were meant to go round and round without getting anywhere and where the end of analysis signalled the death of the omnipotent attempt to stop the progression of time with its inevitable move to separation and death. Being asked to be an 'observer' could describe a capacity to observe herself and the relinquishing of a glass bowl existence. The reference to public executions in the Reign of Terror in France could also be understood as a reference to guilt at and terror of being punished for her excitement at being liberated from her glass bowl existence and from her analyst. All these aspects condense in the dream, with the different fish and the differentiation between 'inside the bowl' and 'outside the bowl'. One can say that the dream which graphically depicts her unconscious understanding of her anxieties and defences sets the scene in its overdetermination for the development of a variety of meanings in subsequent sessions, weeks and months.

The association Beatrice makes to 'les tricotteuses' watching the scene also reminds one of the weaving discussed above. Renunciation does not come easily and without aggression, and 'knitting' in this sense is an attempt to sublimate, to create a something else from the experience of destruction and a something which will be left after the 'murder' of the analyst (the dead fish left in the consulting room) and something to help deal with loss. The dream itself, with its many possible meanings, and the act of dreaming are an important act of 'knitting', of forming a representation with a possible working through.

Eventually, Beatrice could say, "I know that analysis can't solve everything, it shows you patterns which help you to ride the wave, makes you know what to expect and to know yourself better". She added that she felt more "centred". She said that she has to accept that she can never marry me, have babies with me or even go on holiday with me. She added:

> that is very sad, and there will always be sadness in my relationship with you. But that is the human condition. There is always something one can't have. But that also makes one do good things rather than be horrible.

Near the end of her analysis, she then spontaneously represented the process of analysis. It came in the form of a song she wanted to write for me. It was about building sand-castles. She loved to do that as a child:

> First there is nothing and you start to build and it gets more and more elaborate and you imagine all sorts of things, the secret places and passages. Eventually the sea comes and takes it. You know it will happen but you still build the castle, you still get involved with it and carried away in your imagination. When it's gone, there is still the sand and the sea and you know you can start again. You know the wave will come, that time passes and that this is part of life.

Like Camus' Sisyphus she knows about the repetitious process, the progress and the regress, the hope and the disappointment, and therefore can maintain a certain distance from it. She is 'in time' rather than in the timeless hell of eternal remorse and persecution or the idealised timeless glass bowl existence meant to save her from that hell. She knows that good times can follow bad times. "You know that you can start again" conveys that it is a *capacity* which has developed, the capacity for involvement and toleration of loss. As I put it in Chapter 1: "It is the importance of the journey itself, its role as an experience in itself which demarcates psychoanalysis from other forms of therapy" (p. 24). 'Riding the wave' also describes the lessening of a fear of passivity in the face of unconscious processes and of affect. As for Sisyphus, the constructive act and the sense of time are now felt to be in themselves worthwhile and in this Beatrice was representing the process of psychoanalysis.

Marie, the patient who had found it extremely difficult and excruciating to communicate with me in words (Chapter 4), at the end of her analysis also spontaneously offered for the first time a perspective on her analysis.

> It's like if you were writing something, you might have to do it 19 times before something came up that was good and the 19 times would not be a waste. Or like when you're doing a crossword puzzle you think of lots of possible words: bake, cake, steak ... sometimes you don't even notice the right one because you've pronounced it wrong.[2] When you see something, suddenly it changes absolutely everything, everything is different, but then you lose it again and it's very disappointing.

It was the first time Marie showed that she reflected on her analysis and its process. Her creative way of depicting psychoanalysis starts by linking it to a creative activity, writing, which is close to talking. She shows an understanding developed from experience of the nature of the process with its inevitable repetitiveness; she points out the positive aspect of the repetition which, like the creative activity, is not a waste but a valuable part of the process, and she points out the negative aspect, the negative therapeutic reaction, when "you lose it again". I had certainly myself experienced with Marie the feeling of being confronted with a pure struggle between life and death forces. "Sometimes you don't even notice the right one", she says, reflecting now on the difficulty in seeing what is going on at the time and to recognise progress when it is taking place. The 'puzzle' she refers to is her anorexia, her problem over food – "bake, cake, steak". But she has also understood that in her analysis this has centred on her difficulty with words, with speaking. The increasingly cannibalistic sequence is relevant. I could push this further by taking up the 'cross' word but, while I think my patient was often cross when she would not eat or speak, this would misrepresent the underlying fear of her tremendous avidity. It is this libidinal activity (oral/genital) which she was sublimating in her play with the words "bake, cake, steak" reminiscent of the baby's pleasure in babbling. We did not explore her associations to '19' at

238

the time, but I can think now that 19 is the end of the teens and thus marks the passage to adulthood, and represents the move away from the analyst/parent with ending psychoanalysis. The pleasure in the discovery which she also represents also touches on the sublimation of the epistemophilic instinct (Klein).

At this point, when Marie is able to describe the to and fro of the process, she has not 'lost it' but she *knows about* 'losing it' which is what makes the difference. She intuits the negative therapeutic reaction. Like Beatrice she is able to remember, to have an overview, to represent the experience; this capacity for an overview, developed out of an internalisation of the process and a capacity to reflect upon it, fosters a sense of hope.

Marie had been able to mentalise that which had been expressed through the action on her body; she had been able to create in her analysis a space which felt safe enough and separate enough to be able to communicate her experience in words. The ability to communicate meaning through language presupposes a capacity for sublimation and symbolisation. Otherwise words are felt *to be* the milk, nipple or penis which feeds or poisons, deprives or invades, and they no longer act as a sign (in the linguistic sense).

At the time of preparing to leave, Marie was painting a picture of her analysis and of her past with the words she had now learned to use, as a way of preserving that experience. Put another way, she could tolerate separateness and acknowledge the loss of her analysis sufficiently to be able to represent and re-create her experience in words. The wish to repair, to put together the fragments of the analytic experience into a coherent whole, gives impetus to the sublimation in the creative representation. A tapestry has been woven. And it is the capacity to repair and to contain the feelings in a representation which makes leaving possible. This representation is also what makes it possible to have an overview, as one patient who was ending put it, echoing other patients: "Now when I feel depressed I know that it will pass, that it is only temporary in contrast to an earlier belief that this state of mind is the only real one."

Weaving, knitting, the creation of "psychic fabric" (Ithier, 2005) are apt metaphors to describe mourning as opposed to melancholia.

It is striking how both Beatrice and Marie bring in the imagery of the sea, of curiosity and discovery, Beatrice talking of the to and fro of the sea and the engagement with secret places, Marie describing her curiosity about the seaweed uncovered by the tide, the 'lost tribe now discovered'. Psychoanalysis, and these analysands' ability to internalise the experience, fostered and sanctioned their curiosity and developed their 'K links' from experience (Bion, 1962a). Beatrice and Marie now give a representation of a curiosity about their own unconscious, an unconscious grounded in the body, and implying an openness to discoveries in the future. They give a representation of what was and what can be in the future. Both of them also point to the importance of words, Beatrice through writing a song, Marie through her pleasurable play with words. In both representations, time as duration and repetition in its positive aspects are central. In neither does the analyst figure specifically, which suggests the possibility of continuation without that external figure, and the internalisation of the process, a process in which 'it' can be lost and found again.

In the case of another patient, Ross, the representation comes in the form of a dream towards the end of his long analysis. Ross appeared detached and out of touch with his feelings but a dream he had in the middle phase of his analysis about a boy who had to have a bandage taken off and had no skin under the bandage described well what lay behind his apparent detachment. The bandage in fact consisted in a permanent state of resentment. Holding on to grudges made him feel powerful and seemed to be a necessary means of survival; this was part of the 'bandage'/hard skin, as was his preoccupation with creating an anal potency which included making himself unpleasant and me useless. His sadism was as pervasive as his masochism and at times I wondered if I should stop his analysis because I felt that continuing was simply participating in his sadistic pleasure in debasing and defeating me without any hope of change.

Ross hated the ends of sessions to such an extent that he wiped out what had been said and could not remember anything, or even that anything of any importance had been said in the sessions. This consequently made him feel more deprived and more resentful. This also meant that he had no notion of the possibility of being sustained between sessions by a memory of something good, since that had gone. It was a sort of vicious circle because the more he hated his analyst for the fixed endings, the less he could remember, and the less he could feel he had something to sustain him between the sessions, the angrier he felt.

The turning point came one day when Ross could allow himself and trust me enough to regress in the session, 'take off the bandage' and feel attended to. Ross told me that, after the session, he would have to go to an important meeting at work where there would be a large group of people whom he didn't know from a different branch of his firm but that he felt extremely sick and didn't think he could manage this. He thought that maybe he had eaten something bad the evening before. He was in a great panic because he hadn't brought his car due to the fact that he would be taking a train to the meeting. He was expected to give a powerpoint presentation and thought it would damage his career to cancel. Usually Ross was unable to communicate his feelings in a way that I could perceive them. I saw this as failure of projective identification as a communication (Bion, 1962a). It felt impossible to stay connected to what the feelings might be. On this occasion it was different. I could feel his terror and I became very worried about him and wondered what I should do; I didn't know whether I could let him go out in such an ill state at the end of the session. Rather than act on this, I spoke to him about how this resonated with specific experiences in his child-hood which he had not been able to be in touch with before, and described how he might have felt then, and the parallel with the specific situation he would be finding himself in when he left the session which revived and evoked that for him. I was very worried to let him leave. However, he reported the following day that he had felt suddenly better on leaving the session, stopped feeling ill altogether, had gone to the meeting and the rest of the day had been fine.

For the first time Ross had been able to project his feelings of terror and let me contain them for him through my having the ter-rifying experience and putting something into words which could make sense of this experience. I remember thinking that something momentous and unprecedented had taken place. In this experience lay the seeds of a new phase in which Ross grappled with some new-found loving feelings, albeit these were felt to be very danger-ous. My own feelings changed concomitantly from finding Ross a rather offputting, unpleasant, burdensome patient to looking forward to seeing him. It now became possible to see more clearly how he had made himself as unpleasant as possible in order to keep me at bay, in part due to Oedipal anxieties.

241

A next important moment involved the uncovering of something which had not been seen before: an ingrained Oedipal belief that he would one day marry his analyst and his subsequent bitter disillusion. This led to his being openly angry with me for the first time. It seemed suddenly outrageous to him that I had no space in my drive for him to park his car.

For the first time Ross could now speak realistically of plans to end his analysis and we could set a date.

A turbulent phase followed in which Ross had anxiety dreams about falling from heights. There was now a to and fro between dreams with imminent danger, looking over the edge of a cliff and being terrified, and reassuring dreams in which he was managing to get down from a dangerous place, or landing safely in a helicopter.

Then came the dream which represented his analysis. He arrived saying he felt happy today (something he had never said before). In the dream, he is in his childhood home. His father has a hosepipe and he is surprised because in reality his parent's house did not have a garden. His father in the dream shows him how he has an unlimited supply of water from a borehole in the ground. Around the hole the grass is all green.

In a second part of the dream he is looking up at the house, his father's house, and he thinks that he really likes it, "it has many additions, like bits of masonry and ornaments on the façade of the house, and changes to the disposition of the rooms; You could see that it had sort of grown organically rather than it being planned from the beginning." He said he really liked that and he told his father in the dream how much he liked it, it looked Japanese. Then he looked up and saw that there was this tall structure like a tower, decorative, and it was a very nice addition, but then he saw workmen climbing up to fix the TV aerial at the top and suddenly it seemed dangerous with ladders, one on top of the other and gaps between the ladders.

He then remarked how little his father seems to figure in his life and in his analysis, and that this dream seemed in striking contrast to this.

I took up his appreciation of his analysis which had helped him to develop without a pre-ordained plan, organically, and how he felt he now had more of a continuous internal supply which was in identification with a fertilising father. He replied that it was a good representation of the analysis, some bits of the house done, some still in need of being done and some that may never get done. He said the large structure was nice but he worried about how to keep it in good repair, like his worry about what would happen when he had ended analysis.

I thought that the hosepipe represented a good penis which promotes new growth, that he could find both in his father and me and in himself. I wondered if the supply coming from the earth represented the mother who is felt to contain the resources, with the hosepipe linking father and earth mother as 'penis-as-link' rather than faecal penis. I also wondered if the dangerous tower was to do with a dangerous phallic omnipotence, or simply to do with his anxieties about retribution if he is potent.

The dream depicts the process of psychoanalysis and his understanding and internalisation of it; of relevance is that the description he gives, "you could see that it had sort of grown organically rather than it being planned from the beginning", also corresponds to my own understanding of the process of psychoanalysis whereby I have no preconceived ideas about where the patient and I will be going and what to expect, and that it develops as we go along. I would, at the same time, hope that there would be changes to the 'disposition of the rooms' or the discovery of 'new rooms'. Part of the changed disposition of the rooms would include a sense of an internal space with inner resources which would often show also a changed relationship to internal and sometimes external figures. The dream also shows a concern for the future and an anxiety about continuing the 'repair work', a realistic and non-manic understanding that there is never a once-and-for-all resolution, and that he will need to do the ongoing psychic work on his own, or get more help if necessary. I wondered why no woman/mother figured directly in the dream, except indirectly, perhaps indicating that rivalry or envy was still overshadowing valuing the maternal figure, who as 'mother earth' was unconsciously also experienced as omnipotent and omnipresent. The fact that his father, who had so far figured little was here someone who could provide help and show him what to do, seemed important.

In these different ways the analysands I discuss in this chapter were showing a deep understanding of the psychoanalytic process, based on their own experience which they had come to represent consciously or unconsciously, each in their own way. Faced with the need to renounce, they found a creative way of verbally representing the psychoanalytic process.

243

The representation itself is that of a creative process. It seems to me to be an important moment even as the patient may be struggling with severe anxieties. Depending on one's model, one can talk about a greater capacity for sublimation or a capacity to symbolise, to repair the object, the capacity to play, the development of a transitional space, the development of an internal space. While in her earlier work, Klein describes sublimation as the libidinal cathexis of ego-tendencies,[3] in her later work, when she becomes less committed to classical theory, the notion of reparation as central to maturational processes takes over with its stress on a complex process in which anxiety and guilt play a central part.[4] In both classical and Kleinian models, the idea of renunciation is important but in the Kleinian perspective it is the process of mourning the object involved in a successful renunciation which leads to sublimation via symbol formation.[5] If Marie is able to say at the end of her analysis "I want to eat you" it is because she no longer feels that to speak is to eat me and that she can now distinguish the phantasy from the action, and the word from the action.

The psychoanalytic process facilitates the development of a space (mental/transitional) which is promoted by the analyst's containing function, her capacity to reflect rather than react, and to dialogue with herself in the service of the analysis as described in the previous chapter. In so far as this capacity to reflect in the service of the analysis evokes an Oedipal situation (Britton, 1989), impediments will come about as a result of feelings of hatred and of defences erected against knowledge of this 'primal scene', interfering with progress towards termination. These issues will often come to the fore again towards the end of a psychoanalysis.

Our aims, after all, are modest although they can be far-reaching. The new fabric may not always seem so different and yet is very different. I understand the aim of psychoanalysis to be greater freedom from pathological ways of dealing with psychic pain, greater freedom from internal constraints, and greater freedom to relate to others. I take it as a given that a psychoanalytic way of thinking is antithetical to the notion of once-and-for-all absence of conflict or pain. The 'talking cure' initiates a process rather than concludes one.

The patients whom I describe in this chapter, each in their own way, through an act of integration and symbolisation came to represent the *process* of psychoanalysis. The representation was of the ebb and flow of progress and regression as a constant feature of life, of time as necessary for working through, for thinking, for waiting, for tolerating. It is the toleration of time (which brings frustration, absence, loss) which leads to representation; and the representation itself is of that temporality, a temporality which encompasses destructive and constructive forces.

Importantly, all these analysands mentioned 'pleasure', in one way or another, which gave a meaning to their life. Greater capacity for enjoyment and greater sense of being grounded (in reality) are two central aspects that are mentioned in my experience when patients end their analysis.

A greater ability to dream in the sense Bion gives it makes acceptance of interminability of the process more possible. Bion writes of the "felt need to convert the conscious rational experience into dream", emphasising that "the felt need is *very* important; if it is not given due significance and weight, the true dis-ease of the patient is being neglected" (Bion, 1992, p. 184).

I do not discuss here the indications for, or limitations of, psychoanalysis. I subscribe to Green's view that, in spite of the limitations of psychoanalysis, it is the best we have got (Green, 2010) or as Bion put it, we have to make "the best of a bad job" (1979a).

My aim was simply to discuss the spontaneous representation of the *process* of psychoanalysis which I see as an indication of a changed relationship to time and therefore a manifestation of a greater readiness to end. It is of course not always possible to reach this point, and this point is usually not the one patients thought they were coming for, since it does not remove the bad times, and the 'new fabric' can also be a disappointing one. Sometimes more help is needed at a later time. Psychoanalysis is unique in providing a treatment, the positive outcome of which may differ widely from the outcome which the patient requested. The sickness the patient suffers from is often one the patient cannot recognise. If psychoanalysis does not have as a primary goal to take away symptoms, and in that sense is not a simple therapy, it does aim to add a 'something more'. Rather than removing symptoms, it aims to make a person 'alive' and not just 'surviving'. If there is a consistency in descriptions from people who have completed an analysis, it is around the experience of this 'something more', a greater depth of feeling and experience. Often it comes through the sense of being more 'grounded', 'more centred', 'more real'. It may be felt to come at the cost of a loss of illusions and aspirations and the loss of extreme states, something which is given up not without regret. The psychoanalyst too needs to be able to 'ride the wave' if she or he is to sustain a cathexis of the analytic enterprise. Anzieu suggests that it is Freud's innate confidence in the superiority of life instincts over death instincts which made him able to act as a psychotherapist to his patients (Anzieu, 1986, p. 581).

We may often feel, like Sisyphus, condemned to a hopeless task with our patients in which the work of the previous day or the previous term is forever undone. It is the overview, the awareness of the process and the relinquishment of omnipotence which can make us able to wait through the bad times and enjoy the ordinariness of the small rewards we get from our work, and to bear disappointment. The long and difficult and incomplete journey is worth the effort.

Notes

1 There has been a confusion between the English 'representation' and the French 'representation'; the former usually refers to a graphic image while the latter has a wider usage. Here I am using 'representation' in a wider sense to mean idea and image.
2 It was not in fact specified that it was 'steak' and I thought it might also be 'stake', as in 'condemned to the stake', the feared punishment for that cannibalism.
3 Early analysis (1923) in *Love, Guilt and Reparation* (Klein, 1932a).
4 For a discussion of 'The sublimation debate' between Anna Freud and Kleinians see Hinshelwood (1997).
5 Segal writes:

> One of Freud's greatest contributions to psychology was the discovery that sublimation is the outcome of a successful renunciation of an instinctual aim; I would like to suggest here that such a successful renunciation can happen only through a process of mourning, This giving up of an instinctual aim, or object, is a repetition and at the same time a reliving of the giving up of the breast. It can be successful, like this first situation, if the object to be given up can be assimilated in the ego, by the process of loss and internal restoration. I suggest that such an assimilated object becomes a symbol within the ego. Every aspect of the object, every situation that has to be given up in the process of growing, gives rise to symbol formation. In this view, symbol formation is the outcome of a loss; it is a creative act involving the pain and the whole work of mourning.
>
> (Segal, 1977, p. 196)

Bibliography

Abraham, G. (1976) "The Sense and Concept of Time in Psychoanalysis". *International Review of Psychoanalysis*, 3: 461–472.

Abraham, K. (1924) "A Short Study of the Development of the Libido, Viewed in the Light of Mental Disorders". In *Selected Papers of Karl Abraham, M.D.*, trans. D. Bryan and A. Strachey. London: Hogarth Press (1942), pp. 418–501.

Aisenstein, M. (2007) "On Therapeutic Action". *Psychoanalytic Quarterly*, 76S: 1443–1461.

Aisenstein, M. and Smadja, C. (2010) "Conceptual Framework from the Paris Psychosomatic School: A Clinical Psychoanalytic Approach to Oncology". *International Journal of Psycho-Analysis*, 91: 621–640.

André, J. (1995) *Aux origines féminines de la sexualité*. Paris: PUF. Coll. (2004) *Petite Bibliothèque de psychanalyse*. Paris: PUF.

Anzieu, D. (1979) "The Sound Image of the Self". *International Review of Psychoanalysis*, 6: 23–36.

Anzieu, D. (1986) Introduction. *The International Psycho-Analytical Library*. London: The Hogarth Press and the Institute of Psycho-Analysis.

Aulagnier, P. (1975) *La violence de l'interprétation. Du Pictogramme à l'énoncé*. Presses Universitaires de France; trans. A. Sheridan (2001) *The Violence of Interpretation: From Pictogram to Statement*. New Library of Psycho-analysis. London: Routledge.

Aulagnier, P. (2015) "Birth of a Body, Origin of a History". *International Journal of Psycho-Analysis*, 96: 1371–1401. Translated from 'Naissance d'un corps, origine d'une histoire' in *Corps et histoire*. Paris: Les Belles Lettres (1986), pp. 99–141.

Avzaradel, J.R. (2011) "On the Construction of Thinking". *International Journal of Psycho-Analysis*, 92: 833–858.

Balint, E. (1973) "Technical Problems Found in the Analysis of Women by a Woman Analyst: A Contribution to the Question 'What Does a Woman Want?'" *International Journal of Psycho-Analysis*, 54: 195–201.

Barale, F. and Minazzi, V. (2008) "Off the Beaten Track: Freud, Sound and Music. Statement of a Problem and Some Historico-critical Notes". *International Journal of Psycho-Analysis*, 89: 937–957.

Baranger, M. (1993) "The Mind of the Analyst: From Listening to Interpretation", *International Journal of Psycho-Analysis*, 74: 15–24.

Baranger, M. and Baranger, W. (1961) "La situacíon analítica como campo dinámico". *Revista Uruguaya de Psicoanálisis*, 4(1): 3–54.

Baranger, M. and Baranger, W. (1969) *Problemas del campo psicoanalítico.* Buenos Aires: Ediciones Kargieman.

Baranger, M. and Baranger, W. (2008) "The Analytic Situation as a Dynamic Field". *International Journal of Psycho-Analysis*, 89: 795–826.

Baranger, M., Baranger, W. and Mom, J. (1983) "Process and Non-process in Analytic Work". *International Journal of Psycho-Analysis*, 64: 1–15.

Baranger, M., Baranger, W. and Mom, J. (1988) "The Infantile Psychic Trauma From Us to Freud: Pure Trauma, Retroactivity and Reconstruction". *International Journal of Psycho-Analysis*, 69: 113–128.

Barrows, K. (1999) "Ghosts in the Swamp". *International Journal of Psycho-Analysis*, 80: 549–561.

Barzilai, S. (1995) "Models of Reflexive Recognition". *Psychoanalytic Study of the Child*, 50: 368–382.

Bassin, D. (1982) "Woman's Images of Inner Space". *International Journal of Psycho-Analysis*, 9: 191–205.

Battin, D. and Mahon, E. (2003) "Symptom, Screen Memory, and Dream: The Complexity of Mental Representation and Disguise". *Psychoanalytic Study of the Child*, 58: 246–266.

Bayle, G., Dahan-Soussy, E. and Nayrou, F. (2010) *L'Inconscient Freudien: Recherche, écoute, métapsychologie.* Paris: Presses Universitaires de France.

Beebe, B., Lachmann, F.M. and Jaffe, J. (1997) "Mother–Infant Interaction Structures and Presymbolic Self- and Object Representations". *Psychoanalytic Dialogues*, 7: 133–182.

Bégoin, J. (1994) "Eléments masculins et éléments féminins de la croissance psychique". *Revue Française de Psychanalyse*, 58: 1707–1711.

Bene, A. (1973) "Transference Patterns in a Case of Anorexia Nervosa". Unpublished.

Berlin, I.N., Boatman, M.J., Sheimo, S.L. and Szurek, S.A. (1951) "Adolescent Alternation of Anorexia and Obesity". *American Journal of Orthopsychiatry*, 21: 387–419.

Bernardi, B.L. de (2008) "Introduction to the Paper by Madeleine and Willy Baranger: The Analytic Situation as a Dynamic Field". *International Journal of Psycho-Analysis*, 89: 773–784.

Bernstein, D. (1990) "Female Genital Anxieties, Conflicts and Typical Mastery Modes". *International Journal of Psycho-Analysis*, 71: 151–167.

Bianchedi, E.T. de (2005) "Whose Bion? Who is Bion?" *International Journal of Psycho-Analysis*, 86: 1529–1534.

Bick, F. (1968) "Experience of the Skin in Early Object Relations". International Journal of Psycho–Analysis, 49: 484–486.

Bion, W.R. (1956) "Development of Schizophrenic Thought". *International Journal of Psycho-Analysis*, 37: 344–346.

Bion, W.R. (1957a) "Attacks on Linking". *International Journal of Psycho-Analysis*, 40: 308–315.

Bion, W.R. (1957b) "Differentiation of the Psychotic from the Non-Psychotic Personalities". *International Journal of Psycho-Analysis*, 38: 266–275.

Bion, W.R. (1958) "On Hallucination". *International Journal of Psycho-Analysis*, 39: 341–349.

Bion, W.R. (1959) "Attacks on Linking". *International Journal of Psycho-Analysis*, 40: 308–315.

Bion, W.R. (1961) *Experiences in Groups And Other Papers*. London: Tavistock.

Bion, W.R. (1962a) "The Psycho–Analytic Study of Thinking". *International Journal of Psycho-Analysis*, 43: 306–310.

Bion, W.R. (1962b) *Learning from Experience*. London: Tavistock.

Bion, W.R. (1963) *Elements of Psycho-Analysis*. London: Heinemann.

Bion, W.R. (1965a) "Transformations: From Learning to Growth". In W.R. Bion (1977) *Seven Servants*. New York: Aronson, pp. 1–183.

Bion, W.R. (1965b) *Transformations*. London: Heinemann.

Bion, W.R. (1970) *Attention and Interpretation: A Scientific Approach to Insight in Psycho-Analysis and Groups*. London: Tavistock.

Bion, W.R. (1973/1974) "Brazilian Lectures". In C. Mawson (ed.) (2014) *The Complete Works of W.R. Bion*, Vol. VII. London: Karnac, pp. 1–197.

Bion, W.R. (1979a) "Making the Best of a Bad Job". In W.R. Bion *Clinical Seminars and Four Papers*. Abingdon: Fleetwood, pp. 247–257.

Bion, W.R. (1979b) *Clinical Seminars and Four Papers*. London: Karnac. Reprinted 1994.

Bion, W.R. (1992) Cogitations. London: Karnac.

Birksted-Breen, D. (1986) "The Experience of Childbirth: A Developmental View". *Free Associations*, 4.

Birksted-Breen, D. (1989) "Working with an Anorexic Patient". *International Journal of Psycho-Analysis*, 70: 29–40.

Birksted-Breen, D. (1993) *The Gender Conundrum*. New Library of Psychoanalysis. London and New York: Routledge.

Birksted-Breen, D. (1996) "Phallus, Penis and Mental Space". *International Journal of Psycho-Analysis*, 77: 649–657.

Birksted-Breen, D. (1999) Unpublished paper. Rome.

Birksted-Breen, D. (2003) "Time and the Après-coup". *International Journal of Psycho-Analysis*, 84: 1501–1515.

Birksted-Breen, D. (2006) "The Work of Interpretation". *Bulletin of the British Psychoanalytical Society*.

Birksted-Breen, D. (2008) "Introductory Forward". In D. Tuckett (ed.) *Psychoanalysis Comparable and Incomparable*. New Library of Psycho-analysis. London: Routledge, pp. 1–4.

Birksted-Breen, D. (2009) "Reverberation Time, Dreaming and the Capacity to Dream". *International Journal of Psychoanalysis*, 90: 35–51.

Birksted-Breen, D. (2010) "Is Translation Possible?" *International Journal of Psycho-Analysis*, 91: 687–694.

Birksted-Breen, D. (2012) "Taking Time: The Tempo of Psychoanalysis". *International Journal of Psycho-Analysis*, 93: 819–835.

Birksted-Breen, D., Flanders, S. and Gibeault, A. (2010) *Reading French Psychoanalysis*. The New Library of Psychoanalysis Teaching Series. Abingdon: Routledge.

Birksted-Breen, D., Mariotti, P. and Ferro, A. (2008) "Work in Progress: Using the Two Step Method". In D. Tuckett (ed.) *Psychoanalysis Comparable and Incomparable*. New Library of Psychoanalysis. London: Routledge, pp. 167–207.

Blass, R.B. (2006) "A Psychoanalytic Understanding of the Desire For Knowledge As Reflected in Freud's *Leonardo da Vinci and a Memory of his Childhood*". *International Journal of Psycho-Analysis*, 87: 1259–1276.

Blass, R.B. (2011) "On the Immediacy of Unconscious Truth: Understanding Betty Joseph's Here and Now Through Comparison with Alternative Views of it Outside and Within Kleinian Thinking". *International Journal of Psychoanalysis*, 92: 1137–1157.

Blass, R.B. (2015) "Acknowledging the Acts of Choice that Underlie Differences between Analytic Approaches as a Step Towards Meaningful Dialogue Between Them". *IPA Congress IJP Panel*.

Bleger, J. (1967) "Psycho-Analysis of the Psycho-Analytic Frame". *International Journal of Psycho-Analysis*, 48: 511–519.

Bleger, J. (2013) *Symbiosis and Ambiguity: A Psychoanalytic Study*. New York: Routledge.

Blum, H.P. (1976) "Masochism, the Ego Ideal, and the Psychology of Women". *Journal of the American Psychoanalytic Association*, 24(Suppl): 157–193.

Blum, H.P. (2005) "Psychoanalytic Reconstruction and Reintegration". *Psychoanalytic Study of the Child*, 60: 295–311.

Bohleber, W. (2002) "The Restoration of Psychoanalysis in Germany After 1945: Some Focal Points in the Development of Clinical Theory". *Psychoanalysis and History*, 4: 5–20.

Bohleber, W. (2007) "Remembrance, Trauma and Collective Memory: The Battle for Memory in Psychoanalysis". *International Journal of Psycho-Analysis*, 88: 329–352.

Bolognini, S. (1994) "Transference: Erotised, Erotic, Loving, Affectionate". *International Journal of Psycho-Analysis*, 75: 73–86.

Bonaparte, M. (1940) "Time and the Unconscious". *International Journal of Psycho-Analysis*, 21: 427–468.

Boris, H. (1984) "The Problem of Anorexia Nervosa". *International Journal of Psycho-Analysis*, 65: 315–322.

Boris, H. (1987) "Tolerating Nothing". *Contemporary Psychoanalysis*, 23: 351–365.

Boschan, P. (1990) "Temporality and Narcissism". *International Review of Psycho-Analysis*, 17: 337–349.

Botella, C. (2014), "On Remembering: The Notion of *Memory without Recollection*". *International Journal of Psychoanalysis*, 95: 911–936.

Botella, C. and Botella, S. (2001) *La Figurabilité Psychique*. Lausanne, Paris: Delachaux and Niestlé. *Psychic Figurability*, trans. A. Weller. New Library of Psychoanalysis. London: Routledge (2005).

Botella, C. and Botella, S. (2013) "Psychic Figurability and Unrepresented States". In H.B. Levine, D. Scarfone and G.B. Reed *Unrepresented States and the Construction of Meaning*. London: Karnac, pp. 95–121.

Botella, S. (2010) "De la mémoire du Ça". In G. Bayle, Dahan-Souss and F. Nayrou (eds) *L'Inconscient Freudien: Recherche, écoute, métapsychologie*. Paris: Presses Universitaires de France, pp. 161–170.

Braunschweig, D. and Fain, M. (1971a) "L'ombre phallique". In D. Braunschweig and M. Fain (2013) *Eros et Antéros – Réflexions psychanalytiques sur la sexualité*; trans. R. Bowlby (1993) "The Phallic Shadow". In D. Birksted-Breen *The Gender Conundrum: Contemporary Psychoanalytic Perspectives on Femininity and Masculinity*. New Library of Psychoanalysis. London: Brunner-Routledge, pp. 130–144.

Braunschweig, D. and Fain, M. (1971b) *Éros and antéros. Réflexions psychanalytiques sur la sexualité*. Paris: Payot.

Braunschweig, D. and Fain, M. (1975) *La nuit, le jour. Essai psychanalytique sur le fonctionnement mental.* Paris: PUR.

Brazilai, S. (1995) "Models of Reflexive Recognition". *Psychoanalytic Study of the Child,* 50: 368–382.

Breen, D. (1975) *The Birth of a First Child: Towards an Understanding of Femininity.* London: Tavistock.

Breen, D. (1981) *Talking with Mothers.* Reprinted 1999. London: Free Association Books.

Breen, D. (1993) *The Gender Conundrum.* New York: Routledge.

Brenner, C. (2000) "Brief Communication: Evenly Hovering Attention". *Psychoanalytic Quarterly,* 69: 545–549.

Breuer, J. and Freud, S. (1893) "On The Psychical Mechanism of Hysterical Phenomena". In The Standard Edition of the Complete Psychological Works of Sigmund Freud, Volume II (1893–1895): Studies on Hysteria, pp. 1–17.

Britton, R. (1989) "The Missing Link: Parental Sexuality in the Oedipus Complex". In R. Britton, M. Feldman and E. O'Shaughnessy (eds) *The Oedipus Complex Today.* London: Karnac, pp. 83–101.

Britton, R. (1994) "Publication Anxiety: Conflict Between Communication and Affiliation". *International Journal of Psycho-Analysis,* 75: 1213–1224.

Britton, R. (1995) "Psychic Reality And Unconscious Belief". *International Journal of Psycho-Analysis,* 76: 19–23.

Britton, R. (1997) "Psychic Reality And Unconscious Belief: A Reply To Harold B. Gerard". *International Journal of Psycho-Analysis,* 78: 335–339.

Britton, R. (1998a) "Introduction: Projective Identification". In R. Britton *Belief and Imagination: Explorations in Psychoanalysis.* New Library of Psychoanalysis. London: Routledge, pp. 1–7.

Britton, R. (1998b) *Belief and Imagination: Explorations in Psychoanalysis.* London: Routledge.

Britton, R. (2000) "Hyper–Subjectivity and Hyper–Objectivity in Narcissistic Disorders". *Fort Da,* 6B: 53–64.

Britton, R. (2003) *Sex, Death and the Superego.* London: Karnac.

Britton, R. and Steiner, J. (1994) "Interpretation: Selected Fact or Overvalued Idea?" *International Journal of Psycho-Analysis,* 75: 1069–1078.

Britton, R., Chused, J., Ellman, S., Likierman, M. and Bergman, A. (2006) "Panel I: Contemporary Views on Stages versus Positions". *Journal of Infant, Child and Adolescent Psychotherapy,* 5: 268–281.

Bronstein, C. (2015) "Finding Unconscious Phantasy in the Session: Recognizing Form". *International Journal of Psycho-Analysis,* 96: 925–944.

Brown, L.J. (1985) "On Concreteness". *Psychoanalytic Review*, 72: 379–402.

Bruch, H. (1974) *Eating Disorders, Obesity, Anorexia Nervosa and the Person Within*. London: Routledge & Kegan Paul.

Burgner, M. and Edgcumbe, R. (1975) "The Phallic-Narcissistic Phase". *Psychoanalytic Study of the Child*, 30: 161–180.

Busch, F. (2011) "The Workable Here and Now and the Why of There and Then". *International Journal of Psycho-Analysis*, 92: 1159–1181.

Caldwell, L. and Joyce, A. (2011) *Reading Winnicott*. London: Routledge.

Campbell, D. (1993) "The Role of the Father in Pre-Suicide States". *O*, 29(11), December.

Carlson, D.A. (2002) "Free-Swinging Attention". *Psychoanalytic Quarterly*, 71: 725–750.

Carpy, D.V. (1989) "Tolerating the Countertransference: A Mutative Process". *International Journal of Psycho-Analysis*, 70: 287–294.

Casement, P.J. (1982) "Some Pressures on the Analyst for Physical Contact During the Re-Living of an Early Trauma". *International Review of Psycho-Analysis*, 9: 279–286.

Cassorla, R.M. (2001) "Acute Enactment as a 'Resource' in Disclosing a Collusion Between the Analytical Dyad". *International Journal of Psycho-Analysis*, 82: 1155–1170.

Cassorla, R.M. (2005) "From Bastion to Enactment: The 'Non-Dream' in the Theatre of Analysis". *International Journal of Psycho-Analysis*, 86: 699–719.

Cassorla, R.M. (2008) "The Analyst's Implicit Alpha-Function, Trauma and Enactment in the Analysis of Borderline Patients". *International Journal of Psycho-Analysis*, 89: 161–180.

Cavell, M. (2000) "Reasons, Causes, and the Domain of the First-Person". In P. Fonagy, R. Michels and J. Sandler (eds) *Changing Ideas In A Changing World: The Revolution in Psychoanalysis: Essays in Honour of Arnold Cooper*. London: Karnac, pp. 207–213.

Ceglie, G.R. di (2013) "Orientation, Containment and the Emergence of Symbolic Thinking". *The International Journal of Psycho-Analysis*, 94: 1077–1091.

Chasseguet-Smirgel, J. (1964) *Female Sexuality*. London: Virago.

Chasseguet-Smirgel, J. (1976a) "Freud and Female Sexuality – The Consideration of Some Blind Spots in the Exploration of the 'Dark Continent'". *International Journal of Psycho-Analysis*, 57: 275–286.

Chasseguet-Smirgel, J. (1976b) "Freud and Female Sexuality". *International Journal of Psycho-Analysis*, 57: 94–134.

Chasseguet-Smirgel, J. (1984) "The Femininity of the Analyst in Professional Practice". *International Journal of Psycho-Analysis*, 65: 169–178.

Chasseguet-Smirgel, J. (1988) "A Woman's Attempt at a Perverse Solution and its Failure". *International Journal of Psycho-Analysis*, 69: 149–161.

Chasseguet-Smirgel, J. (1992) "Some Thoughts on the Psychoanalytic Situation". *Journal of the American Psychoanalytic Association*, 40: 3–25.

Chervet, B. (2009) "L'après-coup. La tentative d'inscrire ce qui tend a disparaître". *Revue Françise de Psychoanalyse*.

Chianese, D. (2007) *Constructions and the Analytic Field*. New Library of Psychoanalysis. Abingdon: Routledge.

Chiesa, M., Fonagy, P. and Holmes, J. (2003) "When Less is More". *International Journal of Psycho-Analysis*, 84: 637–650.

Chused, J.F. (2007) "Little Hans 'Analyzed' in the Twenty-First Century". *Journal of the American Psychoanalytic Association*, 55: 767–778.

Civitarese, G. (2005) "Fire at the Theatre". *International Journal of Psycho-Analysis*, 86: 1299–1316.

Civitarese, G. (2015) "Transformations in Hallucinosis and the Receptivity of the Analyst". *International Journal of Psycho-Analysis*, 96: 1091–1116.

Cooper, A. (2005) *The Quiet Revolution in American Psychoanalysis: Selected Papers of Arnold M. Cooper*. New York: Brunner-Routledge.

Corel, A. and Good, M.I. (2010) "A Clinical View on the Directions of Time: Here and Now, the Past in the Present, from the Present to the Past". *International Journal of Psycho-Analysis*, 91: 1220–1223.

Cournut-Janin, M. and Cournut, J. (1993) "La castration et le féminin dans les deux sexes". *Revue Française de Psychanalyse*, 57: 1353–1558.

Crisp, A. (1973) *Primary Anorexia Nervosa or Adolescent Weight Phobia*. Unpublished.

Da Rocha Barros, E.M. (2011) "Exploring Core Concepts: Sexuality, Dreams and the Unconscious". *International Journal of Psycho-Analysis*, 92: 270–272.

Da Rocha Barros, E.M. and Da Rocha Barros, E.L. (2011) "Reflections on the Clinical Implications of Symbolism". *International Journal of Psycho-Analysis*, 92: 879–901.

Denis, A. (1995) "Temporality and Modes of Language". *International Journal of Psycho-Analysis*, 76: 1109–1119.

Denis, P. (2011) "Composition et décomposition de la pulsion: emprise, satisfaction, et destructivité". *Canadian Journal of Psychoanalysis*, 19: 298–320.

Donnet, J.-L. (1995) *Le divan bien tempéré*. Paris: PUF.

Donnet, J.-L. (2001) "From the Fundamental Rule to the Analysing Situation". *International Journal of Psycho-Analysis*, 82: 129–140.

Donnet, J.-L. (2005) *La situation analysante*. Paris: Presses Universitaire de France.

Donnet, J.-L. (2010) "De L'attention en égal suspens à l'écoute métapsychologique". In G. Bayle, Dahan-Souss and F. Nayrou (eds) *L'Inconscient Freudien: Recherche, écoute, métapsychologie*. Paris: Presses Universitaires de France, pp. 129–140.

Donnet, J.-L. and Green, A. (1973) *L'enfant de Ça. Psychanalyse d'un entretien. La Psychose Blanche*. Paris: Editions de Minuit.

Doolittle, H. (1956) *Tribute to Freud*. London: Pantheon Books (1971).

Duparc, F. (2001) "The Countertransfererence Scene in France". *International Journal of Psycho-Analysis*, 82: 151–169.

Eagle, M.N. (2000) "A Critical Evaluation of Current Conceptions of Transference and Countertransference". *Psychoanalytic Psychology*, 17: 24–37.

Elise, D. (1998) "The Absence of the Paternal Penis". *Journal of the American Psychoanalytic Association*, 46: 413–442.

Eoche-Duval, B. (2009) *"Humain/Déshumain: Pierre Fédida, la parole de l'œuvre* by Pierre Fédida *et al* Paris". *International Journal of Psycho-Analysis*, 90: 930–936.

Erikson, E.H. (1964) "Woman and Inner Space". In E.H. Erikson *Identity, Youth and Crisis*. New York: Norton (1968), pp. 261–294.

Etchegoyen, H. (1991) *The Fundamentals of Psychoanalytic Technique*. London: Karnac.

Faimberg, H. (2005) *The Telescoping of Generations*. New Library of Psychoanalysis. London: Routledge.

Faimberg, H. (2014) "The Paternal Function in Winnicott: The Psychoanalytic Frame". *International Journal of Psycho-Analysis*, 95: 629–640.

Faimberg, H. and Corel, A. (1990) "Repetition and Surprise: A Clinical Approach to the Necessity of Construction and its Validation". *International Journal of Psycho-Analysis*, 71: 411–420.

Fain, M. (1971) "Prélude à la vie fantasmatique". *Revue Française de Psychanalyse*, 35: 291–364.

Fajrajzen, S. (2014) "The Compulsion to Confess and the Compulsion to Judge in the Analytic Situation". *International Journal of Psycho-Analysis*, 95: 977–993.

Falstein, E.I., Feinstein, S.C. and Judas, I. (1956) "Anorexia in the Male Child". *American Journal of Orthopsychiatry*, 26: 751–772.

Farber, S.K., Jackson, C.C., Tabin, J.K. and Bachar, E. (2007) "Death and Annihilation Anxieties in Anorexia Nervosa, Bulimia and Self Mutilation". *Psychoanalytic Psychology*, 24: 289–305.

Feldman, M. (2007) "The Illumination of History". *International Journal of Psycho-Analysis*, 88: 609–625.

Ferro, A. (1993) "The Impasse Within a Theory of the Analytic Field: Possible Vertices of Observation". *International Journal of Psycho-Analysis*, 74: 917–929.

Ferro, A. (1996) "Carla's Panic Attacks: Insight And Transformation". *International Journal of Psycho-Analysis*, 77: 997–1011.

Ferro, A. (1999) *The Bi-Personal Field*. London and New York: Routledge.

Ferro, A. (2002a) "Some Implications of Bion's Thought". *International Journal of Psycho-Analysis*, 83: 597–607.

Ferro, A. (2002b) "Superego Transformations Through the Analyst's Capacity for Reverie". *Psychoanalytic Quarterly*, 71: 477–501.

Ferro, A. (2006) "Clinical Implications of Bion's Thought". *International Journal of Psycho-Analysis*, 87: 989–1003.

Ferro, A. (2009) "Transformations in Dreaming and the Characters in the Psychoanalytic Field". *International Journal of Psycho-Analysis*, 90: 209–230.

Ferro, A. and Basile, R. (2004) "The Psychoanalyst as Individual". *Psychoanal. Q*, 73: 3–19.

Flanders, S. (2015) "On Piera Aulagnier's 'Birth of a Body, Origin of a History'". *International Journal Psychoanalysis*, 96: 1403–1415.

Fonagy, P. (1999) "Memory and Therapeutic Action". *International Journal of Psycho-Analysis*, 80: 215–223.

Fonagy, P. (2006) "Psychosexuality and Psychoanalysis: An Over View". In P. Fonagy, R. Krause and M. Leuzinger-Bohleber (eds) *Identity, Gender and Sexuality 150 years after Freud*. London: Karnac, pp. 1–20.

Fonagy, P. (2008) "A Genuinely Developmental Theory of Sexual Enjoyment and its Implications for Psychoanalytic Technique". *Journal of the American Psychoanalytic Association*, 56: 11–36.

Fonagy, P. and Target, M. (1996) "Playing with Reality: I. Theory of Mind and the Normal Development of Psychic Reality". *International Journal of Psycho-Analysis*, 77: 217–233.

Fonagy, P. and Target, M. (2004) "Playing with the Reality of Analytic Love: Commentary on Paper by Jody Messler Davies 'Falling in Love with Love'". *Psychoanalytic Dialogues*, 14: 503–515.

Freedman, N. and Lavender, J. (2002) "On Desymbolisation". *Psycho-analysis and Contemporary Thought*, 25: 165–199.

Freud, A. (1937) The Ego and the Mechanisms of Defence. London: Hogarth Press and the Institute of Psychoanalysis.

Freud, S. (1892) "Draft G Melancholia from Extracts From The Fliess Papers". In *The Standard Edition of the Complete Psychological Works of Sigmund Freud, Volume I (1886–1899): Pre-Psycho-Analytic Publications and Unpublished Drafts*, pp. 200–206.

Freud, S. (1896) "Letter 52 from Extracts from the Fliess Papers". In *The Standard Edition of the Complete Psychological Works of Sigmund Freud, Volume I (1886–1899): Pre-Psycho-Analytic Publications and Unpublished Drafts*, pp. 233–239.

Freud, S. (1897) "Letter 692 from Extracts from the Fliess Papers". In *The Standard Edition of the Complete Psychological Works of Sigmund Freud, Volume I (1886–1899): Pre-Psycho-Analytic Publications and Unpublished Drafts*, pp. 259–260.

Freud, S. (1900) "The Interpretation of Dreams". In *The Standard Edition of the Complete Psychological Works of Sigmund Freud, Volume IV (1900): The Interpretation of Dreams (First Part)*, pp. ix–627.

Freud, S. (1905) "Three Essays on the Theory of Sexuality". In *The Standard Edition of the Complete Psychological Works of Sigmund Freud, Volume VII (1901–1905): A Case of Hysteria, Three Essays on Sexuality and Other Works*, pp. 123–246.

Freud, S. (1909) "Letter from Sigmund Freud to Karl Abraham, February 18, 1909". In *The Complete Correspondence of Sigmund Freud and Karl Abraham 1907–1925*, pp. 82–84.

Freud, S. (1910) "Five Lectures on Psychoanalysis". In *The Standard Edition of the Complete Psychological Works of Sigmund Freud, Volume XI (1910): Five Lectures on Psycho-Analysis, Leonardo da Vinci and Other Works*, pp. 1–56. London: Hogarth.

Freud, S. (1912) "Recommendations to Physicians Practising Psycho-Analysis". In *The Standard Edition of the Complete Psychological Works of Sigmund Freud, Volume XII (1911–1913): The Case of Schreber, Papers on Technique and Other Works*, pp. 109–120.

Freud, S. (1913) "On Beginning the Treatment (Further Recommendations on the Technique of Psycho-Analysis I)". In *The Standard Edition of the Complete Psychological Works of Sigmund Freud, Volume XII (1911–1913): The Case of Schreber, Papers on Technique and Other Works*, pp. 121–144.

Freud, S. (1914) "Remembering, Repeating and Working-Through (Further Recommendations on the Technique of Psycho-Analysis II)". In *The Standard Edition of the Complete Psychological Works of Sigmund*

Freud, Volume XII (1911–1913): The Case of Schreber, Papers on Technique and Other Works, pp. 145–156.

Freud, S. (1915a) "Observations on Transference-Love (Further Recommendations on the Technique of Psycho-Analysis III)". In *The Standard Edition of the Complete Psychological Works of Sigmund Freud, Volume XII (1911–1913): The Case of Schreber, Papers on Technique and Other Works*, pp. 157–171.

Freud, S. (1915b) "The Unconscious". In *The Standard Edition of the Complete Psychological Works of Sigmund Freud, Volume XIV (1914–1916): On the History of the Psycho-Analytic Movement, Papers on Metapsychology and Other Works*, pp. 159–215.

Freud, S. (1920) "Beyond the Pleasure Principle". *The Standard Edition of the Complete Psychological Works of Sigmund Freud, Volume XVIII (1920–1922): Beyond the Pleasure Principle, Group Psychology and Other Works*, pp. 1–64.

Freud, S. (1921) "Group Psychology and the Analysis of the Ego". In *The Standard Edition of the Complete Psychological Works of Sigmund Freud, Volume XVIII (1920–1922): Beyond the Pleasure Principle, Group Psychology and Other Works, Standard Edition*, 18, pp. 65–144.

Freud, S. (1922) "Letter from Sigmund Freud to Arthur Schnitzler, May 14, 1922". In *Letters of Sigmund Freud 1873–1939*, pp. 339–340.

Freud, S. (1923) "Two Encyclopaedia Articles". In *The Standard Edition of the Complete Psychological Works of Sigmund Freud, Volume XVIII (1920–1922): Beyond the Pleasure Principle, Group Psychology and Other Works*, pp. 233–260.

Freud, S. (1925a) "A Note Upon the 'Mystic Writing-Pad'". In *The Standard Edition of the Complete Psychological Works of Sigmund Freud, Volume XIX (1923–1925): The Ego and the Id and Other Works*, pp. 225–232.

Freud, S. (1925b) "Some Psychical Consequences of the Anatomical Distinction between the Sexes". In *The Standard Edition of the Complete Psychological Works of Sigmund Freud, Volume XIX (1923–1925): The Ego and the Id and Other Works*, pp. 241–258.

Freud, S. (1933) "New Introductory Lectures On Psycho-Analysis". In *The Standard Edition of the Complete Psychological Works of Sigmund Freud, Volume XXII (1932–1936): New Introductory Lectures on Psycho-Analysis and Other Works*, pp. 1–182.

Freud, S. (1937) "Analysis Terminable and Interminable". In *The Standard Edition of the Complete Psychological Works of Sigmund Freud, Volume XXIII (1937–1939): Moses and Monotheism, An Outline of Psycho-Analysis and Other Works*, pp. 209–254.

Freud, S. (1938) "An Outline of Psycho-Analysis". *The Standard Edition of the Complete Psychological Works of Sigmund Freud, Volume XXIII (1937–1939): Moses and Monotheism, An Outline of Psycho-Analysis and Other Works*, pp. 139–208.

Freud, S. (1942) "Untranslated Freud – *(7) Two Encyclopædia Articles (1922)*". *International Journal of Psycho-Analysis*, 23: 97–107.

Freud, S. (1943) "Untranslated Freud – *(8) Remarks Upon the Theory and Practice of Dream-Interpretation (1923)*". *International Journal of Psycho-Analysis*, 24: 66–71.

Freud, S. (2014) [1914] "Remembering, Repeating and Working-Through (Further Recommendations on the Technique of Psycho-Analysis II)". In *The Standard Edition of the Complete Psychological Works of Sigmund Freud, Volume XII (1911–1913): The Case of Schreber, Papers on Technique and Other Works*, pp. 145–156.

Gabbard, G.O. (1995) "Countertransference: The Emerging Common Ground". *International Journal of Psycho-Analysis*, 76: 475–485.

Gaddini, E. (1969) "On Imitation". *International Journal of Psycho-Analysis*, 50: 475–484.

Galenson, E. and Roiphe, H. (1976) "Some Suggested Revisions Concerning Early Female Development". *Journal of the American Psychoanalytic Association*, 24S: 29–57.

Gibeault, A. (1988) "Du féminin et du masculin". In *Les Cahiers du Centre de Psychanalyse et de Psychotrapie*, nos 16–17. [Gibeault, A. (1988) "On the feminine and the masculine: afterthoughts on Jacqueline Cosnier's Book *Destins de la féminité*", in D. Birksted-Breen (ed.) (2003) *The Gender Conundrum: Contemporary Psychoanalytic Perspectives on Femininity and Masculinity*. London and New York: Routledge, 1993, pp. 166–185.]

Gillespie, W.H. (1969) "Concepts of Vaginal Orgasm". *International Journal of Psycho-Analysis*, 50: 495–497.

Giuffrida, A. (2008) "Is Anatomy Destiny? Metapsychological Proposals on the Femininity of Women". *The Italian Psychoanalytic Annual*, 2: 109–121.

Glasser, M. (1979) "Some Aspects of the Role of Aggression in the Perversions". In I. Rosen (ed.) *Sexual Deviation*. Oxford: Oxford University Press, pp. 278–305.

Glasser, M. (1985) " 'The Weak Spot' – Some Observations on Male Sexuality". *International Journal of Psycho-Analysis*, 66: 405–414.

Gordon, R. (1993) *Bridges, Metaphor for Psychic Processes*. London: Karnac.

Gray, P. (1982) "'Developmental Lag' in the Evolution of Technique for Psychoanalysis of Neurotic Conflict". *Journal of the American Psychoanalytic Association*, 30: 621–655.

Green, A. (1974) "Surface Analysis, Deep Analysis (The Role of the Preconscious in Psychoanalytical Technique)". *International Review of Psycho-Analysis*, 1: 415–423.

Green, A. (1975) "The Analyst, Symbolization and Absence in the Analytic Setting (On Changes in Analytic Practice and Analytic Experience) – In Memory of D.W. Winnicott". *International Journal of Psycho-Analysis*, 56: 1–22.

Green, A. (1977) "The Borderline Concept". In P. Hartocollis (ed.) *Borderline Personality Disorders*. New York: International University Press, pp. 15–44.

Green, A. (1980) "Passions and Their Vicissitudes". In *On Private Madness*. London: Hogarth, 1986. [(1980) *Passions et destins des passions. In: La folie privée*. Paris: Gallimard, 1990.]

Green, A. (1986) *On Private Madness*. London: The Hogarth Press.

Green, A. (1993) *Le travail du négatif*. Paris: Editions Minuit.

Green, A. (1995) "Has Sexuality Anything to do with Psychoanalysis?", *International Journal of Psycho-Analysis*,76: 871–883.

Green, A. (1997a) "Opening Remarks to a Discussion of Sexuality in Contemporary Psychoanalysis". *International Journal of Psycho-Analysis*, 78: 345–350.

Green, A. (1997b) "The Intuition Of The Negative In Playing And Reality". *International Journal of Psycho-Analysis*, 78: 1071–1084.

Green, A. (1998) "The Primordial Mind and the Work of the Negative". *International Journal of Psycho-Analysis*, 79: 649–665.

Green, A. (1999) "Passivité-passivation: jouissance et détresse". *Revue Française de Psychanalyse*, 63, no. 5, Spécial congrès. Paris: PUF.

Green, A. (2000a) "Commentary". *Journal of the American Psychoanalytic Association*, 48: 57–66.

Green, A. (2000b) "The Central Phobic Position: A New Formulation of the Free Association Method". *International Journal of Psycho-Analysis*, 88: 1441–1456.

Green, A. (2002a) *Time in Psychoanalysis: Some Contradictory Aspects*. London: Free Association Books.

Green, A. (2002b) *Idées directrices*. Paris: PUF.

Green, A. (2005) *Key Ideas for a Contemporary Psychoanalysis: Misrecognition and Recognition of the Unconscious*. New Library of Psychoanalysis. London: Routledge.

260

Green, A. (2010) "Vie et mort de l'inconscient freudien". In G. Bayle, Dahan-Souss and F. Nayrou (eds) *L'Inconscient Freudien: Recherche, écoute, métapsychologie*. Paris: Presses Universitaires de France, pp. 151–159.

Green, A. (2011) *Illusions et Desillusions du Travail Psychanalytique*. Paris: Odile Jacob. [*Illusions and Disillusions of Psychoanalytic Work*. London: Karnac.]

Green, A. (2012a) "On Construction in Freud's Work". *International Journal of Psycho-Analysis*, 93: 1238–1248.

Green, A. (2012b) *La Clinique Contemporaine*. Montreuil: Edition Ithaque.

Greenacre, P. (1953) "Certain Relationships Between Fetishism and Faulty Development of the Body Image". *Psychoanalytic Study of the Child*, 8: 79–98.

Greenberg, D.E. (1990) "Instinct and Primary Narcissism in Freud's Later Theory: An Interpretation and Reformulation of 'Beyond the Pleasure Principle'". *International Journal of Psycho-Analysis*, 71: 271–283.

Grinberg, L. (1962) "On a Specific Aspect of Countertransference Due to the Patient's Projective Identification". *International Journal of Psycho-Analysis*, 43: 436–440.

Grinberg, L. (1980) "The Closing Phase of the Psychoanalytic Treatment of Adults and the Goals of Psychoanalysis 'The Search for Truth about One's Self' ". *International Journal of Psycho-Analysis*, 61: 25–37.

Grinberg, L. (1987) "Dreams and Acting Out". *Psychoanalytic Quarterly*, 56: 155–176.

Grinberg, L. (1995) "Nonverbal Communication In The Clinic With Borderline Patients". *Contemporary Psychoanalysis*, 31: 92.

Grinberg, L. and Grinberg, R. (1981) "Modalities of Object Relationships in the Psychoanalytic Process". *Contemporary Psychoanalysis*, 17: 290–320.

Grossman, W.I. and Stewart, W.A. (1976) "Penis Envy: From Childhood Wish to Developmental Metaphor". *Journal of the American Psychoanalytic Association*, 24(Suppl.): 193–212.

Grotstein, J.S. (2005) " 'Projective Transidentification': An Extension of the Concept of Projective Identification". *International Journal of Psycho-Analysis*, 86: 1051–1069.

Grunberger, B. (1964) "Outline for a Study of Narcissism in Female Sexuality". In J. Chasseguet-Smirgel (ed.) *Female Sexuality*. London: Virago, 1981, pp. 68–83.

Gubrich-Simitis, I. (1997) *Early Freud, Late Freud*. New Library of Psychoanalysis. London: Routledge.

Gyler, L. (2010) *The Gendered Unconscious*. London: Routledge.

Hartocollis, P. (1974) "Origins of Time: A Reconstruction of the Ontogenetic Development of the Sense of Time Based on Object-Relations Theory". *Psychoanalytic Quarterly*, 43: 243–261.

Hartocollis, P. (1980) "Time and the Dream". *Journal of the American Psychoanalytic Association*, 28: 861–877.

Head, H. (1920) *Studies in Neurology*. London: Oxford University Press.

Heimann, P. (1950) "On Counter-Transference". *International Journal of Psycho-Analysis*, 31: 81–84.

Hinshelwood, R.D. (1997) "The Elusive Concept Of 'Internal Objects' (1934–1943): Its Role In The Formation Of The Klein Group". *International Journal of Psycho-Analysis*, 78: 877–897.

Hinshelwood, R.D. (2008) "Melanie Klein and Countertransference: A Note on Some Archival Material". *Psychoanalytical History*, 10: 95–113.

Hinz, H. (2012) "Constructions in Psychoanalysis: On the 'Assured Conviction of the Truth of a Construction". *International Journal of Psycho-Analysis*, 93: 1266–1283.

Hock, U. (2014) "Plea for the Unity of the Freudian Theory of Memory". *International Journal of Psycho-Analysis*, 95: 937–950.

Hoffman, I.Z. (2006) "The Myths of Free Association and the Potentials of the Analytic Relationship". *International Journal of Psycho-Analysis*, 87: 43–61.

Horney, K. (1926) "The Flight from Womanhood. The Masculinity Complex in Women as Viewed by Men and by Women". In K. Horney (1967) *Feminine Psychology*, edited by Harold Kelman. New York: Norton & Co, pp. 54–70.

Hughes, A., Furgiuele, P. and Bianco, M. (1985) "Aspects of Anorexia Nervosa in the Therapy of Two Adolescents". *Journal of Child Psychotherapy*, 11(1): 17–32.

"Introductory Memoir" (1989) In M. Tonnesmann (ed.) *About Children and Children-No-Longer: Collected Papers 1942–80*. London: Routledge.

Irigaray, L. (1985) *The Speculum of the Other Woman*, trans. B.C. Till. Ithaca, NY: Cornell University Press.

Isaacs, S. (1948) "The Nature and Function of Phantasy". *International Journal of Psycho-Analysis*, 29: 73–97.

Ithier, B. (2005) "La fonction métaphorisante de l'interprétation comme sublimation du lien". *Revue Française de Psychanalyse*, 69(5): 1739–1745.

Ithier, B. (2016) "The Arms of the Chimera". *International Journal of Psycho-Analysis*, doi: 10.1111/1745-8315.12401.

Jacobs, T.J. (1999) "Countertransference Past And Present". *International Journal of Psycho-Analysis*, 80: 575–594.

Jessner, J. and Abse, D.W. (1960) "Regressive forces in anorexia nervosa". *British Journal of Medical Psychology*, 33: 301–312.

Jones, E. (1927) "The Early Development of Female Sexuality". *International Journal of Psycho-Analysis*, 8: 459–472.

Jones, E. (1935) "Early Female Sexuality". *International Journal of Psycho-Analysis*, 16: 263–273.

Joseph, B. (1985) "Transference: The Total Situation". *International Journal of Psycho-Analysis*, 66: 447–454. Also in E.B. Spillius and M. Feldman, M. (1989) *Psychic Equilibrium and Psychic Change*. London: Routledge.

Kestemberg, E., Kestemberg, J. and Decorbert, S. (1972) *La Faim et le Corps*. Paris: PUF.

Kestenberg, J.S. (1980) "The Three Faces of Femininity". *Psychoanalytic Review*, 67: 313–335.

Khan, M.R. (1964) "Ego Distortion, Cumulative Trauma, and the Role of Reconstruction in the Analytic Situation". *International Journal of Psycho-Analysis*, 45: 272–279.

King, P. (1989) "Paula Heimann's Quest for her Own Identity as a Psychoanalyst: An Introductory Memoir". In M. Tonnesmann (ed.) *About Children and Children-No-Longer, Collected Papers 1942–80. Paula Heimann*. London: Tavistock/Routledge, pp. 1–7.

Klauber, J. (1981) *Difficulties in the Analytic Encounter*. London: Free Association Books.

Kleeman, J.A. (1976) "Freud's Views on Early Female Sexuality in the Light of Direct Child Observation". *Journal of the American Psychoanalytic Association*, 24S: 3–26.

Klein, M. (1923) "Early Analysis". In M. Klein (1975) *Love, Guilt and Reparation: And Other Works 1921–1945*. London: Hogarth Press, pp. 77–105.

Klein, M. (1926) "Infant Analysis". *International Journal of Psycho-Analysis*, 7: 31–63.

Klein, M. (1928) "Early Stages of the Oedipus Conflict". *International Journal of Psycho-Analysis*, 9: 167–180.

Klein, M. (1932a) "The Oedipus Complex in the Light of Early Anxieties. In M. Klein (1975) *Love, Guilt and Reparation: And Other Works 1921–1945*. London: Hogarth Press, pp. 344–369.

Klein, M. (1932b) "The Effects of Early Anxiety-Situations on the Sexual Development of the Boy". In M. Klein (1980) *The Psychoanalysis of Children*. London: Hogarth Press, pp. 240–278.

Klein, M. (1932c) "The Psycho-Analysis of Children". *The International Psycho-Analytical Library*, 22: 1–379. London: Hogarth Press.

Klein, M. (1946) "Notes on Some Schizoid Mechanisms". *International Journal of Psycho-Analysis*, 27: 99–110.

Klein, M. (1952) "The Origins of Transference". *International Journal of Psycho-Analysis*, 33: 433–438.

Klein, M. (1961) *Narrative of a Child Analysis*. London: Hogarth Press.

Klein, M. (1975) *Envy and Gratitude*. London: Hogarth Press.

Kohon, G. (1987) "Fetishism Revisited". *International Journal of Psycho-Analysis*, 68: 213–229.

Kohut, H. (1968) "The Psychoanalytic Treatment of Narcissistic Personality Disorders – *Outline of a Systematic Approach*". *Psychoanalytic Study of the Child*, 23: 86–113.

Kris, E. (1956) "The Personal Myth – A Problem in Psychoanalytic Technique". *Journal of the American Psychoanalytic Association*, 4: 653–681.

Kristeva, J. (2007) " 'Speech in Psychoanalysis' From Symbols to the Flesh and Back". In D. Birksted-Breen, S. Flanders and A. Gibeault (2010) *Reading French Psychoanalysis*. New Library of Psychoanalysis. London: Routledge, pp. 421–433.

Künstlicher, R. (2001) "Human Time and Dreaming". *Scandinavian Psychoanalytic Review*, 24: 75–82.

Kurth, F. and Patterson, A. (1968) "Structuring Aspects of the Penis". *International Journal of Psycho-Analysis*, 49: 620–628.

Lacan, J. (1966) *Écrits*. London: Tavistock.

LaFarge, L. (2012) "The Screen Memory and the Act of Remembering". *International Journal of Psycho-Analysis*, 93: 1249–1265.

Lander, J. (1953) "Meetings of the New York Psychoanalytic Society". *Psychoanalytic Quarterly*, 22: 469–470.

Laplanche, J. (1974) "Panel on 'Hysteria Today' ". *International Journal of Psycho-Analysis*, 55: 459–469.

Laplanche, J. (1980) *Castrations, Symbolisations*. Paris: PUF.

Laplanche, J. (1992) "Transference: Its Provocation by the Analyst". In D. Birksted-Breen, S. Flanders and A. Gibeault (eds) (2010) *Reading French Psychoanalysis*. The New Library of Psychoanalysis Teaching Series. Abingdon: Routledge, pp. 233–250.

Laplanche, J. (1995) "Seduction, Persecution, Revelation". *International Journal of Psycho-Analysis*, 76: 663–682.

Laplanche, J. (1997) "The Theory of Seduction and the Problem of the Other". *International Journal of Psycho-Analysis*, 78: 653–666.

Laplanche, J. (1998a) *Essays on Otherness*. Abingdon: Taylor and Francis.

Laplanche, J. (1998b) *Notes sur l'après-coup. Standing Conference on Psychoanalytical Intracultural and Intercultural Dialogue*. Paris, 27–29 July.

Laplanche, J. (2007) "Gender, Sex, and the Sexual". *Studies in Gender and Sexuality*, 8: 201–219.

Laplanche, J. and Pontalis, J.B. (1967) *The Language of Psycho-Analysis*, trans. D. Nicholson-Smith (1973). New York: Norton.

Laplanche, J. and Pontalis, J.B. (1968) "Fantasy and the Origins of Sexuality". *International Journal of Psycho-Analysis*, 49: 1–18.

Laplanche, J. and Pontalis, J.B. (1973) *The Language of Psychoanalysis*. London: Hogarth Press.

Laub, D. and Lee, S. (2003) "Thanatos and Massive Psychic Trauma: The Impact of the Death Instinct on Knowing, Remembering and Forgetting". *Journal of the American Psychoanalytic Association*, 51: 433–463.

Laufer, E. (2009) "Now and Then". *Psychoanalytic Inquiry*, 29: 277–287.

Laufer, M.E. (1982) "Female Masturbation in Adolescence and the Development to the Relationship to the Body". *International Journal of Psycho-Analysis*, 63: 295–302.

Laufer, M.E. (1986) "The Female Oedipus Complex and the Relationship to the Body". *Psychoanalytic Study of the Child*, 41: 259–277.

Laufer, M.E. (1994) "Formulation of Interpretation – From Truth to Experience". *International Journal of Psycho-Analysis*, 75: 1093–1105.

Laufer, M.E. (1996) "The Role of Passivity in the Relationship to the Body during Adolescence". *Psychoanalytic Study of the Child*, 51: 348–364.

Lawrence, M. (2001) "Figures of Lightness. Anorexia, Bulimia and Psychoanalysis". *International Journal of Psycho-Analysis*, 82: 625–627.

Lawrence, M. (2002) "Body, Mother, Mind". *International Journal of Psycho-Analysis*, 83: 837–850.

Le Guen, C. (2008) *Dictionnaire Freudien*. Paris: Presses Universitaires de France.

Leach, E. (1953 [1961]) "Cronus and Chronos". In S. Hugh-Jones and J. Laidlaw (eds) (2001) *The Essential Edmund Leach*. New Haven, CT: Yale University Press, pp. 174–181.

Leach, E. (1955 [1961]) "Time and False Noses". In S.Hugh-Jones and J. Laidlaw (eds) (2001) *The Essential Edmund Leach*. New Haven, CT: Yale Univesity Press, pp. 182–185.

Lefebvre, H. (2000) *La production de l'espace*. Paris: Anthropos.

Lemma, A. (2009) "Being Seen or Being Watched? A Psychoanalytic Perspective on Body Dysmorphia". *International Journal of Psycho-Analysis*, 90: 753–771.

Lemma, A. (2013) "The Body One has and the Body One is: Understanding the Transsexual's Need to be Seen". *International Journal of Psycho-Analysis*, 94: 277–292.

Lerner, H.E. (1976) "Parental Mislabeling of Female Genitals as a Determinant of Penis Envy and Learning Inhibitions in Women". *Journal of the American Psychoanalytic Association*, 24S: 269–283.

Lester, E.P. (1976) "On the Psychosexual Development of the Female Child". *Journal of the American Academy of Psychoanalysis*, 4: 515–527.

Leuzinger-Bohleber, M. (2008) "Biographical Truths and their Clinical Consequences: Understanding 'Embodied Memories' in a Third Psychoanalysis with a Traumatized Patient Recovered from Severe Poliomyelitis". *International Journal of Psycho-Analysis*, 89: 1165–1187.

Levine, H.B. and Friedman, R.J. (2000) "Intersubjectivity and Interaction in the Analytic Relationship". *Psychoanalytic Quarterly*, 69: 63–92.

Lewin, B.D. (1946) "Sleep, the Mouth and the Dream Screen". *Psychoanalytic Quarterly*, 15: 419–434.

Lewin, B.D. (1955) "Dream Psychology and the Analytic Situation". *Psychoanalytic Quarterly*, 24: 169–199.

Lewkowicz, D. (1989) "The Role of Temporal Factors in Infant Behavior and Development". In I. Levin and D. Zakay (eds) *Time and Human Cognition: A Life-Span Perspective*. Amsterdam: North-Holland, pp. 9–62.

Lichtenberg, J.D. (2003) "Communication in Infancy". *Psychoanalytic Inquiry*, 23: 498–520.

Limentani, A. (1991) "Neglected Fathers in the Aetiology and Treatment of Sexual Deviation". *International Journal of Psycho-Analysis*, 72: 573–584.

Litowitz, B. (2013) "From Switch-Words to Stich-Words". *International Journal of Psycho-Analysis*, 95: 3–13.

Lucas, R. (2001) "On Lawrence's 'Loving Them to Death'". *International Journal of Psycho-Analysis*, 82: 601–602.

Mahon, E. and Battin, D. (1981) "Screen Memories and Termination". *Journal of the American Psychoanalytic Association*, 29: 939–942.

Makari, G.J. (1997) "Current Conceptions Of Neutrality And Abstinence". *Journal of American Psychoanalytical Assessments*, 45: 1231–1239.

Mancia, M. (2003) "Dream Actors in the Theatre of Memory: Their Role in the Psychoanalytic Process". *International Journal of Psycho-Analysis*, 84: 945–952.

Mancia, M. (2004) *Sentire le paroli*. Turin: Bollati Boringhieri. Trans. J. Baggot (2006) *Feeling the Words: Neuropsychoanalytic Understanding of Memory and the Unconscious*. New Library of Psychoanalysis. London: Routledge.

Marty, P. and De M'Uzan, M. (1963) "La 'pensée opératoire'". Revue Française, 27(Suppl.): 345–356.

Masi, F. de (2015) "Delusion and Bi-Ocular Vision". *International Journal of Psycho-Analysis*, 96: 1189–1211.

Matte-Blanco, I. (1988) "Thinking, Feeling, and Being". *New Library of Psycho-Analysis*, 5: 1–336. London and New York: Tavistock/Routledge.

Mayer, E.L. (1985) "Everybody Must Be Just Like Me: Observations on Castration Anxiety". *International Journal of Psycho-Analysis*, 66: 331–349.

McDougall, J. (1974) "The Psychosoma and the Psychoanalytic Process". *International Review of Psycho-Analysis*, 1: 437–459.

McDougall, J. (1978) Plaidoyer pour une certaine anormalité. Paris: Gallimard. [Plea for a Measure of Abnormality. New York: International University Press, 1980.]

McDougall, J. (1985) *Theatres of the Mind*. London: Free Association Books.

McDougall, J. (1993) "Of Sleep and Dream". *International Forum of Psychoanalysis,* 2: 204–218.

McDougall, J. (2000) "Sexuality and the Neosexual". *Modern Psychoanalysis*, 25: 155–166.

Mehler, J.A. and Argentieri, S. (1989) "Hope and Hopelessness: A Technical Problem?" *International Journal of Psycho-Analysis*, 70: 295–304.

Meissner, W.W. (2005) "Gender Identity and the Self: I. Gender Formation in General and in Masculinity". *Psychoanalytic Review*, 92: 1–27.

Meltzer, D.W. (1967) *The Psycho-Analytic Process*. London: Heinemann.

Menzies-Lyth, I. (2004) Personal communication.

Mijolla, A. de (ed.) (2002) *Dictionnaire international de la psychanalyse*. Paris: Caiman-Levy.

Milner, M. (1952) "Aspects of Symbolism in Comprehension of the Not-Self". *International Journal of Psycho-Analysis*, 33: 181–194.

Milner, M. (2011) *On Not Being Able to Paint*. London: Routledge.

Minuchin, S., Rosman, B. and Baker, L. (1978) *Psychosomatic Families: Anorexia Nervosa in Context*. New York: Harvard University Press.

Mitchell, J. and Rose, J. (1982) *Feminine Sexuality*. London: Macmillan.

Mitrani, J. (2001) "Taking the Transference". *International Journal of Psycho-Analysis*, 82: 1085–1104. Also in J. Mitrani (2001) *Ordinary People and Extra-Ordinary Protections*. New Library of Psychoanalysis. Hove: Brunner-Routledge.

Momigliano, L.N. (1988) "The Setting: A Theme with Variations". *Rivista di Psicoanalisi*, 34(4): 604–682.

Money-Kyrle, R. (1968) "Cognitive Development". *International Journal of Psycho-Analysis*, 49: 691–698.

Money-Kyrle, R. (1971) "The Aim of Psychoanalysis". *International Journal of Psycho-Analysis*, 52: 103–106.

Morris, H. (1993) "Narrative Representation, Narrative Enactment, and the Psychoanalytic Construction of History". *International Journal of Psycho-Analysis*, 74: 33–54.

M'Uzan, M. de (1983) "Interpréter: pour qui, pourquoi?" *Revue Francaise Psychoanalyse*, 47: 784–793.

M'Uzan, M. de (1994) *La bouche de l'inconscient*. Paris: Gallimard.

M'Uzan, M. de (1994) *La bouche de l'inconscient* [The mouth of the unconscious]. Paris: Gallimard.

M'Uzan, M. de (2005) *Aux confins de l'identité*. Paris: Gallimard.

M'Uzan, M. de (2007) "The Same and the Identical". *Psychoanalytic Quarterly*, 76: 1205–1220.

M'Uzan, M. de (2009) *L'inquiétante étrangeté ou "je ne suis pas celle que vous croyez"*. Paris: PUF.

M'Uzan, M. de (2010) "The Uncanny, or 'I Am Not Who You Think I Am'". In D. Birksted-Breen, S. Flanders and A. Gibeault (eds) (2009) *Reading French Psychoanalysis*. New Library of Psychoanalysis. London: Routledge, pp. 201–209.

Neyraut, M. (1974) *Le transfert*. Paris: Presses Universitaires de France.

Noel-Smith, K. (2002) "Time and Space as 'Necessary Forms of Thought'". *Free Associations*, 9: 394–442.

Novey, S. (1968). *The Second Look*. Baltimore, MD: Johns Hopkins University Press.

O'Shaughnessy, E. (1992) "Enclaves and Excursions". *International Journal of Psycho-Analysis*, 73: 603–611.

Ogden, T.H. (1994) "The Analytic Third: Working with Intersubjective Clinical Facts". *International Journal of Psycho-Analysis*, 75: 3–19.

Ogden, T.H. (1997a) "Reverie and Interpretation". *Psychoanalytic Quarterly*, 66: 567–595.

Ogden, T.H. (1997b) "Reverie and Metaphor: Some Thoughts on How I Work as a Psychoanalyst". *International Journal of Psycho-Analysis*, 78: 719–732.

Ogden, T. (1999) "The Music of What Happens in Poetry and Psychoanalysis". *International Journal of Psycho-Analysis*, 80: 979–994.

Ogden, T. (2004a) "On Holding and Containing, Being and Dreaming". *International Journal of Psycho-Analysis*, 85: 1349–1364.

Ogden, T. (2004b) "The Analytic Third". *Psychoanal. Q.*, 73: 167–195.

Olmos de Paz (2012) "La Sexualidad Masculina y sus vicisitudes". *Revista de Psicoanalisis de la Asociacion Psicoanalitica de Madrid*, 66: 155–172.

Orgel, S. (2000) "Letting Go". *Journal of the American Psychoanalytic Association*, 48: 719–738.

Palazzoli, S. (1978) *Self Starvation in the Treatment of Anorexia Nervosa.* New York: Jason Aronson.

Parat, C. (1995) "Le phallique féminin". *Revue Française de Psychanalyse*, 59: 1236–1259.

Parens, H., Pollock, L., Stern, J. and Kramer, S. (1976) "On the Girl's Entry into the Oedipus Complex". *Journal of the American Psychoanalytic Association*, 24(Suppl.): 79–109.

Parker, A. (1986) "Mom". *Oxford Literary Review*, 8: 96–104.

Parsons, M. (2000) *The Dove that Returns, the Dove that Vanishes.* The New Library of Psychoanalysis. London: Routledge.

Parsons, M. (2007) "Raiding the Inarticulate: The Internal Analytic Setting and Listening Beyond Countertransference". *International Journal of Psycho-Analysis*, 88: 1441–1456.

Penot, B. (2005) "Psychoanalytical Teamwork in a Day Hospital". *International Journal of Psycho-Analysis*, 86: 503–515.

Perelberg, R. (2008) *Time, Space and Phantasy.* New Library of Psychoanalysis. London: Routledge.

Perelberg, R.J. (1997) "To Be – Or Not to Be – Here: A Woman's Denial of Time and Memory". In J. Raphael-Leff and J. Perelberg (eds) (1998) *Female Experience.* London and New York: Routledge, pp. 60–76.

Perelberg, R.J. (2003) "Full and Empty Spaces in the Analytic Process". *International Journal of Psycho-Analysis*, 84: 579–592.

Perelberg, R.J. (2006) "The Controversial Discussions and *après-coup*". *International Journal of Psycho-Analysis*, 87: 1199–1220.

Perelberg, R.J. (2011) "'A Father is Being Beaten': Constructions in the Analysis of Some Male Patients". *International Journal of Psycho-Analysis*, 92: 97–116.

Perelberg R.J. (2015) "On Excess, Trauma and Helplessness: Repetition and Transformations". *International Journal of Psycho-Analysis*, 96: 1453–1476.

Perelberg, R.J. and Jozef, B. (2002) "Temps et mémoire dans cent ans de solitude". In C. Botella (ed.) *Penser les limites: Ecrits en l'honneur d'André Green.* Paris: Delachaux and Niestlé, pp. 382–390.

Piaget, J. (1954) *The Construction of Reality in the Child.* New York: Basic Books.

Pichon-Riviere, E. (1958) "Referential Schema and Dialectical Process in Spiral as Basis to a Problem of the Past". *International Journal of Psycho-Analysis*, 39: 294 (abstract).

Pines, D. (1982) "The Relevance of Early Psychic Development to Pregnancy and Abortion". *International Journal of Psycho-Analysis*, 63: 311–319.

Pines, D. (1993) *A Woman's Unconscious Use of Her Body: A Psychoanalytic Perspective*. London: Virago.

Pontalis, J.B. (1974) "Dream as an Object". *International Review of Psycho-analysis*, 1: 125–133.

Potamianou, A. (1997) *Hope: A Shield in the Economy of Borderline States*. New Library of Psycho-Analysis. London: Routledge.

Potamianou, A. (2015) "Amnemonic Traces: Traumatic After-Effects". *International Journal of Psycho-Analysis*, 96: 945–966.

Quinodoz, D. (1992) "The Psychoanalytic Setting as the Instrument of the Container Function". *International Journal of Psycho-Analysis*, 73: 627–635.

Quinodoz, J.-M. (1991) *La solitude apprivoisée*. Paris: Presses Universitaire France; trans. P. Slotkin (1993) *The Taming of Solitude*. London and New York: Routledge.

Racker, H. (1953) "A Contribution to the Problem of Counter-Transference". *International Journal of Psycho-Analysis*, 34: 313–324.

Racker, H. (1957) "The Meanings and Uses of Countertransference". *Psychoanalytic Quarterly*, 26: 303–357.

Racker, H. (1958) "Psychoanalytic Technique and the Analyst's Unconscious Masochism". *Psychoanalytic Quarterly*, 27: 555–562.

Rey, H. (1986) "The Schizoid Mode of Being and the Space–Time Continuum (Beyond Metaphor)". *Journal of the Melanie Klein Society*, 4: 12–52.

Rey, H. (1994) *Universals of Psychoanalysis in the Treatment of Borderline and Psychotic Patients*. London: Free Association Books.

Richards, A.K. (1994) "Primary Femininity and Female Genital Anxiety". *Journal of the American Psychoanalytic Association*, 44(Suppl.): 261–281.

Riesenberg-Malcolm, R. (1990) "As If: The Phenomenon of not Learning". *International Journal of Psycho-Analysis*, 71: 385–392. Reprinted in R. Riesenberg-Malcolm and P. Roth (eds) (1999) *On Bearing Unbearable States of Mind*. London: Routledge.

Ripa di Meana, G. (1999) *Figures of Lightness. Anorexia, Bulimia and Psychoanalysis*. London: Jessica Kingsley.

Riviere, J. (1929) "Womanliness as a Masquerade". *International Journal of Psycho-Analysis*, 10: 303–313.

Roiphe, H. and Galenson, E. (1981) *Infantile Origins of Sexual Identity*. New York: International University Press.

Rose, J. (1997) "Distortions of Time in the Transference". *International Journal of Psycho-Analysis*, 78: 453–468.

Rosenfeld, H. (1971) "A Clinical Approach to the Psychoanalytic Theory of the Life and Death Instincts: An Investigation Into the Aggressive Aspects of Narcissism". *International Journal of Psycho-Analysis*, 52: 169–178.

Rosenfeld, H. (1987) *Impasse and Interpretation: Therapeutic and Anti-Therapeutic Factors in the Psychoanalytic Treatment of Psychotic, Borderline, and Neurotic Patients*. New Library of Psychoanalysis. London: Tavistock.

Roth, P. (2001) "Mapping the Landscape: Levels of Transference Interpretation". *International Journal of Psycho-Analysis*, 82: 532–543.

Roth, P. (2009) "Where Else? Considering the Here and Now". *Bulletin of the British Psychoanalytic Society*, 45: 113–122.

Roussillon, R. (2011) *Primitive Agony and Symbolization*. London: Karnac.

Rycroft, C. (1958) "An Enquiry Into the Function of Words in the Psycho-Analytical Situation". *International Journal of Psycho-Analysis*, 39: 408–415.

Sabbadini, A. (1989) "Boundaries of Timelessness. Some Thoughts about the Temporal Dimension of the Psychoanalytic Space". *International Journal of Psycho-Analysis*, 70: 305–313.

Sandler, J. (1983) "Reflections on Some Relations Between Psychoanalytic Concepts and Psychoanalytic Practice". *International Journal of Psycho-Analysis*, 64: 35–45.

Sandler, J. (1990) "On the Structure of Internal Objects and Internal Object Relationships". *Psychoanalytic Inquiry*, 10: 163–181.

Sandler, J. (1993) On Communication from Patient to Analyst: Not Everything is Projective Identification". *International Journal of Psycho-Analysis*, 74: 1097–1107.

Sandler, J. (2003) "On Attachment to Internal Objects". *Psychoanalytic Inquiry*, 23: 12–26.

Sandler, J. and Rosenblatt, B. (1962) "The Concept of the Representational World". *Psychoanalytic Study of the Child*, 17: 128–145.

Sandler, J. and Sandler, A. (1994) "The Past Unconscious and the Present Unconscious". *Psychoanalytic Study of the Child*, 49: 278–292.

Scarfone, D. (2014) "L'impassé , actualité de l'inconscient". *Congrés des psychanalystes de langue française*, Montreal.

Schachter, J. (1992) "Concepts of Termination and Post-Termination Patient–Analyst Contact". *International Journal of Psycho-Analysis*, 73: 137–154.

Schaeffer, J. (1997) *Le refus du féminin*. Paris: PUF.

Schilder, P. (1942) "The Body Image in Dreams". *Psychoanalytic Review*, 29: 113–126.

Schneider, M. (2002) "Feminité". In A. De Mijolla (ed.) *Dictionnaire International de la Psychanalyse*. Paris: Calmann-Levy, pp. 598–600.

Schwartz, H. (1986) "Bulimia: Psychoanalytic Perspectives". *Journal of the American Psychoanalytic Association*, 34(2): 439–463.

Scott, W.M. (1958) "Noise, Speech and Technique". *International Journal of Psycho-Analysis*, 39: 108–111.

Segal, H. (1957) "Notes on Symbol Formation". *International Journal of Psycho-Analysis*, 38: 391–397. Also in *The Work of Hanna Segal*. London: Jason Aronson, 1981, pp. 49–65.

Segal, H. (1962) "The Curative Factors in Psycho-Analysis". *International Journal of Psycho-Analysis*, 43: 212–217.

Segal, H. (1977) *The Work of Hanna Segal: A Kleinian Approach to Clinical Practice*. New York and London: Jason Aronson.

Segal, H. (1981) "The Function of Dreams". In H. Segal *The Work of Hanna Segal: A Kleinian Approach to Clinical Practice*. New York and London: Jason Aronson, pp. 89–100.

Segal, H. (1982) "Early Infantile Development as Reflected in the Psychoanalytical Process: Steps in Integration". *International Journal of Psycho-Analysis*, 63: 15–22.

Segal, H. (1988) "Sweating It Out. Psychoanalytic Study of the Child". *International Journal of Psycho-Analysis*, 43: 167–175.

Segal, H. (1993) "On the Clinical Usefulness of the Concept of Death Instinct". *International Journal of Psycho-Analysis*, 74: 55–61.

Segal, H. (1994) "Phantasy and Reality". *International Journal of Psycho-Analysis*, 75: 395–401.

Segal, H. (2007) *Yesterday, Today and Tomorrow*. New Library of Psychoanalysis. London: Routledge.

Sharpe, E.F. (1940) "Psycho-Physical Problems Revealed in Language: An Examination of Metaphor". *International Journal of Psycho-Analysis*, 21: 201–213.

Sirois, F. (2012) "The Role and Importance of Interpretation in the Talking Cure". *International Journal of Psycho-Analysis*, 93: 1377–1402.

Sirois, F. (2014) "The Personal Myth: A Re-Evaluation". *International Journal of Psycho-Analysis*, 95: 271–289.

Smith, H.F. (1995) "Analytic Listening and the Experience Of Surprise". *International Journal of Psycho-Analysis*, 76: 67–78.

Sodre, I. (1997) "Insight and Après-Coup". *Revue Française de Psychana-lyse*, 61A: 255–262.

Sohn, L. (1985a) "Anorexic and Bulimic States of Mind in the Psychoan-alytic Treatment of Anorexic/Bulimic Patients and Psychotic Patients". *Psychoanalytic Psychotherapy*, 1: 49–56.

Sohn, L. (1985b) "Narcissistic Organization, Projective Identification, and the Formation of the Identificate". *International Journal of Psycho-Analysis*, 66: 201–213.

Sours, J. (1974) "The Anorexia Nervosa Syndrome". *International Journal of Psycho-Analysis*, 55: 567–576.

Spence, D.P. (1982) *Narrative Truth and Historical Truth: Meaning and Inter-pretation in Psychoanalysis*. London and New York: W.W. Norton.

Spillius, E. (1973) "Anorexia in Analysis". Unpublished.

Spillius, E.B. (1992) "Clinical Experiences of Projective Identification". In R. Anderson (ed.) *Clinical Lectures on Klein and Bion*. New Library of Psychoanalysis. London: Routledge, pp. 59–73.

Spillius, E.B. (2004) Melanie Klein Revisited: Her Unpublished Thoughts on Technique". *International Journal of Psycho-Analysis*, 40: 13–28.

Spillius, E.B., Milton, J., Garvey, P., Couve, C. and Steiner, D. (2011) *The New Dictionary of Kleinian Thought*. London: Routledge.

Sprince, M. (1984) "Early Psychic Disturbances in Anorexic and Bulimic Patients as Reflected in the Psychoanalytical Process". *Journal of Child Psychotherapy*, 10: 99–215.

Steiner, J. (1993) *Psychic Retreats*. New Library of Psychoanalysis. London: Routledge.

Steiner, J. (1996) "The Aim of Psychoanalysis in Theory and in Practice". *International Journal of Psycho-Analysis*, 77: 1073–1083.

Steiner, J. (1997) "Introduction". In *Psychoanalysis, Literature and War*. London: Routledge, pp. 1–12.

Steiner, R. (1996) "Letter to the Editor: 'Penis, Phallus and Mental Space'". *Bulletin of the British Psychoanalytic Society*, 32: 11–15.

Stern, D. (1985) *The Interpersonal World of the Infant*. New York: Basic Books.

Stoller, R.J. (1964) "A Contribution to the Study of Gender Identity". *International Journal of Psycho-Analysis*, 45: 220–226.

Stoller, R.J. (1966) "The Mother's Contribution to Infantile Transvestic Behaviour". *International Journal of Psycho-Analysis*, 47: 384–395.

Stoller, R.J. (1975) *Perversion: The Erotic Form of Hatred*. New York: Pantheon.

Stoller, R.J. (1976) "Primary Femininity". *Journal of the American Psychoan-alytic Association*, 24(Suppl.): 59–79.

273

Strachey, J. (1934) "The Nature of the Therapeutic Action of Psycho-Analysis". *International Journal of Psycho-Analysis*, 15: 127–159.

Sullivan, H.S. (1953) *The Interpersonal Theory of Psychiatry*. New York: Norton.

Torras De Beà, E. (1987) "Body Schema and Identity". *International Journal of Psycho-Analysis*, 68: 175–183.

Tuckett, D. (ed.) (2008) *Psychoanalysis Comparable and Incomparable*. New Library of Psychoanalysis. London: Routledge.

Tuckett, D. (2011) "Inside and Outside the Window: Some Fundamental Elements in the Theory of Psychoanalytic Technique". *International Journal of Psycho-Analysis*, 92: 1367–1390.

Tustin, F. (1984) "Autistic Shapes". Meeting of the Applied Section of the British Psycho-Analytical Society, 25 January.

Tutter, A. (2014) "Under the Mirror of the Sleeping Water: Poussin's Narcissus". *International Journal of Psycho-Analysis*, 95: 1235–1264.

Tyson, P. (1982) "A Developmental Line of Gender Identity, Gender Role, and Choice of Love Object". *Journal of the American Psychoanalytic Association*, 30: 61–86.

Urtubey, L. de (1995) "Counter Transference Effects of Absence". *International Journal of Psycho-Analysis*, 76: 683–694.

Urtubey, L. de (1999) *Monographies de Psychanalyse, Interpretation ll: Aux sources de l'interpretation: le contre-transfert*. Paris: Presses Universitaires de France.

Viderman, S. (1979) "The Analytic Space: Meaning and Problems". *Psychoanalytic Quarterly*, 48: 257–291.

Weiss, H. (2013) "The Explosion of the Present and the Encapsulation of Time: Transference Phenomena in the Analysis of a Psychotic Patient". *International Journal of Psycho-Analysis*, 94: 1057–1075.

White, K. (2010) "Notes on 'Bemächtigungstrieb' and Strachey's Translation as 'Instinct for Mastery'". *International Journal of Psycho-Analysis*, 91: 811–820.

Widlöcher, D. (2004) "The Third in Mind". *Psychoanalytic Quarterly*, 73: 197–213.

Williams, G. (1997) "Reflections on Some Dynamics of Eating Disorders: 'No Entry' Defences and Foreign Bodies". *International Journal of Psycho-Analysis*, 78: 927–994.

Winnicott, D.W. (1955) "Metapsychological and Clinical Aspects of Regression within the Psycho-Analytical Set-Up". *International Journal of Psycho-Analysis*, 36: 16–26.

Winnicott, D.W. (1958) "Primary Maternal Preoccupation". In *Collected Papers: Through Paediatrics to Psycho-Analysis*. London: Tavistock, pp. 300–306.

Winnicott, D.W. (1965) *The Maturational Processes and the Facilitating Environment*. London: Hogarth and the Institute of Psychoanalysis. The International Psycho-Analytical Library, vol. 64, pp. 1–276.

Winnicott, D.W. (1967a) "The Location of Cultural Experience". *International Journal of Psycho-Analysis*, 48: 368–372.

Winnicott, D.W. (1967b) "Mirror-Role of Mother and Family in Child Development". In P. Lomas (ed.) *The Predicament of the Family: A Psycho-Analytical Symposium*. London: Hogarth Press and the Institute of Psycho-Analysis (1971) In *Playing and Reality*. London: Tavistock, pp. 111–119.

Winnicott, D.W. (1967c) "The Location of Cultural Experience". *International Journal of Psycho-Analysis*, 48: 368–372.

Winnicott, D.W. (1971) *Playing and Reality*. London: Tavistock.

Winnicott, D.W. (1974) "Fear of Breakdown". *International Review of Psycho-Analysis*, 1: 103–107.

Winnicott, D.W. (1986) "Holding and Interpretation". *International Psycho-Analytic Library*. London: Hogarth Press and the Institute of Psycho-Analysis, 115: 1–194.

Yu, C.K. (2001) "Neuroanatomical Correlates of Dreaming: The Supra-marginal Gyrus Controversy (Dream Work)". *Neuro-Psychoanalysis*, 3: 47–59.

INDEX

Page numbers with "n" attached, for example 169n2, refer to notes.

sexuality *continued*
    noisy sexuality 86, 86–7, 93–8,
    100; 'penis-as-link' 87–8; sexual
    identity and modalities of
    thought 49–68; silent sexuality
    86–8, 98–9, 100; sublimation
    88–9, 92, 100n4; vision, role of
    60–6
Sharpe, Ella 59
Sirois, F. 53
slicing 151–3
Sodre, L. 149–50
Sohn, L. 52
sound 179–81
Sours, J. 103
speech 59–60
Spence, D.P. 45
Spillius, E. 26
splitting 51–2
stasis 2, 4, 8, 153, 175, 183
Steiner, J. 13
Steiner, R. 131, 147, 170, 234–5
Stoller, R.J. 54, 71, 72
Strachey, J. 3, 21, 139–40
subjectification 66
sublimation 88–9, 92, 100n4, 244
Sullivan, H.S. 28
symbols/symbolisation 3, 47, 60, 66,
    88–9, 90, 144, 190, 207, 210,
    217, 226, 227; body image 56–8;
    eating disorders 108–9, 124–5;
    modes of functioning 195;
    phallus/penis 126, 127; and
    sexual identity 62; symbolic
    capacity 5–6, 233–4; symbolic
    equations 189, 199; symbolic
    thinking 192, 198, 199

talking 13–14; as a phallic activity
    91–2; 'talking cure' 3, 21, 244

Target, M. 99, 195
temporality 2–3, 23, 38, 47,
    151–5; ambiguity between past
    and present 4–5; bi-temporality
    183; bidirectional temporality
    143–4; continuity over time
    183; and the continuity/survival
    of the object 145; and dreams
    174–5; *'fort-da'* game 144–5,
    148; freezing of 175; and the
    generativity resulting from
    linking 153; and identity 3–4;
    and the inability to accept
    change 178; instantaneity 146;
    Nachträglichkeit 139–40, 143,
    149; opposition between
    chronological time and
    timelessness of the unconscious
    175–6; 'polytemporal' 226,
    'primary process thinking'
    155–6; primitive temporality
    175, 176–7, 178, 190;
    'projective identification'
    145–6; repetition/non-
    repetition 148; reverberation
    time 147–8, 175, 178–80, 182,
    183, 186, 190, 193, 218;
    reverie 146–8; and rhythms
    176–7; slicing 151–3; tempo
    of psychoanalysis 192–212;
    'theory in practice' 193–4,
    202–3; time and the *après-coup*
    139–57; time as duration
    234–5; timelessness 145, 181;
    togetherness of developmental
    temporality and *après-coup*
    149–51; 'unpicking the
    tapestry' image 151, 235;
    working 'in the transference'
    183–4